The *Historia de sancto Cuthberto*, Manuscript C (Cambridge University Library, ff.1.27), p. 195

HISTORIA DE
SANCTO CUTHBERTO

A History of Saint Cuthbert and
a Record of His Patrimony

Edited by

TED JOHNSON SOUTH

D. S. BREWER

First published 2002
D. S. Brewer, Cambridge

Transferred to digital printing

ISBN 978-0-85991-627-1

D. S. Brewer is an imprint of Boydell & Brewer Ltd
PO Box 9, Woodbridge, Suffolk IP12 3DF, UK
and of Boydell & Brewer Inc.
668 Mt Hope Avenue, Rochester, NY 14620, USA
website: www.boydellandbrewer.com

A CiP catalogue record for this book is available
from the British Library

This publication is printed on acid-free paper

Contents

Illustrations

Acknowledgements

I am, with apologies to Bernard of Chartres, a dwarf dangling precariously from the shoulders of giants; I can't actually see as far as they can, but I do have an unusual perspective. In the fourteen years it has taken me to complete this ascent I have left scuff marks on the backs of three scholars in particular, without any one of whom this volume would not exist. The first, from my days as a graduate student at Cornell, is James J. John, a world-class palaeographer who also proved to be the best and kindest mentor one could wish for. The second, from my year at Durham, is David Rollason, who took an American M.A. student from the archaeology department under his wing and introduced him to St Cuthbert. The third is Simon Keynes, who in a decade-long act of generosity has read and provided detailed comments on successive drafts of this work as I struggled to convert my doctoral research into a publishable monograph.

This work was conceived of from the start as an interdisciplinary project. The skills required for a thorough study of this single small text range from palaeography and codicology through hagiography and Northumbrian history to landscape history and place-name studies. I have therefore picked the brains of specialists in a wide range of fields during the course of my research: for generously sharing their expertise with me I particularly wish to thank Eric Cambridge, Larry Field, Michael Gullick, Alan Piper, David Roffe, John Ruffing, Chris Scull, Victor Watts and Alex Woolf. I am also very grateful to Paul Hyams, whose advice and support were crucial to the success of my first major paper (from which the present volume eventually grew), and to all the regulars at the annual Haskins Society conference, which has always been a welcome source of feedback and new ideas for me. For help and advice during the final preparation of this volume I am indebted to the editors of this series, Andy Orchard and Michael Lapidge.

I am grateful to my students at Western New England College for their energy and enthusiasm over the past ten years; the great pleasure I take from teaching at a small college is ultimately what drives my scholarship. For moral support and keeping me in touch with reality I am particularly thankful to my colleagues John Baick and Bill Mandel. Finally, for sustaining me and enabling me to do what I love throughout these years, I wish to thank my family: Elva, Frances and Ty. I dedicate this volume with love to my wife, Frances, who has been with me every step of the way.

Springfield
January 2001

Abbreviations

AL	*Annales Lindisfarnenses et Dunelmenses*, ed. Levison
AU	*Annals of Ulster*, ed. Mac Airt and Mac Niocaill
ASC	*Anglo-Saxon Chronicle*, trans. Whitelock
BB	*Boldon Book*, ed. Austin
CÆ	*Chronicon Æthelweardi*, ed. Campbell
CMD	*Cronica monasterii Dunelmensis*, ed. Craster, 'Red Book', pp. 523–9
DBY	*Domesday Book: Yorkshire*, ed. Faull and Stinson
FPD	*Feodarium Prioratus Dunelmensis*, ed. Greenwell
GA	*Asserius de rebus gestis Aelfredi*, ed. Stevenson
GPA	*Willelmi Malmesbiriensis monachi gesta pontificum Anglorum*, ed. Hamilton
HE	*Bede's Ecclesiastical History of the English People*, ed. Colgrave and Mynors
HR	*Historia regum*, ed. Arnold, *Symeonis opera* II, 3–283
HSC	*Historia de sancto Cuthberto*
LDE	*Libellus de exordio et procursu istius, hoc est Dunhelmensis, ecclesie*, ed. Rollason
LF	*Liber feodorum: The Book of Fees Commonly Called Testa de Nevill*, ed. Lyte
LVD	*Liber uitæ ecclesiæ Dunelmensis*, ed. Thompson
MSC	*Capitula de miraculis et translationibus sancti Cuthberti*, ed. Arnold, *Symeonis opera* I, 229–61
VCA	*Vita sancti Cuthberti auctore anonymo*, ed. Colgrave, *Two Lives*, pp. 59–139
VCB	*Vita sancti Cuthberti auctore Beda*, ed. Colgrave, *Two Lives*, pp. 141–307
VPN	*Vita prima sancti Neoti*, ed. Lapidge, *Annals of St Neots*, pp. 109–14
VW	*Eddius' Life of St Wilfrid*, ed. Colgrave

Introduction

1. TEXT AND CONTEXT

Brief Description

The *Historia de sancto Cuthberto* is a brief work of around 6,500 words, written in Latin and produced within the community of St Cuthbert in the late Anglo-Saxon or very early Norman period. The *Historia* is important because it is the earliest surviving source for a number of events in the history of the community, including its translation from Lindisfarne to Chester-le-Street, and for a number of miracle stories which became part of later medieval traditions concerning the saint. It also contains a detailed record of land-holdings which is unique for pre-Conquest Northumbria. In fact, the *Historia* is more the history of a monastic community than a traditional saint's life, as its full title – 'a history of St Cuthbert and a record of the places and regions of his ancient patrimony, from the beginning up to the present time' – makes clear.

The text begins with a brief description of St Cuthbert's life (*HSC* 1–3). This is followed by descriptions of the property of Lindisfarne and of royal grants of land to (and occasional confiscations from) St Cuthbert and the community down to the early ninth century (*HSC* 4–12). The text then describes how Bishop Eardulf and Abbot Eadred of Carlisle transported the saint's body from Lindisfarne to Chester-le-Street, how they secured the election of a slave named Guthred as king of York and how Guthred granted to St Cuthbert all the land between the rivers Tyne and Wear (*HSC* 13 and 19b–20). This episode is interrupted in the middle by another, which shifts focus from Northumbria to Wessex, telling how St Cuthbert appeared in a dream to King Alfred and promised him victory over the Vikings (*HSC* 14–19a). The text then turns to a discussion of the lands gained and lost during the early tenth century, while the community was at Chester-le-Street (*HSC* 21–4). The next portion returns to the theme of West Saxon patronage and describes how kings Athelstan and Edmund, mindful of how the saint had aided their ancestor Alfred, each made pilgrimages bearing gifts to Cuthbert's shrine (*HSC* 25–8). This is followed by records of grants and leases from the early eleventh century; presumably these took place after the community had moved again from Chester-le-Street to Durham (an event traditionally dated to 995), though no mention of the move is made in the text (*HSC* 29–32). The final portion of the text jumps back to the ninth century and the time of King Guthred, telling how St Cuthbert aided the king in a

1

victory over an invading army of Scots and how Guthred in turn rewarded the community (*HSC* 33–4).

It can be seen that the *Historia de sancto Cuthberto* does not present the reader with a single continuous narrative, but rather with a series of thematic blocks, each with its own particular focus. There is seldom any attempt to smooth the transitions between these blocks, with the result that the text often shifts its chronological or geographical setting without warning. What holds the *Historia* together is instead a unifying theme. Throughout its length, the text remains focused on the community of St Cuthbert, and more specifically on the land-holdings that anchor the community's temporal power and identity. When historical events are referred to, they are used to explain the acquisition or loss of particular estates. When specific individuals receive attention, it is because they were responsible for the expansion, protection or reduction of St Cuthbert's patrimony.

The Community of St Cuthbert in the Late Saxon Period

The main body of the *Historia* was produced within the community of St Cuthbert in either the tenth or eleventh century; the question of which century will be discussed in detail below. What do we know of the monastic community which produced this text? Unfortunately, there is little mention of the community of St Cuthbert after the time of Bede until we reach the *Historia* itself. We do know that Lindisfarne supported a thriving scriptorium during the eighth century capable of producing deluxe manuscripts like the *Lindisfarne Gospels*; the investment of man-hours and resources, such as the hundreds of lambs required for vellum, represented by this one book alone suggests a stable and prosperous community. We also know that in 793 Lindisfarne had the dubious distinction of suffering one of the first Viking raids on English soil.[1] According to the *Historia*, the monks of St Cuthbert abandoned the monastery of Lindisfarne at some point during the ninth century and eventually settled south of the Tyne at Chester-le-Street. Although the *Historia* does not mention it, later sources record that the community moved again in the late tenth century, shifting from Chester-le-Street to Durham, a more defensible site some seven miles further south.[2]

---

1 This raid is recorded in the *Anglo-Saxon Chronicle* (*ASC* 793 DE) and is also the subject of several letters of Alcuin; see, for example, *English Historical Documents I*, ed. Whitelock, nos. 193 and 194. The impact of this raid continues to be debated; see below, Commentary, *HSC* 20, n. 88.

2 The authoritative source for this period in the history of the community is Symeon of Durham's *Libellus de exordio*, written in the early twelfth century. Symeon dates the seven years of wandering which led the monks from Lindisfarne to Chester-le-Street to 875–83 (*LDE* II.6), and he dates the move from Chester-le-Street to Durham to 995 (*LDE* III.1–2).

The power and influence of the monks of St Cuthbert seems to have increased as that of the Northumbrian kings declined. While there is still debate concerning the relative power of the Northumbrian kings in the later eighth century, it is clear that by the middle of the ninth century, whatever royal authority there was had been overwhelmed by the Viking invasions.[3] In particular, the capture of York by the Danes in 866 seems to have left northern Northumbria in a power vacuum into which the community of St Cuthbert naturally moved. This would explain why in the 880s it was the community, rather than the high reeve at Bamburgh, which apparantly came to terms with the Danes of York and secured the election of King Guthred (*HSC* 13). The later pilgrimages to St Cuthbert's shrine made by kings Æthelstan (*HSC* 26) and Edmund (*HSC* 28) suggest that the community offered the kings a promising political alliance as they moved to consolidate their hegemony in Northumbria.[4] In fact, the continued growth of their patrimony and the decline of royal authority made the monks of St Cuthbert a formidable political and economic force in the region; it was this fact which has led William Kapelle to describe the pre-Conquest community of St Cuthbert as 'the most powerful body of men in the North'.[5]

All of this directly contradicts the claims made by the twelfth-century historian Symeon of Durham, who gives the impression that the community at Lindisfarne was almost entirely destroyed by the Vikings, leaving only a handful of survivors to flee with the body of the saint.[6] Instead, the community seems to have been little diminished by the transition from Lindisfarne to Chester-le-Street. Certainly the community continued to exert control over a substantial amount of property, as the *Historia* itself records. In fact, it was this property which seems to have provided the primary motive for the composition of the *Historia*, as 'a record of the places and regions of [St Cuthbert's] ancient patrimony' (*HSC* 1). The creation of such a record might have seemed particularly important in the tenth century, as the expansion of West Saxon hegemony and the monastic reformation begun by St Dunstan might have appeared to threaten the community's power and its patrimony. It

---

3   Given the dearth of post-Bedan historical evidence, the debate over the strength of Northumbrian kingship has focused primarily on the question of the size of Viking armies. If these were relatively small, as P. Sawyer suggests, they could only have conquered an already fragmented kingdom; see Sawyer, *Age of the Vikings*, pp. 117–28, and *Kings and Vikings*, pp. 93–5. N. P. Brooks, who defends the traditional view, argues for large Viking armies and implies that the kingdoms of East Anglia, Mercia and Northumbria were still powerful on the eve of the invasion; see Brooks, 'Crucible of Defeat'.

4   For a discussion of the political advantages which monastic alliances offered the house of Wessex in the later tenth century, see John, *Orbis Brittaniæ*, pp. 177–80.

5   Kapelle, *Norman Conquest*, p. 31.

6   See *LDE* II.6. For further discussion of Symeon and the seven years' wandering see below, Commentary, *HSC* 20.

would have seemed even more urgent in the eleventh century, when a nearly continuous series of invasions and upheavals culminating in the Norman Conquest threatened long-established property rights.

Sources

What sort of sources did our monastic author have access to when he sat down to compose the *Historia de sancto Cuthberto*? First, he drew, directly or indirectly, on three different early works on the life of St Cuthbert. These three early sources are the anonymous *Vita sancti Cuthberti* (hereafter *Anonymous Life* or *VCA*) produced at Lindisfarne between the years 699 and 705, Bede's prose *Vita sancti Cuthberti* (hereafter *Prose Life* or *VCB*), based in large part on the *Anonymous Life* and written around the year 721, and a much briefer description of Cuthbert's life incorporating new information which Bede included in the fourth book of his *Historia ecclesiastica* (hereafter *HE*), completed in 731. Our text includes information which occurs uniquely in each of these three sources.[7] All additional details concerning Cuthbert's life in the *HSC* seem to derive from elaborations or misinterpretations of these three early sources.[8] In fact, the way in which the *HSC* blends

---

[7]   This can be established with several brief examples. First, the *Historia* sets Cuthbert's vision of St Aidan's death near the river Leader (*HSC* 2), a detail unique to the *Anonymous Life* (*VCA* I.5). After this vision, Cuthbert leaves his sheep to take up the monastic life under Boisil at Melrose (*HSC* 2); this follows Bede's description of events (*VCB* 6 and *HE* IV.27), while the *Anonymous Life* has Cuthbert enter the monastery of Ripon (*VCA* II.2). Boisil then describes Cuthbert's sanctity to King Oswin (*HSC* 3). Although this incident is clearly ahistorical (see next note), it may have been influenced by an episode unique to the *Prose Life* (*VCB* 6), in which Boisil speaks instead to Abbot Eata; both events occur just after Cuthbert's arrival at Melrose. In general, however, the life of Cuthbert in the *HSC* seems to adhere most closely to the brief biography of the saint presented in the *Historia ecclesiastica*. The best example of this is the sequence of events surrounding Cuthbert's consecration as bishop (*HSC* 3); only the *HE* explains that Cuthbert was originally elected as bishop of Hexham and then exchanged sees with Eata, or mentions the attendance of seven bishops at the consecration ceremony (*HE* IV.28).

[8]   The *Historia* does occasionally depart from the details of the three early Lives which seem to have served as its models, but there is little evidence to suggest that in doing so our author was drawing on another source, now lost. Some of the departures in the *HSC* are based on faulty chronology; for example, King Oswin makes a gift to Cuthbert after learning of Cuthbert's vision of St Aidan's death, although Bede states that Oswin died eleven days before Aidan (*HE* III.14). Again, Cedd and Chad are described as being among the seven bishops celebrating Cuthbert's ordination at York although, as Colgrave has pointed out, they would have been dead for twenty-one and fourteen years respectively; see Colgrave, 'Post-Bedan Miracles', p. 307. Other departures seem rooted in misunderstandings of the early Lives; for example, the *Historia* has both Boisil and Cuthbert after him serving as abbot of Melrose rather than as prior under Abbot Eata, and later it confuses the village of Alne in North Yorkshire with the

and occasionally confuses information from the early Lives may suggest that our author was not working directly from these sources, but was instead drawing on a traditional understanding of the saint's life which had developed over time. For history after the time of Bede our author seems to have had little information, relying primarily on the *Anglo-Saxon Chronicle*. References to historical events outside the community itself are brief, and are usually used to set the scene for a miracle story or property transaction.

The *Historia* contains a number of longer miraculous episodes which do not derive from any earlier known works. These include the story of the election of King Guthred (*HSC* 13), the story of King Alfred's dream (*HSC* 15–18), the story of the seven years' wandering and the waves of blood (*HSC* 20), the story of the death of Onlafbald (*HSC* 23), and the story of King Guthred's victory over the Scots (*HSC* 33).[9] It seems likely that some of these stories are based on local traditions and may have been first set down in writing by our author himself. On the other hand, in at least two cases (Alfred's dream and Guthred's victory), there is evidence that the author of the *Historia* incorporated a pre-existing written episode into his own work.[10] In fact, as we shall see below, it may be more accurate to think of the man who composed the *Historia* as a compiler rather than an author, one whose interest was more in organizing existing material than in producing a new narrative.

The main purpose of this anonymous author/compiler, as we have seen, was to record and substantiate the various property claims of the community of St Cuthbert. This process of substantiation included, wherever possible, the placing of each property grant in a convincing historical context. To achieve this aim our author seems to have brought together all the historical and hagiographical evidence he could find. Most importantly, though, our author required information concerning the patrimony of St Cuthbert itself. Frequently, he cites specific details concerning individual grants or leases, such as lists of dependent vills or descriptions of geographical boundaries; it

---

river Aln in Northumberland, near which Bede states that the synod that named Cuthbert as bishop took place (*HE* IV.28). The remaining details which do not occur in the early Lives, such as Cuthbert's habit of positioning his body in the shape of the cross while praying (*HSC* 2), are relatively minor and seem to point to a natural process of embellishment over time rather than to an undiscovered early source.

9   It should be noted, however, that parallel versions of two of these stories, featuring similar plots but different saints, do exit. Another version of King Alfred's dream featuring St Neot rather than St Cuthbert occurs in the *Vita prima sancti Neoti*, while a story similar to Guthred's victory over the Scots, but featuring St Acca of Hexham, occurs in the *Historia regum*. For further discussion see below, Commentary, *HSC* 15–18 and *HSC* 33.

10 Both of these episodes have long been viewed as having originated independently of the rest of the *Historia*, and have therefore traditionally been regarded as later interpolations to the text; see, for example, Craster, 'Patrimony', pp. 178 and 199. For further discussion see below, Commentary, *HSC* 15–18 and *HSC* 33.

5

seems likely that much of this information was drawn from written records rather than from oral tradition alone. However, as Simon Keynes has recently observed:

> We need not imagine that grants of land to the community, whether at Lindisfarne before 883, or at Chester-le-Street from 883 to 995, or at Durham from 995 onwards, were effected or recorded by the transfer of charters into the keeping of the church. It would appear to have been the community's practice to enter important records concerning their lands and men in the blank spaces of their most treasured books, and it is probably material of this kind which lies behind the surviving accounts of the pre-Conquest history of the church of St Cuthbert.[11]

Keynes notes four such treasured books: (1) a lost gospel book decorated with gold and inscribed with 'multis evidenciis et munimentis', described in a list of relics kept in the shrine of St Cuthbert in 1383; (2) *King Æthelstan's Gospel Book* (London, British Library, Cotton Otho B. ix, almost completely destroyed in the Cottonian fire of 1731); (3) the *Liber uitæ Dunelmensis* (London, British Library, Cotton Domitian A. vii); (4) a presentation copy of Bede's *Vitæ Cuthberti* (Cambridge, Corpus Christi College 183).[12] Each of the three surviving books contains records from the tenth and eleventh centuries which have been inserted into blank spaces in the original works. Of these, the most interesting for our present purposes is *King Æthelstan's Gospel*, since it seems to have served as a direct source for the *Historia*. This book, as reconstructed from its description in catalogues written before the Cottonian fire, contained at least four records of manumission from the late tenth or early eleventh century, entered on blank leaves at the beginning and end of the volume. More importantly, it also contained two Old English notes describing the king's gifts to St Cuthbert; these had been inscribed in a blank space preceding the Gospel of St John. Keynes has argued convincingly that 'King Æthelstan's Charter' given in *HSC* 26 is a Latin conflation of these two notes.[13]

Interestingly, the two other surviving 'treasured books' noted by Keynes

---

11 Keynes, *Anglo-Saxon Charters* (forthcoming).

12 The fourteenth-century description of the lost gospel book can be found in *Extracts from the Account Rolls of the Abbey of Durham*, Surtees Society 100 (Durham, 1899) II, 432. For a recent discussion of *King Æthelstan's Gospel*, see Keynes, 'King Æthelstan's Books', pp. 170–9. For a recent discussion of the *Liber uitæ Dunelmensis*, see Gerchow, *Gedenküberlieferung*, pp. 109–54. For recent discussions of CCCC 183 see Keynes, 'King Æthelstan's Books', pp. 180–5, and Rollason, 'St Cuthbert and Wessex'. For further discussion and bibliography on all four volumes, see Keynes, *Anglo-Saxon Charters* (forthcoming).

13 See Keynes, 'King Æthelstan's Books', pp. 175–8; for further discussion of the relationship between the records in *King Æthelstan's Gospel* and 'King Æthelstan's Charter' see below, Commentary, *HSC* 26.

were not used in the same way by the author of the *Historia*. The records in Bede's *Vita S. Cuthberti* would have been of relatively little interest; it contains only a Latin inventory of church goods from the tenth century which has been inscribed on the book's final page. (This page also contains an Old English record of a lease made shortly after the Conquest by Bishop Walcher and the community.) The Durham *Liber uitæ*, on the other hand, contains three grants to St Cuthbert from the late tenth or early eleventh century, as well as a manumission from the later eleventh century; all of these were inscribed on a blank leaf which occurs at the end of the original volume.[14] One of these grants is by man, Earl Northman, who is also mentioned in the *Historia* (*HSC* 31); nevertheless, none of these grants is described in the *Historia*. Gerchow has suggested that the leaf containing the three grants may not have been incorporated into the *Liber uitæ* until a series of additions to the manuscript were begun under Bishop William of St Calais late in the eleventh century;[15] if true, this might explain how these grants escaped our author's notice.

The evidence of these three surviving manuscripts suggests that it was the practice of the community to preserve its important 'business records' by inscribing them in gospels and other treasured books. In fact, one of the chief reasons for the creation of the *Historia* itself may have been to gather the information scattered among these various books into a single, easily accessible text. Although the surviving records surveryed above all date from the tenth century and later, it is certainly possible that other treasured books which have not survived, particularly the lost gospel identified by Keynes, might have also held records from an earlier period. Thus, although Craster assumed that it was only 'from about 900 . . . [that] the author of the *Historia* had written evidences to draw upon',[16] and that earlier records had been lost in the seven years' wandering, this would not have been the case if those records were inscribed in books; certainly the monks of St Cuthbert took precious volumes like the *Lindisfarne Gospels* with them in their wanderings.[17] At any rate, we know that the author of the *Historia* was able to make use of records preserved in *King Æthelstan's Gospel*, and it seems likely that his sources also included records similarly inscribed in at least one other treasured book, the lost gospels, which contained a number of early records.

We should note that while the author of the *Historia* seems to have had

---

14 Keynes dates the first grant, by Earl Thored, to the late tenth century, and places the other two grants, by earls Northman and Ulfcytel, in the early eleventh; see Keynes, *Anglo-Saxon Charters* (forthcoming). Gerchow dates all three grants to the last quarter of the tenth century; see Gerchow, *Gedenküberlieferung*, p. 120.

15 Gerchow argues that this leaf (*LVD* fol. 47) differs from the original portion of the *Liber uitæ* in terms of vellum, trimming and binding; see Gerchow, *Gedenküberlieferung*, pp. 120–1.

16 Craster, 'Patrimony', p. 199; see also *ibid.*, p. 190.

17 Sawyer notes that ten Lindisfarne manuscripts, including the *Lindisfarne Gospels*, have survived to the present day; see Sawyer, *Kings and Vikings*, p. 94.

access to relatively early records as well as to local traditions concerning the patrimony of St Cuthbert, there are several reasons for handling the information preserved in the *Historia* with caution. First, our author seems to have been quite uncritical in selecting and recording information from all the sources before him. There are numerous cases in which information given in one section of the *Historia* contradicts that given in another, and much of this confusion can probably be traced to conflicts between sources which our author has made no attempt to rectify.[18] Other difficulties, such as the *Historia's* unique reference to two very similar battles at Corbridge, may have been caused by references to the same event in two different sources.[19] Furthermore, the records used by our author may themselves have been composed some time after the transactions they describe. For example, Keynes suggests on stylistic grounds that the two Old English records in *King Athelstan's Gospel* which served as the basis for 'Æthelstan's Charter' (*HSC* 26) were probably not written until the second half of the tenth century, and thus date from a time after Æthelstan's death.[20] Finally, our author may have taken certain liberties with the records available to him. Again, the best example of this is 'Æthelstan's Charter', which is presented as if it were a *verbatim* copy of the text of a royal document. In fact, if Keynes is correct, our author combined elements of two different Old English records and then translated the result into Latin in order to produce this 'charter'.

Post-Conquest Durham Texts

Given the relative silence of the late Saxon period, the first half-century after the Norman Conquest saw the production of a remarkable number of historical and hagiographical texts at Durham, including the *Cronica monasterii Dunelmensis*, the *Miracula sancti Cuthberti*, the *Libellus de exordio*, and the *Annales Lindisfarnenses et Dunelmenses*. The earliest of these, the *Cronica monasterii Dunelmensis*, no longer survives but has been reconstructed by Edmund Craster based on passages preserved in later sources. [21] Craster dates the composition of this text between 1072 and 1083.[22] The *Cronica* covers much of the same material described in the *Historia* (particularly *HSC* 8, 11, 12–13 and 26–32), often compressing information that appears in the *HSC*

---

18 To give one example, *HSC* 19b states that the vills of Castle Eden and *Twilingatun* were both purchased for the community by Abbot Eadred, while *HSC* 21 states that these two vills were given to the community after Eadred's death by Tilred of Heversham and Bernard the priest respectively.

19 See below, Commentary, *HSC* 22 and *HSC* 24.

20 See Keynes, 'King Æthelstan's Books', pp. 176–8. For further discussion see below, Commentary, *HSC* 26.

21 See Craster, 'Red Book', pp. 520–3.

22 See *ibid.*, pp. 529–31.

but sometimes providing additional details. It seems most likely, as Craster originally asserted, that the *Cronica* was composed after the *Historia* and derived a large part of its information from it.[23] The author of the *Cronica* also seems to have had access to one or more earlier sources (quite possibly using some of the same source material as the author of the *Historia* but drawing additional detail from it) and used them to embellish upon some of the *HSC*'s later episodes, particularly those concerning kings Guthred, Athelstan, Edmund and Cnut.[24]

The *Miracula sancti Cuthberti*, the earliest versions of which had appeared by the beginning of the twelfth century, originated as a collection of seven miracles of St Cuthbert; soon an account of the saint's translation to his new cathedral in 1104 had been added, and by the end of the century the list of miracles had grown to twenty-one. The first four of the original seven miracles in the *Miracula* also occur as episodes in the *Historia* (*HSC* 14–18, 20, 22–3 and 33), and Colgrave has shown that the miracles in the *MSC*, while considerably more elaborate, are based directly on the *HSC* and show no signs of recourse to other sources.[25]

Colgrave has also shown that Symeon of Durham drew on both the *HSC* and the early *MSC* when he composed the *Libellus de exordio et procursu istius, hoc est Dunhelmensis, ecclesie* (long known as the *Historia Dunelmensis ecclesiæ*)[26] in the early twelfth century.[27] Symeon includes virtually every episode from the *HSC* in his history. He assigns specific dates to the various events described in the *HSC* and elaborates on many details, but generally his sources for these episodes seem to have been limited to the *HSC* itself. One notable exception to this is Symeon's description of the seven years' wandering (*LDE* II.10–12), which introduces a number of elements (such as the loss and recovery of the Lindisfarne Gospels and a description of St Cuthbert's seven bearers) which derive neither from the *HSC* nor from any other known source.

Another source which provides dates for many of the events described in

---

23 Craster remarked that 'the earlier portions of the chronicle exhibit obvious borrowing from the *Historia*' (Craster, 'Red Book', p. 530).
24 The *Cronica* includes every royal grant mentioned in the *HSC* starting with a brief reference to the Bowmont Water grant (here more plausibly ascribed to Oswiu rather than Oswin, as in *HSC* L), omitting only the grants by King Ecgfrith (*HSC* 5–7). The *Cronica* also includes a detailed version of Guthred's rise from slavery to kingship (*HSC* 12–13), the grants by Styr and Snaculf (*HSC* 29–30) and Bishop Aldhun's forced lease to the three earls (*HSC* 31). The *Cronica* shows the most divergence from the *Historia* in its treatments of *HSC* 13, 26, 28 and 32; for detailed discussions of these episodes, see Commentary below.
25 See Colgrave, 'Post-Bedan Miracles', pp. 321–4.
26 See Rollason, 'Symeon's Contribution', p. 1.
27 For the interrelationship of episodes in the *HSC*, *MSC* and *LDE*, see Colgrave, 'Post-Bedan Miracles', pp. 321–24.

the *HSC* is the *Annales Lindisfarnenses et Dunelmenses*. Although the *Annales* were originally thought to have been begun in the ninth century or earlier, Levison has shown their pre-Conquest entries to be the work of a single twelfth-century scribe.[28] The *Annales* present no new information for the late-Saxon period, and their entries seem to derive either from the *HSC* itself or from other twelfth-century sources such as Symeon's *Libellus de exordio*. In fact, Gullick has suggested that the scribe of the pre-Conquest entries in the *Annales* was none other than Symeon himself, and has placed the *Annales* amongst the scribe's later works.[29]

Finally, a number of incidents described in the *HSC* are also recorded in the early twelfth-century *Historia regum*. Although it is attributed in one of its manuscripts to Symeon of Durham, the author and place of production of the *HR* continue to be hotly debated. P. H. Blair has distinguished three distinct divisions within this work: an historical miscellany covering events down to 887, probably assembled in the tenth century (*HR*i); a brief compilation of Northern chronicles from 888 to 957, dating from the eleventh century (*HR*ii); and a chronicle from 848 to 1129 based primarily on John of Worcester and probably composed in Durham in the earlier twelfth century (*HR*iii).[30] Lapidge has refined this model by suggesting that *HR*i was composed by Byrhtferth of Ramsey in the late tenth or early eleventh century.[31] There is ongoing debate as to whether the final compilation of the text took place at Hexham, Sawley, Fountains or Durham.[32] All three divisions of the *Historia regum* contain references to events also described in the *HSC*; however, those in *HR*i duplicate passages found in later portions of the *HR* and intrude into a section otherwise based on Asser, and are most likely the work of a later compiler.[33] A description of the property of Lindisfarne in

28 See Levison, *Annales Lindisfarnenses*, pp. 475–7.
29 Gullick, 'Durham Martyrology Scribe', p. 105. Symeon's dates are uncertain; he entered the community at Durham in the early 1090s and was cantor in or shortly after 1126.
30 See Blair, 'Observations', p. 117. *HR*i contains §§ 1–79, *HR*ii contains §§ 80–5, and *HR*iii contains §§ 86–214 of the complete work. Blair further observes that the original portions of *HR*iii, which show a clear Durham interest, were most likely the work of Symeon of Durham (p. 117).
31 See Lapidge, 'Byrhtferth of Ramsey', esp. pp. 118–19. Lapidge suggests that *HR*i be labelled as Byrhtferth's 'Historical Miscellany' or 'Historical Compilation'.
32 Arnold and James argued that the *HR* had been written at Hexham; see Arnold, *Symeonis Opera* II, x, and James, *Descriptive Catalogue* I, 323. More recent scholarship, encouraged by the discovery of an erased Sawley *ex libris* on the second folio of the manuscript, has favoured Sawley; see e.g. Blair, 'Observations', pp. 72–6 and 118, and Dumville, 'Two Cambridge Books', p. 440, n. 9. Baker, however, has argued that parts at least of the *HR*'s parent volume originated at Fountains (Baker, 'Scissors and Paste', pp. 98–103), while Meehan has argued that parts show a strong Durham connection (Meehan, 'Durham Manuscripts', pp. 440–2).
33 *HR*i 75 includes a reference to the seven (here nine) years' wandering (*HSC* 20) which

*HR*iii 89 seems to be based on an otherwise unknown source.[34] An entry in *HR*ii 82 referring to nine years of wandering (rather than seven) may derive from a source independent of the *HSC* or may simply be the result of scribal error. The remaining entries concerning the community of St Cuthbert in *HR*ii and *HR*iii seem to derive directly from the *HSC* or from a common parent source.[35]

This brief survey of Durham historical texts leads to two general observations. First, it is remarkable how much of the traditionally accepted history of the pre-Conquest community of St Cuthbert, including major events like the transition from Lindisfarne to Chester-le-Street, can be traced back no farther than the *Historia de sancto Cuthberto* itself. This is particularly significant when we consider the rather unusual nature of the *HSC* as an historical source. It is important to remember that the author's primary goal throughout the *Historia* was to document and substantiate the property claims of the community of St Cuthbert. Although our author does sometimes present these claims without any narrative embellishment (particularly in *HSC* 29–32), he more regularly places his charters and leases in some historical context. Thus, for example, King Oswin's supposed grant of the Bowmont Water estate is explained as a response to Cuthbert's miraculous vision of St Aidan (*HSC* 3), and King Ceolwulf's grant of Warkworth is linked to his abdication and entry into the monastery at Lindisfarne (*HSC* 8). In some cases our author's explanation seems plausible (as with Ceolwulf), while in others it is clearly unhistorical (as with Oswin), but in almost every case we are left wondering whether he is drawing on a pre-existing source when he describes the background of a particular transaction, or whether he is simply adjusting to the demands of his narrative and giving his audience a reasonable explanation based on the facts he knows. Clearly, one of our author's main goals is to strengthen his community's property claims by placing them in a convincing historical context. Given the specific purpose of the *Historia* and the unverifiability of much of the information contained within it, it can be unsettling to realize how much of the traditionally accepted history of the community of St Cuthbert after the time of Bede, as presented by Symeon of Durham and other twelfth-century authors, depends on this one source.

Second, it is worth observing that, ignoring the *Historia* itself for a moment, there is an almost complete dearth of sources written within and

is very similar to *HR*ii 82; *HR*i 76 refers to Alfred's dream (*HSC* 16) in a passage identical to *HR*iii 96; and *HR*i 78 refers to the election of King Guthred (*HSC* 13) in a brief interlinear addition, while the full story of Guthred's election is given in *HR*iii 98.
34 For the text of this property list, see below, Appendix I.1.
35 These passages refer to King Alfred's dream (*HR*iii 96), the election of King Guthred (*HR*iii 98) and King Athelstan's visit to Chester-le-Street (*HR*ii 83 and *HR*iii 107). For a complete discussion of the relationship between episodes in the *HR* and the *HSC*, see below, Commentary, *HSC* 13, *HSC* 15–8 and *HSC* 26.

about the community of St Cuthbert between the age of Bede and the Norman Conquest; this is followed by a veritable explosion of historical writing which coincides with the Norman refoundation of the monastic community under Bishop William. Given the uncertainty of the *Historia*'s own date of production, it is worth asking whether *Historia* represents a lone tenth-century exception to this pattern, as has generally been assumed, or whether it is better understood in the context of the sudden renewal of interest in the history of the community in the later eleventh century.

Parallel Sources

Although the combination of spiritual and temporal preoccupations in the *Historia* is striking, it is not unique. By the eleventh century, a number of English saints' lives and monastic chronicles had begun to incorporate records of property transactions and lists of holdings into their narratives. Arguably the earliest parallel to the *Historia* is a work of the late tenth or early eleventh century, the *Libellus quorundam insignium operum beati Æthelwoldi episcopi*.[36] The *Libellus*, like the *Historia*, presents cartulary information in a narrative format as it gives an estate-by-estate description of St Æthelwold's restoration of the abbey of Ely. However, unlike the *Historia,* there is no real hagiographical component to the *Libellus*; there are no miracles and virtually no description of St Æthelwold's life or character, and the work is structured as a property register rather than a saint's life, with each chapter devoted to a different grant or estate.

Somewhat closer in content to the *Historia* is a portion of Hemming's *Cartulary* entitled 'Codicellus possessionum huius æcclesiæ'.[37] The 'Codicellus', written in the late eleventh century, is similar to the *Libellus operum Æthelwoldi* in that, after a brief introduction, it proceeds estate by estate through the various properties lost by the community of Worcester after the invasion of the Danes. Now, however, the tone is more narrative; particulars surrounding the acquisition or confiscation of specific properties are often given, and although no explicit miracles are described, several

---

36 The *Libellus* was translated from a vernacular source at the instigation of Bishop Hervey (1109–31). Blake speculates that this source had itself been compiled from a collection of informal Old English records shortly after the time of the events described, some time in the last quarter of the tenth century; see Blake, *Liber Eliensis*, pp. i, xxxiv and li–liii. Material from the *Libellus* was in turn incorporated in the twelfth-century *Liber Eliensis*, where it makes up the first forty-nine chapters of Book II.

37 The 'Codicellus' is contained on fols. 119–34 of Hemming's *Cartulary* (London, British Library, Cotton Tiberius A.xiii); see Hearne, *Hemingi chartularium*, pp. 248–88. For a complete discussion of the manuscript, see Ker, 'Hemming's Cartulary'.

object lessons concerning the bad ends of those who unjustly seize church property are drawn.[38]

Another work from the late eleventh century, 'De ampliatione huius coenobii per Ælwinum abbatem', also incorporates cartulary material into its narrative, but like the *Historia* it presents itself as a biography rather than a property register.[39] 'De ampliatione' is a life of Æthelwig, abbot of Evesham (1059–77), which focuses on three main aspects of its subject's life. It begins with Æthelwig's political life, describing his consecration as abbot and his dealings with King William and his fellow bishops, then tells of his piety and almsgiving, and concludes with a description of the lands which Æthelwig acquired for the abbey. The work's only miracle story also has to do with the abbey's property; it describes how, during the time of Æthelwig's predecessor Manni, a noblewoman named Aldith stole certain relics of St Ecgwin from the abbey, but confessed her crime after the saint appeared to her in a series of visions. Aldith was allowed to retain the relics until her death, and Æthelwig eventually recovered them from her son.[40]

Perhaps the closest parallel to the structure of the *Historia*, however, can be found in another work ascribed to Hemming and contained in his *Cartulary*: a very brief life of Wulfstan, bishop of Worcester (1062–95), entitled 'Quomodo Wlstanus episcopus per singulos gradus episcopatus apicem conscenderit'.[41] Here, as in the *Historia*, descriptions of specific grants of land are interwoven with details from the subject's life. Wulfstan's piety and humility are first described, and these attract the attention of Count Leofric and his wife and son, who grant him three estates. This in turn brings Wulfstan to the attention of Archbishop Aldred and leads to his consecration as bishop, which is followed by the acquisition of three more estates. Finally, Wulfstan's way of life as bishop brings him to the attention of King William, who grants him eight further properties.

Although it is far from comprehensive, this brief survey of textual parallels to the *Historia* allows us to make two significant observations. First,

38 The case of Viscount Rawulf is typical: 'Later Rawulf de Beornegia seized this [vill of *Witlæge*] for himself from the monastery by force; but shortly thereafter he was imprisoned, losing not only that vill but also all his land, God having thus rendered proper vengeance for himself' (*Hemingi Chartularium*, ed. Hearne, pp. 256–7).
39 'De ampliatione' is preserved as a chapter in the thirteenth-century *Chronicon abbatiæ de Evesham* by Thomas of Marlborough (Macray, *Chronicon de Evesham*, pp. 87–96); both Darlington and Gransden argue that it originally existed as a separate work written shortly after Æthelwig's death. See Darlington, 'Æthelwig', pp. 1–10; see also Gransden, *Historical Writing*, pp. 87 and 89.
40 See Macray, *Chronicon de Evesham*, pp. 91–2.
41 Hearne, *Hemingi Chartularium*, pp. 403–8. The text was apparently written shortly after Wulfstan's death in 1095. The *Cartulary* actually contains two versions of the text, the first written in Old English and the second, containing a few additional elaborations, in Latin.

although the tradition of institutional history as opposed to strict hagiography can be traced back to Bede's *Vita abbatum* in the early eighth century, the habit of incorporating the precise details of grants and leases in such works seems to first occur (ignoring the *Historia* itself) in the late tenth or early eleventh century with the *Libellus operum Æthelwoldi*. Second, a number of more specific traits characteristic of the *Historia* – the hagiographical format, the interweaving of narrative background and cartulary information, the protection of a community's property by God and its patron saint – only begin to occur elsewhere in works of the later eleventh century.

In her typology of Anglo-Saxon hagiography, Antonia Gransden describes the late eleventh century as a period whose defining characteristic is 'the authors' anxiety to define the rights and possessions of the saint's (or other ecclesiastic's) see or monastery', a phrase which suits the *Historia* admirably.[42] The anxiety Gransden describes is presumably explained by the desire to confirm or reassert traditional claims to property in the wake of the political upheaval and territorial confiscations which accompanied the Norman Conquest. It is noteworthy that even a work primarily concerned with the earlier depredations of the Danes, Hemming's 'Codicellus', was in fact written in the aftermath of the Conquest, suggesting that monastic communities felt a strong need to substantiate all of their prior property claims before they could be swept aside by Norman reorganization. Dating based on comparative sources such as these can hardly be conclusive, but this evidence, like that of the Durham histories, does suggest that we take a long, hard look at the supporting arguments behind the tenth-century date traditionally ascribed to the *Historia*.

2. SURVIVING MANUSCRIPTS

The original manuscript of the *Historia de Sancto Cuthberto* does not survive; the text is preserved in three later copies. The earliest surviving copy, here referred to as O, is from the late eleventh century and is preserved at Oxford (Oxford, Bodleian Library, Bodley 596). The next, here referred to as C, dates from the later twelfth century and is preserved in Cambridge (Cambridge, University Library, Ff. 1. 27). The last manuscript, here referred to as L, is a mid-fifteenth-century copy now in London (London, Lincoln's Inn Library, Hale 114). Only the London manuscript contains the complete

---

42 Gransden contrasts this with the hagiography of the tenth and early eleventh centuries, which she characterizes as being absorbed in the progress of the monastic revival, a trait conspicuously absent in the *Historia*. Gransden nevertheless accepts the traditional tenth-century date for the *Historia*, though this conflicts with her own typology. See Gransden, *Historical Writing*, p. 69; see also pp. 76–7 and 88.

text; the first folio in the Oxford manuscript is missing, while the Cambridge text stops short. The London text also contains a concluding section (*HSC* 34) not found in either of the earlier manuscripts.

Manuscript O

The earliest known surviving copy of the *HSC* is contained on folios 203r–206v in a collection of miscellaneous works bound together in the seventeenth century and currently preserved in the Bodleian Library, Oxford, catalogued as Bodley 596.[43] The text is incomplete: the first folio of the *Historia*, along with the final folios of Bede's metrical *Vita Cuthberti* which precede it, is missing, and the text now begins in mid-sentence in the middle of *HSC* 8.[44]

The main script of O is best described as an early Gothic textual script of Anglo-Norman type.[45] Continental influence shows in the script's shading and angularity and in its tendency toward pointed rather than rounded tops (especially in the letters *c*, *e*, and *o*), while the treatment of the letter *a* (which, in the initial position, tends to have a pronounced head and be taller than its neighbours) and the relatively wide space between lines of text are more reflective of English practice. Michael Gullick has recently identified this script as the hand of the Durham Martyrology scribe, and has further argued convincingly that this scribe was Symeon of Durham himself.[46]

Parent volume

The volume now catalogued as Bodley 596 was bound together only in 1605. The majority of the volume (fols. 1–174) consists of works in various fifteenth-century hands, but its final portion (fols. 175–214), which includes the *Historia*, contains a series of texts copied in the late eleventh or early twelfth century. This portion of Bodley 596 consists of Bede's prose *Vita S. Cuthberti* (175r–200v), the beginning of his metrical *Vita S. Cuthberti* (201r–202v), the *Historia de sancto Cuthberto* (203r–206v) and a life and

---

[43] Bodley 596 is described in Madan and Craster, *Summary Catalogue*, entry 2376 D, pp. 335–6.

[44] The assumption that the missing portion of the *HSC* consisted of a single folio is supported by the fact that the surviving pages of the manuscript average 750 words per page, and that the missing portion of the text is approximately 1500 words long.

[45] This description is based on the criteria put forward by B. Bischoff, 'La nomenclature des livresques du IXe au XIIIe siècle', in *Nomenclature des écritures livresques du IXe au XVIe siècle: Premier colloque international de paléographie latine* (Paris, 1954), pp. 7–14.

[46] See Gullick, 'Durham Martyrology Scribe', p. 93, and 'Hand of Symeon of Durham', pp. 14–15.

office of St Julianus, bishop of Le Mans (206v–214v).[47] Earlier catalogues made various distinctions between the Bedan material, the *Historia*, and the Julian material; in fact, the codicological details of all three works are very similar.[48] The dimensions of the text space are the same (roughly 190 x 110 mm), the text is presented in single columns of thirty-eight lines, rulings have been inscribed with a stylus and no prickings are visible. These similarities suggest that this early portion of Bodley 596 actually originated as a single volume.

Date of production

According to Gullick, the Bedan material in Bodley 596 belongs to the first stage of Symeon of Durham's work as a scribe, and is 'datable to some years either side of 1100'.[49] Although the script of the *Historia* is somewhat more compressed than that of the preceding Bedan material in Bodley 596, and although it is written in a slightly lighter ink, it does appear to be the work of the same scribe. The script of the *Historia* is also very similar to a portion of Digby 175, which Gullick judges to be one of the scribe's earliest extant works.[50] Gulick considers the *Historia* to be a slightly later addition to Bodley 596, though still in Symeon's hand and not of noticeably later date.[51]

Place of production and later provenance

If Gullick is correct in identifying the Durham Martyrology scribe as Symeon of Durham, then the *Historia* was almost certainly copied at Durham, where Symeon joined the monastic community in the early 1090s.[52] Interestingly enough, however, O's later history was connected not with Durham, but with Canterbury. The first page of the early portion of Bodley 596 (175r) bears the inscription 'Liber Sancti Augustini Cantuarie', and a

---

47 The Julian material seems an odd intrusion in what is otherwise a collection of Cuthbertine texts. It is probably explained by the fact that Bishop William of St Calais, the Norman appointee who reformed the community at Durham in the late eleventh century, had formerly been abbot of St Vincent at Le Mans, and may have brought material concerning St Julianus with him to Durham.

48 Madan and Craster dated the hand of Bede's *Lives* to the early twelfth century and the hands of the *Historia* and the Julian material to the eleventh: Madan and Craster, *Summary Catalogue*, p. 335. Colgrave placed the Bedan material and the *HSC* together in the early twelfth century and believed that this part of the volume was probably written in Durham, while he ascribed the Julian material to a later hand; see Colgrave, *Two Lives*, p. 24.

49 Gullick, 'Hand of Symeon of Durham', p. 15.

50 See Gullick, 'Durham Martyrology Scribe', p. 97, and 'Hand of Symeon of Durham', p. 24.

51 See Gullick, 'Hand of Symeon of Durham', p. 24, where he dates the *Historia* to s. xi/xii. He suggests that the *Historia* is the result of 'a near-contemporary addition or even a different scribal campaign'; Michael Gullick, personal correspondence, 28 June 1997.

52 See Gullick, 'Hand of Symeon of Durham', p. 18.

volume fitting its description is recorded in a late medieval catalogue for the library of St Augustine's, Canterbury.[53] It is worth noting that another manuscript by the Martyrology scribe, Durham, Cathedral Library, B.II.22, a copy of Augustine's *De ciuitate dei*, also has a Canterbury connection. The text contains marginal notation typically used by Archbishop Lanfranc and his circle; Gullick observes that 'powerful hints in DCL B.II.22 of a close dependence upon a Canterbury exemplar may mean either that the manuscript was copied at Durham from a borrowed exemplar or that the scribe copied the manuscript away from Durham, perhaps at Canterbury itself'.[54]

Manuscript C

The second oldest copy of the *Historia* is contained on pages 195–202 of a collection of works of historical interest bound together no earlier than the fifteenth century and now in the Cambridge University Library, catalogued as Ff. 1. 27.[55] This copy of the text omits the final five sections included in manuscripts O and L (*HSC* 29–33). Since the next text in the volume follows the *HSC* on the same page, there is no chance that these final sections were written on an additional page which has since been lost. Aside from the missing sections, the text of C is virtually identical to that of O. The fact that C contains an abbreviated version of the text has led to the widespread conclusion that C represents an earlier redaction of the text than O and L.

The text has been copied in a single hand, and its main script can best be described as English early Gothic. This script conforms to Ker's 'mid-century hand', which was most common in the period c. 1140–70. Ker defines this hand's characteristic forms:

> The backward-leaning, trailing-headed *a*; the ample 8–like *g*, the lower part of which is made in, it seems, three separate strokes, the third of them rising to or towards the base of the upper, o-like part; final *t* with a downward tick at the end of the headstroke; *x* with long left-hand lower stroke curling neatly round the base of a preceding letter; vertical strokes finished by means of a horizontal or slightly sloping angular foot.[56]

Our script displays all of these traits, although the tick at the end of the final *t* is generally quite small and the third stroke in the tail of the *g* is usually a nearly invisible hairline.

---

[53] See James, *Ancient Libraries*, pp. 238 and 517. James dates this catalogue to the late fifteenth century. Colgrave, while apparently relying on James, dates it to the fourteenth century; see Colgrave, *Two Lives*, p. 25.

[54] Gullick, 'Durham Martyrology Scribe', p. 101.

[55] CUL Ff. 1. 27 is described in Hardwick, *Catalogue of Manuscripts* II, 318.

[56] Ker, *English Manuscripts*, p. 35.

Parent manuscript

Ff. 1. 27, like Bodley 596, consists of works from two distinct periods. Text C occurs in the first part of the volume (pp. 1–236), which contains a number of texts in different twelfth-century hands, including copies of Gildas' *De excidio Britanniae*, a heavily revised version of the 'Nennian recension' of the *Historia Brittonum*, Bede's *De temporibus*, the *Libellus de exordio* and several shorter works concerning the churches of Durham, Lindisfarne and Hexham. Except for a fourteenth-century continuation of Gildas which occupies pp. 41–72, the various texts on pp. 1–236 are codicologically similar and were most likely produced together.[57] The same codicological characteristics also occur in one half of Cambridge, Corpus Christi College 66, which also dates from the twelfth century and concentrates on the Northumbrian church. The other half of this volume, like the later half of Ff. 1. 27, consists of fourteenth-century material connected with Bury St Edmunds. The traditional interpretation, originally voiced by M. R. James, is that two early books, one from the twelfth century and the other from the fourteenth, were split in two in the sixteenth century and recombined to form CUL Ff. 1. 27 and CCCC 66.[58] However, Meehan has recently argued that the two volumes 'should instead be regarded . . . as having been conceived in sections which were combined at an early date into a single volume'.[59]

Date of production

The question of the date and provenance of CUL Ff. 1. 27 is the subject of an ongoing debate which also involves two other Cambridge volumes, Corpus Christi College Mss. 66 and 139. As noted above, the early portion of Ff. 1. 27 has generally been assumed to have originated as part of a single volume which also included material now in CCCC 66. This material in CCCC 66 includes a page containing the inscription 'Sancte Marie de Salleia' in a hand of the late twelfth or early thirteenth century. Traces of the Sawley *ex libris* have also been discovered in CCCC 139; furthermore, the text of the *Historia Brittonum* in Ff. 1. 27 is based directly on the version in

---

57 Here I disagree with Hardwick's *Catalogue* II, 318, which extends this part of the volume to include pp. 237–52. These later pages are written on heavier vellum with a different page-size and pattern of ruling, in hands probably belonging to the thirteenth century.

58 See James, *Descriptive Catalogue* I, 323. See also Ker, *Medieval Libraries*, p. 97, n. 3, and Dumville, 'Two Cambridge Books', p. 427.

59 Meehan, 'Durham Manuscripts', p. 444. For a recent response to this argument see Norton, 'History, Wisdom and Illumination'.

60 For the Sawley *ex libris* in CCCC 139 see Blair, 'Observations', p. 118; for the relationship between the two texts of the *Historia Brittonum*, see Dumville, 'Corpus Christi Nennius', pp. 373 and 376; for scribal similarities, see Blair, 'Observations', p.

CCCC 139, and several scholars have suggested that some of the same scribes worked on both volumes.[60]

Dumville has argued that Ff. 1. 27 can date from no earlier than 1202–1207, since this is the date of a legal controversy over Wedale which is mentioned in the text of the *Historia Brittonum* in Ff. 1. 27, and which originated as an added note in CCCC 139.[61] However, as Baker has pointed out, CCCC 139 is not a homogeneous manuscript but a collection of four main sections written separately, and Meehan has suggested that Ff. 1. 27 originated in the same way.[62] Caution therefore suggests that individual texts within these manuscripts be dated independently when possible. In the case of the *Historia de sancto Cuthberto*, the most important link is not with the *Historia Brittonum* but with the copy of the *Historia regum* in CCCC 139. This particular text can be dated between 1164 and 1175.[63] This is in turn significant because one of the hands responsible for the *Historia regum* is identical with the hand that copied the *HSC* in Ff. 1. 27, which suggests that it was produced at about the same time. Scribal practices in C also support a date near the end of the third quarter of the twelfth century. Our scribe uses a cup-shaped abbreviation mark, which Ker notes was increasingly being replaced by a straight horizontal mark by 1170.[64] On the other hand, C's pages are laid out in double columns and ruled in ink, a habit that only began to dominate the earlier pattern of single columns ruled with a stylus at around the same date.[65] We should also recall that the script of C conforms to all the major characteristics of Ker's 'mid-century hand', which was most common in the third quarter of the twelfth century. The weight of the evidence therefore suggests a date for C in the later twelfth century rather than the early thirteenth, at about the time that the same scribe worked on the copy of the *Historia regum* in CCCC 139.

76, n. 1, Dumville, 'Corpus Christi Nennius', p. 371, n. 4, and Meehan, 'Durham Manuscripts', p. 442.

61 Dumville, 'Corpus Christi Nennius', p. 377. Dumville's model is that 'the text of the *Historia [Brittonum]* in CCCC 139 was thus a living document from the time it was written [in 1164–66, following Blair] until very shortly after the production of the greater text in Ff. 1. 27, perhaps half a century later' (p. 378). He has continued to support this date for the whole of Ff. 1. 27 in later writing; see Dumville, 'Two Cambridge Books', p. 427.

62 Baker, 'Scissors and Paste', pp. 85–6; Meehan, 'Durham Manuscripts', p. 444.

63 Blair dates the *Historia regum* to 1164 on the basis of information given in its *incipit*; see Blair, 'Observations', p. 78. Baker, following Offler, points out that the *incipit* could be copied from an exemplar, and further suggests a *terminus ante quem* of 1175, which is the date of death for Richard, abbot of Whitby, who is mentioned in the *HR* annal for 1074; see Baker, 'Scissors and Paste', p. 96.

64 See Ker, *English Manuscripts*, p. 39.

65 *ibid.*, p. 41.

Place of production

Debate continues over whether Ff. 1. 27, CCCC 66 and CCCC 139 were produced at Sawley or at Durham. Even Meehan, who argues that Ff. 1. 27 probably did not originate as a single volume with CCCC 66, agrees that they 'were combined at an early date into a single volume',[66] which seems tacitly to suggest that the Sawley *ex libris* in CCCC 66 applies to Ff. 1. 27 as well. This means that all three volumes were at Sawley by the end of the twelfth or the beginning of the thirteenth century; the only question is whether they were also produced there, or were received as gifts shortly after their production. Blair argued for a Sawley provenance for CCCC 139 on the basis of the 'pronounced Yorkshire interest' of its texts.[67] Dumville, by dating the production of Ff. 1. 27 / CCCC 66 to the early thirteenth century, automatically concluded that it had been produced at Sawley.[68] Meehan and Norton, however, have both pointed out a number of links between the texts in these volumes and others known to have been produced at Durham; each has also noted the poverty of Sawley during the period in question, and suggested that the rich decoration of CCCC 66 makes it unlikely to have been the product of a Cistercian scriptorium.[69] The question remains unresolved, though it is perhaps easier to imagine that this copy of the *HSC*, along with the rest of Ff. 1. 27, was produced in Durham and then sent to Sawley as a gift, than to assume that a substantial quantity of Durham historical material had somehow been sent to Sawley and copied there.

Manuscript L

The last of the three surviving copies of the *Historia* is contained on six and a half folios (153r–159r) of a volume of Northumbrian historical material which has remained intact since its production in the fifteenth century, and which is now in the library at Lincoln's Inn, London, catalogued as Hale 114.[70] The text of L is more complete than those of either O or C, since it contains both the lost sections at the beginning of O (*HSC* 1–8), the final sections which do not appear in C (*HSC* 29–33) and a colophon (*HSC* 34) which does not occur in either O or C. In general, the text of L conforms to those of the other manuscripts, but it does omit several sentences and phrases, and at one point (*HSC* 3) its readings differ substantially from those of C.

Manuscript L is the work of a single hand, the same hand responsible for

---

66 Meehan, 'Durham Manuscripts', p. 444.
67 Blair, 'Observations', p. 72.
68 See Dumville, 'Corpus Christi Nennius', p. 371.
69 See Meehan, 'Durham Manuscripts', pp. 441–6, and Norton, 'History, Wisdom and Illumination'.
70 For a description of this volume, see Craster, 'Red Book', pp. 504–7.

all seven of the short works that comprise the second half of Hale 114. The script is best described as an English Secretary Hand with Anglicana affinities.[71] The script displays the Secretary Hand's simplified forms of *a* and *d*, its tapering vertical strokes and its tendency to splay, but it lacks that hand's typically broken minims and horned bows, and it occasionally uses the Anglicana's double-bowed *a*.

Parent volume

Craster describes Hale 114 as 'two manuscripts bound within one cover'.[72] The first half of this double manuscript contains a text from the early fifteenth century, the *Libellus de exordio et statu ecclesie Dunelmensis* by John Wessington, Prior of Durham. The second half, in a different hand, consists of seven shorter works concerning St Cuthbert and Lindisfarne, including the *Historia*. Craster's division of the manuscript into two halves is borne out by the codicological evidence; the quires containing the *Libellus* are numbered while the rest are not, and their pages are more regularly ruled, with single bounding lines on all four sides extending right to the edge of the page. However, page dimensions and the average size of the written space are the same in both halves, and the volume's foliation, in what Craster identifies as a fifteenth-century hand, is continuous.[73] The available evidence thus suggests that the two halves of Hale 114 were bound together in a single volume soon after their production, some time in the fifteenth century.[74]

Hale 114 has been identified by Craster as the Red Book of Durham, which is described in a Durham catalogue of 1663 as a volume 'containing royal charters and privileges granted to the bishop of Durham, once called the Red Book, most carefully kept in the chancel at Durham, but recently lost most negligently by the servants and officials of the lord bishop Thomas Morton [Bishop of Durham 1632–47]'.[75] The first page of Hale 114 contains the signatures of Thomas Swalwell (Chancellor of the Cathedral 1497–99) and John Barnes (Chancellor of the Cathedral 1577); inside the front cover is

---

71 This categorization is based on the script characteristics suggested by M. B. Parkes, *English Cursive Book Hands 1250–1500* (Oxford, 1969).

72 Craster, 'Red Book', p. 505.

73 *ibid.*, p. 505.

74 Craster dates the hands of both halves of the Red Book to the first quarter of the fifteenth century; see Craster, 'Red Book', p. 504. Ker accepts Craster's description without comment, dating the book as a whole to the fifteenth century; see Ker, *Medieval Manuscripts*, pp. 131–2.

75 'libri continentis chartas regum et priuilegia episcopis Dunelmensibus concessa, qui olim dicebatur Liber Ruber, in cancellaria Dunelmensi diligentissime custoditus, sed nuper a seruis et officiariis domini Thomae Mortoni episcopi negligentissime deperditus.' From Bishop Cosin's book of transcripts, ed. J. Raine in *Historiæ Dunelmensis scriptores tres*, Surtees Society 9 (Durham, 1839), p. ccccxxii. For further discussion see Craster, 'Red Book', pp. 504–7.

a note in the hand of Sir Matthew Hale '4 Ap. 1657. bought of Mr. Washington pro 30s.' This date, notes Craster, 'agrees with the tradition that the Red Book disappeared from Durham between 1632 and 1647'.[76]

Date of production

If we compare the hand of L with those of dated manuscripts, we find that it has the most affinity with works produced in the middle of the first half of the fifteenth century. If we examine a work from early in the century, London, British Library, Harley 631, written in 1408, we find L's *b, d, h* and *l* with looped ascenders, its *x* with an exaggerated tail, simple *a*, 6–shaped final *s*, and circular *z* for *et*.[77] But Harley 631 does not contain our 'reverse *e*' or figure-8 *g* (the horned *g* is used instead); the single *i* is not normally dotted, and the 2–shaped *r* is used only following a facing bow; all of these traits mark the Harley manuscript as an earlier work than L. If we turn to London, British Library, Add. 36983, written in 1442, we find all of these features ('reverse *e*', figure-8 *g*, single dotted *i*, 2–shaped *r* used independently of facing bows), and we further note the disappearance of earlier habits that still occasionally appear in L, such as the v-shaped *r* and double-bowed *a*.[78] Most of L's distinctive traits first appear around 1420; London, British Library, Royal 17 C. VIII, written in 1418, contains the independent 2–shaped *r* and figure-8 *g*, and uses an unlooped *d* while favouring other letters with looped ascenders,[79] while London, BL Add. 14251, written in 1421, contains the 'reverse *e*' and figure-8 *g*.[80] In both of these manuscripts, older letter forms (such as the v-shaped *r*, horned *g* and double-bowed *a*) coexist beside newer ones, just as they do in L.

Place of production

There is no reason to doubt that Hale 114 was copied at Durham; Ker describes it as 'from and doubtless written at Durham Cathedral Priory.'[81] The volume consists exclusively of texts of Durham interest, and though its earliest history is unknown, it was certainly at Durham within a century of its production, as the signature of Thomas Swalwell demonstrates. If it was indeed copied at Durham, then its scribe should have had access to much earlier copies of his texts. The possibility therefore exists that L, despite its relatively late date, might actually preserve the earliest surviving version of

---

[76] Craster, 'Red Book', p. 504.
[77] Reproduced in Watson, *Dated Manuscripts*, pl. 317.
[78] Reproduced *ibid.*, pl. 451.
[79] Reproduced *ibid.*, pl. 351.
[80] Reproduced *ibid.*, pl. 364.
[81] Ker, *Medieval Manuscripts*, p. 131.

the *Historia*.[82] This brings us to the question of how the texts in our three manuscripts compare to one another and which one is in fact closest to the lost original.

Comparison of Texts

As we have seen, the complete text of the *Historia* is preserved in only one manuscript, L. The first eight and a half sections of the text are missing in O, presumably because a folio was lost from the manuscript at some point, while the text of C concludes with *HSC* 28. L also includes a final section (*HSC* 34) which does not occur in either O or C. Despite these differences, when we compare those portions of the text common to all three manuscripts, what is most striking is their overall similarity. After we eliminate minor differences which can be ascribed to the idiosyncracies of individual scribes (for example, O's fondness for the *ae*- dipthong, C's attempts to incorporate Anglo-Saxon letter forms and L's tendency to update place names), what remains is generally limited to the odd change in phrasing (most commonly in C) or omission of a word or line (most commonly in L). The only substantial difference in content amongst the texts occurs in *HSC* 3, where C and L provide significantly different readings; this will be discussed in detail below.

As for which manuscript should be accorded primacy as containing the earliest surviving version of the text, claims have been made for all three. Manuscript C stands out in two ways. First, it is unique in including letter-forms intended to reproduce the Old English ash, eth, thorn, and wynn, as well as variant forms of the letters *r* and *s* borrowed from Anglo-Saxon minuscule; however, both of the other manuscripts also contain spelling variations caused by Anglo-Saxon letter forms, suggesting that they too are based directly or indirectly on an exemplar written in an Anglo-Saxon hand.[83] Second, as we have seen, the text of C concludes with *HSC* 28, describing a visit to St Cuthbert's shrine by King Edmund which probably took place in 944. Since *HSC* 29–32 describe grants from the reigns of Ethelred and Cnut, scholars have traditionally assumed that the text in C was completed in the mid-tenth century, while the text in O and L dates from nearly a century later.[84] This question will be explored in detail in the next section; for the moment, it should simply be noted that a textual comparison reveals no compelling evidence that C derives from a different exemplar than O and L. Aside from the missing sections, the texts of O and C are virtually identical,

---

[82] This was certainly the view taken by Craster when he rediscovered L; see Craster, 'Red Book', p. 507.

[83] For further discussion, see below, pp. 25–6 and 39.

[84] See, for example, Craster, 'Patrimony', pp. 177–8.

with differences limited to minor variations in spelling, and several unusual spellings are common to both texts, which suggests that the exemplars they were copied from were very close to one another, if not identical.[85]

As for L, Craster believed that 'There is little doubt that it was transcribed from a lost exemplar, said to be written in a very ancient hand, named the prior's book, for the readings, which are in some respects superior to those of the thirteenth-century Cambridge manuscript, agree at all points'.[86] In fact, as we have seen above, the texts in all three manuscripts are remarkably similar, and there are only two instances in which the readings of C and L diverge significantly. The first of these concerns *HSC* 3, where C and L repeatedly differ in phrasing and occasionally in content. In addition to avoiding two important contradictions of Bede made in C (namely the designation of Boisil as abbot rather than prior of Melrose and an apparent confusion between King Oswin and King Oswiu), the variant readings in L are often much closer to models in Bede than the readings in C. A good example of this is seen when Cuthbert is brought before the synod which wishes to elect him bishop; C simply has the saint taken from Farne by the people and led away, while L, like the *Prose Life*, has Cuthbert drawn weeping from the island, with the king and bishops likewise crying.[87]

We might assume that L, being closer to Bede and therefore more likely to be historically correct, preserves readings which have somehow become garbled in C. In fact, L's increased adherence to Bede in these divergent passages seems to go against the rest of the *Historia*, which often contradicts or confuses information in Bede; for example, the reference to bishops Chad and Cedd at Cuthbert's consecration, or the confusion of the vill of Alne in Yorkshire with the river Aln in Northumberland, both in *HSC* 3. The readings in C, although they may be ahistorical, are more consistent with the rest of the text than those in L. In the case of the weeping withdrawal from Farne, L refers to 'the king and the bishop', yet no bishop has yet been mentioned in the text. This could conceivably be a reference to Archbishop Theodore; however, he is never called anything but 'Archbishop Theodore' in the rest of the *HSC*. Although this reference to a bishop thus makes little sense in the context of the *Historia*, it does make sense in the context of the *Prose Life*, where Bede has Bishop Trumwine weeping with the King (*VCB* 24). It thus

---

85 These unusual spellings include *paludas* for *paludes* in *HSC* 15 (corrected in both manuscripts), *paganissimum* for *paganismum* in *HSC* 17 (corrected in C), *helemosinarii* for *elemosinarii* in *HSC* 18 (corrected in O), and *turribulum* for *turibulum* in *HSC* 19 (corrected in O).

86 Craster, 'Red Book', p. 507. For a discussion of the Prior's Book see below, pp. 26–7.

87 Bede writes that 'at length this same king [Ecgfrith] himself, together with the most holy Bishop Trumwine, as well as many other religious and powerful men, sailed to the island; they all knelt down and adjured him in the name of the Lord, with tears and prayers, until at last they drew him, also shedding many tears, from his sweet retirement and led him to the synod' (*VCB* 24).

seems more likely to me that C represents the original text of the *Historia* in this case, and that the variant passages in L are the work of a later redactor attempting to bring the text into conformity with the accepted history of St Cuthbert as presented by Bede.

The second area of divergence between C and L occurs in the rendering of place-names. L does contain at least two readings that do indeed seem superior to those in C, namely *Greatadun* for *Grstatadun* (*HSC* 3) and *Suthgedling* for *Suthgedluit* (*HSC* 6). Nevertheless, these must be balanced against a much larger number of place-names where the readings in L are clearly inferior to those in C, either because of simple error or because L attempts to update names to their late medieval equivalents, such as *Perstun* for *Pacrestun* (*HSC* 3) or *Ganford* for *Gegnford* (*HSC* 9). L's tendency to interpret and update names also calls into question the validity of readings like *Suthgedling*, since these may simply be the result of scribal guesswork. In short, I find very little textual evidence to support Craster's assertion that L contains readings superior to those of the other manuscripts and preserves the text of a very early exemplar; if L was copied directly from an early exemplar in the Prior's Book, the scribe seems to have taken a number of liberties with the original text.

This brings us to O, which claims respect both by virtue of being the earliest of our three manuscripts to be copied and by being the most trustworthy; if we compare unique readings in all three manuscripts, we discover that O diverges least from the other two texts, followed by C, with L showing the greatest number of unique readings.[88] Although impressive, these facts are not enough in themselves to establish O as the earliest surviving text. The equivocal results of this comparison make the task of reconstructing the relationship between the three surviving manuscripts particularly difficult; nevertheless, it is to this problem that we must now turn if we wish to date the original composition of the *Historia*.

3. STEMMA AND DATE OF COMPOSITION

There is clear evidence that the earliest surviving manuscript copy, O, is not the original manuscript of the *Historia*. All three copies, including O, contain scribal errors in personal and place-names caused by the misreading of letters written in an insular script. From this we can conclude that all three copies

---

[88] Out of a total of some 240 unique readings (those readings in which one text disagrees with both of the others) in that portion of the text preserved in all three manuscripts (*HSC* 9–28), roughly 15% occur in O, 35% in C, and 45% in L. Of these unique readings, some 60% have to do with variations in spelling, while the remaining 40% are variations in word order, usually involving the addition, omission or substitution of a single word.

descend from an earlier exemplar which was presumably written in an Anglo-Caroline script, but which utilized an insular script for proper names. In O, the scribe has twice written *Tere* for *Tese* (the river Tees), mistaking the long-stemmed insular *s* for a Gothic *r* (*HSC* 9 and 24). The scribe of O has also mistaken the Old English wynn for a Gothic *p* and then corrected it to a *w* in *Wudacestre* (*HSC* 11). Confusions between *d* and *th* caused by the Old English eth also occur in all three manuscripts, including O.

The date of the *HSC*'s composition thus presents a problem; all that can initially be said is that it had reached its final form before O was produced around the year 1100. It is equally difficult to determine which of the three surviving copies of the *HSC* is closest to the original text. The construction of a stemma for the *Historia* is complicated by the fact that none of the three surviving texts has been copied directly from either of the others. O is palaeographically the earliest of the three, and therefore cannot have been copied from either of the others. C contains a number of unique readings caused by the Old English eth and wynn which do not occur in O, and therefore it cannot have been copied from O. L contains additional material found in neither C or O (in *HSC* 3 and 34), and it also contains unique readings caused by the eth and wynn which do not derive from either of the earlier manuscripts.[89]

There is tantalizing evidence for the possible existence of a fourth copy of the *Historia*, now lost, which may have served as the exemplar for all three surviving copies. References to a volume containing much the same information as the *Historia* occur in the marginal notes of a fifteenth-century manuscript, London, British Library, Cotton Claudius D. iv. This volume contains a copy of the *Libellus de exordio et statu ecclesie cathedralis Dunelmensis*, a history of the community of St Cuthbert apparently written by John Wessington, prior of Durham 1416–46, and an appendix containing extracts of earlier texts concerning the history of the community.[90] Both the *Libellus* and its appendix contain substantial portions of text that are identical with sections of the *Historia*.[91] In four cases, these passages are accompanied by marginal notation which states that they are taken from a volume called the prior's book.[92] The most extensive note states that these passages are

---

[89] These unique readings include *Werkeworde* for *Werceworthe* (*HSC* 8) and *Dyrpente* for *Dyrwente* (*HSC* 24).

[90] For a complete description of this volume see Craster, 'Red Book', pp. 513–14.

[91] As Craster has noted, the *Libellus* incorporates *HSC* 4–5, 8, 21–2, 26–7 and 33 within its text; see Craster, 'Red Book', p. 517, n. 2. Additional passages, including *HSC* 23, 28 and 34, occur in the appendix to the *Libellus* (British Library, Cotton Claudius D.iv, fols. 89–113).

[92] The four marginal notes inscribed in Cotton Claudius D. iv, one in the text of the *Libellus* itself and three in its appendix, are as follows: (1) fol. 23v, opposite the text of *HSC* 22: 'In finem libri prioris de uita sancti Cuthberti de manu ualde antiqua'; (2) fol. 95, introducing a lengthy passage from *HSC* 21–23: 'Ex libro priore de sancti

26

taken from the end of the prior's book on the life and miracles of St Cuthbert, in very ancient writing.

This description of the text and its parent volume does not seem to fit any of the surviving copies of the *Historia*, which suggests that a fourth copy of the *HSC* once existed at Durham and survived into the fifteenth century. The reference to ancient writing suggests a manuscript written at least in part in an insular script, which we have already deduced our exemplar of the *Historia* must have been. Craster thought there was little doubt that L had been copied directly from this Prior's Book;[93] in fact, given the similarities among our three surviving manuscripts and the fact that none were copied from any of others, it is possible that all three were copied from an exemplar in the Prior's Book at different times. If this is true, it also increases the likelihood that all three surviving copies of the text were in fact produced at Durham. This hypothetical exemplar in the Prior's Book brings us closer to the original text of the *Historia*; we are still left, however, with the question of when and in what order that text was composed.

Model I (tenth-century)

The text of the *HSC* has traditionally been dated to the mid-tenth century. The argument for this date was most fully articulated by Edmund Craster. Following J. H. Hinde, Craster based his date on the fact that C ends with *HSC* 28, which describes King Edmund's visit to Chester-le-Street, while O contains additional material (*HSC* 29–32) from the reign of Cnut.

> One may draw the conclusion that the Cambridge manuscript, although later in date than the Oxford version and inferior in its readings, represents an older text which lacked the final paragraphs and ended with the account of King Edmund's visit to St Cuthbert's shrine in or about 945. And inasmuch that the author states in his opening paragraph that he is bringing his history down to his own time, it would follow that this original composition dates to about this year.[94]

This dating scheme depends on the assumption that the *Historia* was not a uniform composition, but was added to at various times. Besides assuming that the charters from Cnut's time (*HSC* 29–32) are a later addition, Craster was also forced to assume a second interpolation. This is the story of St

---

Cuthberti uita et miraculis de scriptura ualde antiqua, in fine libri ad tale signum Ø'; (3) fol. 95v, introducing the complete text of *HSC* 26–28: 'Ex libro priore ad tale signum Ø et concordat cum libro magnis altaris'; (4) fol. 102v, introducing the complete text of *HSC* 33–4: 'Ex libro priore, quomodo terra scotos uiuos absorbebat'.
93 See Craster, 'Red Book', p. 507.
94 Craster, 'Patrimony', pp. 177–8.

I: TENTH-CENTURY MODELS

MODEL IA

MODEL IB

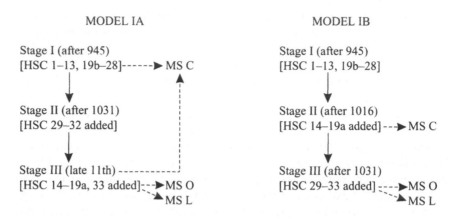

II: ELEVENTH-CENTURY MODELS

MODEL IIA

MODEL IIB

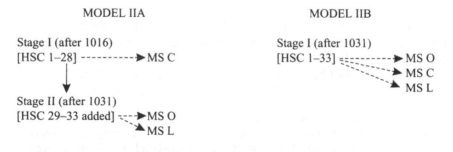

Fig. 1   Possible stemmata for the *HSC*

Cuthbert's appearance to King Alfred in a dream (*HSC* 14–19a). In this episode, Alfred's victory at Edington (*Ethandune*) in 878 has been confused with Cnut's victory at Ashingdon/Ashdon (*Assandun*) in 1016, and therefore 'the story is an interpolation which cannot be earlier than the reign of Cnut, and may well be later'.[95] Craster therefore concluded that the *Historia* was written in a series of stages:

> No part of it was written before 945 [when the original text consisting of *HSC* 1–13 and 19b–28 was composed] . . . Then comes a half century for which there is a blank; and it was only after the bishop's seat had been transferred from Chester-le-Street to Durham that the *Historia* and the

[95] Craster, 'Patrimony', p. 178.

Liber uitæ began to be treated in the manner of chartularies and that dioc-esan documents were registered in them [*HSC* 29–32]. The latest entry of a grant in the *Historia* is that of King Cnut's gift in or about 1031. It was probably not till quite late in the eleventh century that the *Historia* received two further additions; both made with the object of exalting St Cuthbert; the one an interpolation that tells of the saint's protection of King Alfred [*HSC* 14–19a], the other being the final paragraph which describes the earthquake-miracle reputed to have happened in King Guthred's time [*HSC* 33].[96]

Craster thus postulated three stages in the production of the *HSC*: stage I, written shortly after 945 and consisting of the 'original text' (*HSC* 1–13 and 19b-28); stage II, written shortly after 1031 and describing property transac-tions from the time of Cnut (*HSC* 29–32); and stage III, written late in the eleventh century and consisting of two miracles of St Cuthbert, one involving King Alfred (*HSC* 14–19a), the other King Guthred (*HSC* 33). (See fig. 1.Ia.) This three-stage model is directly dictated by Craster's dating scheme. If the main text was produced in the mid-tenth century, then the sections from Cnut's time must have been added later, since they date from the early eleventh century. Similarly, the episode describing Alfred's dream must also be a later interpolation, since it contains an anachronistic reference to Cnut's battle at *Assandun*. Because of his belief that the earliest part of the *Historia* dates from the tenth century, then, Craster was forced to postulate that the present text was produced in a very haphazard way. Originally written as a saint's life, it was set aside for half a century, then used for a time as a cartulary, and finally, after another half-century, chosen as a convenient place to record two additional miracle-stories about St Cuthbert.

Although it has been widely accepted, Craster's dating-scheme does have weaknesses. First, there is the assumption that C is based on an earlier version of the text than O. While this is the most logical explanation for C's omission of *HSC* 29–32, it troubles me that, except for the missing sections, there are no substantial differences between C and O which would suggest that they were copied from different exemplars. The fact that they share a number of unusual variant spellings, later corrected by one or both scribes, suggests that their exemplars must have been close to one another, if not identical.[97] Although this certainly doesn't prove that C was not copied from an earlier version of the text, it does perhaps suggest that we should look for further evidence beyond the missing sections.

Second, Craster's scheme requires the assumption that the *Historia* was the product of several different authors or copyists working at different periods. This model of production seems to me to ignore the essential

---

96 Craster, 'Patrimony', p. 199.
97 See above, n. 85.

thematic unity of the *HSC*. At bottom, such a model rests on the assumption that there is a clear distinction between narrative episodes on the one hand and property records like those in *HSC* 29–32 on the other, and that the author of a saint's life would not willingly insert such records into his work. However, we have seen that the incorporation of documents and charters into hagiographical texts was not particularly unusual, at least not by the later eleventh century.[98] In the case of the *Historia*, the presentation of documents in *HSC* 29–32 is fully in keeping with the author's concern to document the holdings of the community of St Cuthbert as completely and convincingly as possible. Descriptions of earlier grants are peppered throughout the text, and in *HSC* 26 the author has already recorded in its entirety a purported charter of King Æthelstan.

Third and most importantly, Craster's stemma involves us in a logical contradiction (see fig. 1.Ia). C contains Alfred's dream (*HSC* 14–19a), which according to Craster's scheme was not added until more than a century after the creation of C's exemplar. In order for Craster's model to work, then, the scribe of C must have had access to copies of both the original text and to an expanded text containing Alfred's dream. But the expanded text must have also included Cnut's charters, since according to Craster's model they were added to the text before the dream. We must therefore assume that the scribe of C copied material from the expanded text, yet carefully noted where the original text ended and refused to borrow from the expanded text beyond that point. This seems unlikely. The alternative is that the scribe of C found an independent copy of the Alfred-episode and chose to add it to the *Historia*. But if this is the case, how do we explain the fact that he chose to insert it in the middle of his text, in exactly the same awkward position as in O?

It is possible to adjust Craster's stemma to eliminate its logical contradictions while retaining a tenth-century date for the original production of the *Historia*. This can be done by assuming that Alfred's dream was added to the original text before C was copied, rather than after.[99] This still gives us an original text consisting of *HSC* 1–13 and 19b–28, written after 945 but before 995 (the traditional date of the community's move to Durham, which is never mentioned in the text), but now the Alfred-episode (*HSC* 14–19a) is added first, producing the text in C; after this the eleventh-century records and Guthred's dream (*HSC* 29–33) are added to the text, producing the text in O. (See fig. 1.Ib.) The Alfred-episode must have been added some time after 1016 (the date of the battle of *Assandun*), probably in the mid-eleventh century, while the eleventh-century records must have been added after 1031 (the likely date of Cnut's visit to Durham), most likely in the second half of

---

98 See above, pp. 12–14. See also Rollason, *Saints and Relics*, pp. 196–214, and Gransden, *Historical Writing*, pp. 87–91.
99 This model owes much to Professor Simon Keynes; it evolved out of a long-distance discussion of Craster's model via letter and e-mail, 1991–7.

the eleventh century. According to this model, the bulk of the *Historia* would originally have been produced some time in the second half of the tenth century, although the earliest surviving version of the text, C, dates only from the mid-eleventh.

This stemma eliminates the major difficulties of Craster's scheme. However, it still assumes that the text was produced in at least three different stages by a number of different authors or copyists, and that neither the Alfred-episode nor the eleventh-century records are integral to the original text. This model assumes Alfred's dream to be an interpolation for two reasons: (1) it presumes that the original text dates from the tenth century, yet Alfred's dream must date from the eleventh century, because of the *Assandun* anachronism; (2) it presumes that Alfred's dream is a later interpolation because it interrupts the flow of the text. Both of these assumptions will work, but both can be questioned. First, the assumption of a tenth-century date of composition is based solely on the missing sections in C, as noted above. More importantly, the textual evidence for the interpolation of the Alfred-episode is equivocal. First, this is not the only point where the logic of the text is interrupted. *HSC* 11 should logically follow *HSC* 8, since both describe the gifts of King Ceolwulf, and *HSC* 12 continues the story of the Danish invasions from *HSC* 10, ignoring the intrusion of *HSC* 11. No one has yet suggested that either of these episodes are later interpolations; instead, it seems that our author was trying to incorporate material from a number of different sources, and occasionally lost track of or had difficulty with his narrative logic. Second, it can be argued that Alfred's dream is integral to the basic structure of the second half of the *Historia* and cannot be explained as a later interpolation. This episode explains the roots of West Saxon patronage for St Cuthbert, and sets the stage for the visits of Athelstan and Edmund to the saint's shrine (*HSC* 25–8). The main narrative pattern which holds the second half of the *Historia* together – the reverence of the West Saxon kings for St Cuthbert and the way this reverence is passed from one king to the next – is thus introduced and shaped by the Alfred episode.

Furthermore, if one eliminates Alfred's dream from the original text, several loose ends occur. *HSC* 21 begins by stating 'Then Edward, long wisely taught by his father, succeeded to the kingdom and wisely ruled it'. This would seem to be a reference to the end of the Alfred-episode, which states that Alfred summoned his son Edward 'and admonished him diligently to love God and St Cuthbert and to trust in them just as he himself had always trusted' (*HSC* 19a). Edward's father, Alfred, is not even named in *HSC* 21; it is assumed that the reader knows his story and his relation to Edward from the previous episode. Similarly, *HSC* 25 tells of how King Edward instructed his son Æthelstan 'to love St Cuthbert and honour him above all saints, revealing to him how he had mercifully succoured his father King Alfred in poverty and exile, and how he had boldly aided him against all enemies.' Again the author seems to be referring to the Alfred episode, which describes

31

how Alfred 'hid in the Glastonbury marsh in great poverty', and how St Cuthbert appeared to him there and promised him aid against his Viking enemies (*HSC* 14). In short, if the Alfred episode is a later interpolation, then it seems that significant portions of the rest of the *Historia* (especially *HSC* 24–8) must have been reworked at the same time.

Model II (eleventh-century)

If we accept that the Alfred's Dream episode is indeed integral to the main body of the *Historia*, two important results occur. First, we can now treat *HSC* 1–28 as a unified whole, produced by a single author in a single campaign. Second, since this initial campaign now includes *HSC* 16 with its anachronistic reading of *Assandun*, we must assume that the *Historia* was initially composed some time after 1016, the date of the battle of *Assandun*.[100] (See fig. 1.IIa.) I believe that this conclusion, although it represents a radical departure from the traditional interpretation, deserves consideration for a number of reasons. First, it produces a straightforward stemma which accounts for the known facts in a simpler way than the tenth-century models and which acknowledges the essential unity of the *Historia*. Second, an eleventh-century date would bring the *Historia* closer in time to the other late-Saxon texts we have surveyed which combine narrative history and property records in a similar way. Third, there are elements in those portions of the text which all scholars agree to be original (i.e. *HSC* 1–13 and 19b–28) that seem more likely to date from the eleventh century than from the tenth. The vill of Norham, described in *HSC* 9, is rendered as *Northam* in all three manuscripts, but a list of saints' resting-places which itself most likely dates

---

100 The alternative here is to argue that *Assandun* is actually the result of later scribal error and that *HSC* 1–28 was composed as a single unit in the mid-tenth century; see Simpson, 'The King Alfred/St. Cuthbert Episode', pp. 397–8. Simpson argues that this mid-tenth-century version of the text is preserved in C, and that the later material in *HSC* 29–33 was added in the mid-eleventh century to produce O. This means, however, that the *Assandun* error must have been made independently by at least two different scribes, since the parent texts of C and O would have already diverged before the error could have taken place, some time after 1016. Such a coincidence is difficult to believe. Simpson argues that Alfred's Dream was composed in the mid-tenth century primarily because it echoes several formulæ found in royal documents of that period, and because the episode would have been 'politically meaningful' at that time (p. 400). This assumption is open to question; however, even if we accept that the Alfred's Dream episode was composed in the mid-tenth century, this does not imply that it was incorporated in the *Historia* at this time. As I hope I have shown, the *Historia* seems to have been assembled from a number of pre-existing sources; although each of these sources can provide us with a date *ante quem non* for its production, none of them can, by themselves, tell us when the final work was actually composed.

from the tenth century gives it the earlier name of *Ubbanford*.[101] Similarly, the two sources on which 'Æthelstan's Charter' (*HSC* 26) is based seem themselves to date from no earlier than the later tenth century, which suggests that the *Historia* must be later still.[102]

There is one obvious difficulty with this eleventh-century model. This is the fact that it brings the initial date of production for the *HSC* beyond 995, the traditional date for the translation of St Cuthbert's body (and the see) from Chester-le-Street to Durham. If the *Historia* was indeed produced after this event, why is there no mention of it in the text? There are no firm answers to this question, but possibilities do exist. First, the earlier translation of the saint from Lindisfarne to Chester-le-Street is only mentioned in the *Historia* because it is associated with a miracle (Cuthbert prevents his body from being taken to Ireland by swamping the boat with three waves of blood) and with the grant of 'all the land between the Tyne and the Wear' to the community by King Guthred of York. Our author has a clear purpose in mind, and ignores material that does not bear directly on St Cuthbert's patrimony.

Second, it is worth noting that the author of the *Historia* seems to have thought of himself more as a compiler than an original composer, and that most of his work seems based on pre-existing sources of one kind or another. It was only with Symeon's *Libellus de exordio* in the early twelfth century that the miraculous story of St Cuthbert's translation to Durham really appears to have taken shape; without an existing source like this to work from, and given that the move had no immediate impact on the saint's patrimony, it may never have occurred to our author to describe the saint's translation to Durham in his own words. The move to Durham may not have

---

101 For the text of this list of resting-places, titled *Secgan be þam Godes sanctum þe on Engla lande aerost reston*, see Liebermann, *Die heiligen Englands*, pp. 9–19. Rollason states that the *Secgan* was only completed in its present form in or shortly after 1031; see Rollason, 'Resting-places', p. 68. However, he also notes that the information in the first half of the text, which includes the reference to St Cuthbert's resting-place at *Ubbanford*, generally seems to date from the pre-Viking period, and he suggests that the *Ubbanford* entry originated in the mid-ninth century while St Cuthbert's body was actually at Norham (p. 68). If this is correct, all we can be certain of is that the change from *Ubbanford* to Norham took place sometime between the late ninth century and the late eleventh, when Norham was referred to in a record of the activities of Bishop William of St Calais recorded in the *Liber uitae Dunelmensis* (*LVD* 50r).

102 These are a pair of Old English records which were inscribed in *King Æthelstan's Gospels* (Cotton Otho B. ix). The first of these was a diploma in official language recording Æthelstan's gift of the Gospels to St Cuthbert, which Keynes suggests 'was written some time later in the tenth century': Keynes, 'King Æthelstan's Books', p. 176. The second was a note listing Æthelstan's other gifts to the saint, which Keynes states 'must have been contemporary with [the preceding diploma] or later still' (p. 178). For further discussion of this point see above, pp. 6 and 8, and below, Commentary, *HSC* 26.

seemed particularly momentous in the first century after it took place, and may have even been considered another temporary change, with hopes for an eventual return to Lindisfarne. For whatever reason, we know that another author/compiler working in the later eleventh century ignored the move to Durham in just the way we are hypothesizing: the *Cronica monasterii Dunelmensis*, which chronicles the history of the community of St Cuthbert from the ninth century down to the time of William the Conqueror and which, like the *Historia*, concentrates on the saint's property, makes absolutely no mention of the translation.[103]

If we accept that the initial version of the *Historia*, consisting of *HSC* 1–28, was not composed before the mid-eleventh century, another question arises. Why should we still assume that *HSC* 29–33, which dates from the mid- or late eleventh century itself, is necessarily a later addition? Two reasons have traditionally been given for treating this portion of the text as a later addition: first, the character of the text seems to change at this point from narrative to cartulary; and second, the text of C ends with *HSC* 28. The first reason no longer seems very substantial; we have seen how cartulary material is interspersed throughout the *Historia*, and we have noted that the mood and focus of *HSC* 29–33 are perfectly in keeping with the rest of the text, continuing to concentrate on the patrimony of St Cuthbert and the saint's ability to protect that patrimony. The second point, however, is much more puzzling: why should C stop with *HSC* 28?

We have already seen that in other respects the text of C is not demonstrably earlier than that of O. The possibility that C represents an incomplete copy rather than an earlier version of the text should therefore be considered. Examination of CUL Ff. 1. 27 shows that C is written on the last four leaves of a twelve-leaf quire.[104] The text which follows C (Æthelwulf's *De abbatibus*) begins on a new quire and appears to be the work of a different scribe.[105] Our scribe therefore seems to have reached the end of his assigned quire before he reached the end of his copy. To have added an additional leaf to his quire would have been awkward and created difficulties during binding. Instead, our scribe could conceivably have chosen to solve his problem by ending his copy of the *Historia* at a relatively logical stopping

---

103 For the text of the *Cronica,* see Craster, 'Red Book', pp. 523–9. Craster dates its composition to shortly after 1072 (p. 530).

104 The hand and ink of the first four leaves of this quire, which contain the final chapters of Symeon's *Libellus de exordio*, are similar to those of C, while the middle four leaves, containing *De Ranulpho episcopo*, are in a different hand and darker ink. It thus seems likely that this portion of the volume originated as a standard eight-leaf quire consisting of four folded bifolios containing the end of the *LDE* and the *Historia*, and that an additional pair of bifolios containing *De Ranulpho episcopo* were then inserted in the middle to create a twelve-leaf quire.

105 *De abbatibus* is written in a different hand and darker ink than the *Historia* and the presentation of the text is more elaborate, including decorative colored initials.

point and filling the remaining space with a short text (a vernacular poem on Durham) that left only two blank lines at the end of his quire. If for this or any other reason the scribe of C did stop before he reached the end of his exemplar, then it is possible that the *Historia* as originally written included at least *HSC* 1–32, and was therefore written at some point after 1031 (the most likely date of Cnut's grant in *HSC* 32), probably in the second half of the eleventh century. (See fig.1.IIb.)

Finally, even if we assume that *HSC* 29–32 was part of the original text, we are left with the problem of *HSC* 33–4. This is the only episode in the work that is seriously out of chronological order; logically, it should follow the story of King Guthred's election in *HSC* 13. We have evidence that this episode existed independently of the *Historia*, for a separate copy of it is preserved in a volume now in Paris.[106] We have also seen that although the author of the *Historia* brought together material from a variety of sources, he always attempted to arrange it in more or less chronological order; the fact that this is not the case with this episode suggests that it may be a later addition. On the other hand, Guthred's Dream is certainly not the only portion of the text which may have had an independent existence before being incorporated into the *Historia*, and this alone does not prove it to be a later addition to the text. Furthermore, *HSC* 33–4 was included in the text of the *Historia* as it existed in the lost Prior's Book, which we have speculated may have served as the exemplar for our surviving texts.[107] If the *Historia* was indeed composed in the second half of the eleventh century, and if O was copied in the last decade of that century from the Prior's Book, which had itself been produced earlier (although the Prior's Book text could have conceivably been the original archetype of the *Historia*), this leaves a relatively small window of opportunity within which material could have been added to the text. It therefore seems that if this final portion of the text was not part of the *Historia* as initially compiled by our author, it must have been appended shortly afterwards, either by our author himself or by a fellow scribe.

Summary

The stemma and date of production we choose thus depends on our conception of the structure of the *Historia* – are Alfred's dream and the eleventh-century charters integral to the text or later interpolations, and did the original text consist of *HSC* 1–13 and 19b–28, *HSC* 1–28 or *HSC* 1–32? If the Alfred-episode is an interpolation, then the traditional tenth-century date is probably correct, although later in the century seems more likely than

---

106 Paris, Bibliothèque Nationale, Fonds Latin 5362.
107 For the Prior's Book and its contents, see above, pp. 26–7.

Craster's date of shortly after 945; if only the eleventh-century charters are interpolated, then the text must date from after 1016, probably mid-century; and if neither group is interpolated, then the text must date from after 1031 and is probably a work of the later eleventh century. Each of these three models is plausible, and each has its weaknesses. To me, the key question is whether or not the Alfred-episode is a later interpolation. I am inclined to see it as an integral part of the second half of the *Historia*, and I believe that its intrusive appearance can be explained by the way in which the text was assembled from a variety of existing sources. I am therefore hesitant to accept the traditional date of production in the mid-tenth century, and am open to the possibility that the *Historia* is a product of the mid to late eleventh century. What is now required, it seems to me, is further stylistic analysis of the text to help determine whether it better fits a tenth- or eleventh-century context.

4. PREVIOUS SCHOLARSHIP AND THE PRESENT EDITION

Previous Scholarship

The *Historia de sancto Cuthberto* first received attention when it was edited and printed by Roger Twysden in his *Decem scriptores*, published in 1652. At this time only the Cambridge manuscript was known; Twysden's text thus concludes with King Edmund's visit to Cuthbert's shrine (*HSC* 28), since C terminates at this point. Twysden was followed by J. H. Hinde, who included the *HSC* in the first of two volumes devoted to Symeon of Durham and his sources, published by the Surtees Society in 1868.[108] Hinde made use of the Oxford manuscript (which had just been rediscovered by James Raine) as well as the Cambridge text and included modern identifications of place-names in his footnotes. Hinde's omission of the London manuscript was explained by Edmund Craster in his own description of Hale 114: 'Mr. Hodgson Hinde made inquiries for the Lincoln's Inn manuscript for the purposes of his edition, but was misinformed as to its contents and so made no use of it.'[109]

The most recent edition of the *Historia* was produced by Thomas Arnold for his own volumes on Symeon of Durham, published in the Rolls Series between 1882 and 1885.[110] Arnold was also limited to the Oxford and Cambridge manuscripts, and he relied on Hinde for his place-name identifications. Although Arnold's edition is generally agreed to be inferior to

---

108 Hinde, *Symeonis opera* I, 138–52.
109 Craster, 'Red Book', p. 507.
110 Arnold, *Symeonis opera* I, 196–214.

Hinde's, it is his edition which first subdivided the text into sections, a scheme which has generally been accepted by later scholars. In all three surviving manuscripts, the text is presented as a single unit without any internal divisions; Arnold divided the text into 33 sections or chapters. For the sake of convenience, I have followed Arnold's scheme in the present edition, adding one additional section-number (*HSC* 34) to cover the final section found in the London manuscript which Arnold, like Hinde, failed to consult.

It was Edmund Craster who rediscovered the third copy of the *Historia* during his study of Hale 114, sometimes called the 'Red Book of Durham'.[111] Although Craster referred to place-name variants from this third text in his later discussion of the *Historia* as evidence for the property holdings of the community of St Cuthbert, the complete text of L has never before been published. With his later study, 'The Patrimony of St Cuthbert', Craster focused scholarly attention on the *Historia* as a source of detailed information on property holding and set the tone for later examinations of the text.[112]

A number of authors have followed Craster in using the *Historia* primarily as a source of charters and leases relating to the property holdings of the community of St Cuthbert.[113] Place-name evidence from the *Historia* has also been used by local historians as a starting point for detailed regional studies within County Durham.[114] Other scholars have gone further, using the estates described in the *HSC* to develop a comparative model for land--holding in late Anglo-Saxon Northumbria.[115] Finally, the *HSC* represents a unique source for the history of the Viking kingdom of York, and reconstructions of the reigns of kings Guthred and Rægnald in particular rely heavily on it.[116] In short, the *Historia* has suffered from a piecemeal approach; it has been treated as a valuable source for historical information of various kinds, but little effort has been made to understand the text as part of a larger hagiographical tradition or to approach the work as a unified whole. Bertram Colgrave, in his study of the later miracle tradition surrounding St Cuthbert, has shown that later collections of Cuthbertine miracles developed around a core of four miracles which first appear in the *Historia*, and that later

---

[111] See Craster, 'Red Book'.

[112] See Craster, 'Patrimony'.

[113] C. R. Hart, for example, has included material from the *HSC* in his study of Northumbrian charters; see Hart, *Early Charters*, pp. 118–42. David Hall has extended Craster's research and carried out an exhaustive study of the community's property; see Hall, *Community of St. Cuthbert*.

[114] See, for example, Roberts, 'Rural Settlement in County Durham', and Clack and Gill, 'Land Divisions of County Durham'.

[115] Recent examples include Morris, 'Northumbria and the Viking Settlement'; Barrow, *Kingdom of the Scots*, ch. 1; Kapelle, *Norman Conquest*, ch. 3.

[116] See, for example, Smyth, *Scandinavian York*, chs. 3 and 6.

versions of these miracles seem to rely on the *HSC* as their only source.[117] To date, however, no one has attempted to systematically explore the sources from which the *HSC* in turn derived its information. This is one of the problems the present study is intended to address.

The Present Edition

Section numbers

Although the original text of the *Historia* was not subdivided into sections or paragraphs, I have for convenience retained the section numbers introduced by Arnold, with two additions. I have distinguished section 19b to mark the point at which the Alfred-episode concludes and the text returns to the activities of Abbot Eadred, and I have added section 34, the colophon from manuscript L.

Main text and variant readings

Given the fact that all three surviving copies of the text are remarkably similar and that none has been copied from either of the others, I have operated on the assumption that all three were probably copied directly from the same exemplar. It seems likely that this exemplar resided in a lost Durham volume called the Prior's Book.[118] I have attempted to reconstruct the text of this lost exemplar by generally preferring any reading which two of the three surviving texts have in common. In the small number of cases where all three texts differ or where only two texts contain the passage in question, I have assigned priority based on the overall trustworthiness of each text. Since O contains the lowest number of unique readings, suggesting that its scribe was the most careful of the three in copying from the common exemplar, I have regularly given preference to its readings. I have also generally given preference to C in the first eight sections which are missing in O; since L contains by far the highest number of unique readings, I have given preference to its readings only in cases where the other texts seem garbled, particularly in the case of place names.[119]

Unrecorded variants

There are a number of minor variations in spelling which have not been noted in the present edition. These fall into two general groups, the first of which contains variations which are phonetic in origin. The *æ-* dipthong is particularly problematic; in the two earlier manuscripts it is distinguished

---

117 See Colgrave, 'Post-Bedan Miracles', esp. pp. 308–9 and 321–4.
118 For a discussion of the Prior's Book see above, pp. 26–7.
119 For percentages of unique readings in each text see above, n. 88.

(regularly in O, less regularly in C) by an *e-caudata* or 'hooked *e*', while L does not distinguish it at all, simply replacing *æ* with *e*. The letters *i* and *y* and the letters *u*, *uu* and *w* are often used interchangeably in all three manuscripts. Spelling variations caused by double consonants, the aspirate *h* and confusion between *c* and the soft *t* (particularly common in L) have also been ignored.

The second group of unrecorded variants consists of differences caused by the misreading of Anglo-Saxon letter-forms. These confusions occur regularly in personal and place-names, which were apparently written in an Anglo-Saxon minuscule script in the original archetype of the text. Confusion between *d* and *th* is common, caused by difficulties in distinguishing the Old English eth from the letter *d*. This is further confused in C by the fact that the scribe generally uses the eth itself rather than *th*, occasionally placing it where a *d* is in fact called for. C also reproduces the Old English wynn by using the letter *p*, and occasionally reproduces the capital ash by using an ampersand-like sign. Other confusions in C include the Anglo-Saxon *s* mistaken for *r* (this also occurs twice in O), Anglo-Saxon *r* mistaken for *n*, and Anglo-Saxon *f* mistaken for *p*.[120]

---

[120] Misspellings in C caused by Anglo-Saxon letter-forms include *Commer* for *Commes* (*HSC* 21), *Wertun* for *Westun* (*HSC* 26), *Uffentun* for *Uffertun* (*HSC* 26), *Reophoppas* for *Reofhoppas* (*HSC* 26), and *Ileclip* for *Ileclif* (*HSC* 9). Misspellings in O include *Pudacestre* for *Wudacestre* (*HSC* 11, later corrected) and *Tere* for *Tese* (*HSC* 9 and *HSC* 24). Misspellings in L include *Werkeworde* for *Werkeworthe* (*HSC* 8) and *Dyrpente* for *Dyrwente* (*HSC* 24).

Text and Translation

List of Sigla: Surviving Manuscripts of the
Historia de sancto Cuthberto

C   Cambridge, University Library, Ff. 1. 27 (Durham or Sawley, s. xii²; provenance Sawley), pp. 195–202.

L   London, Lincoln's Inn Library, Hale 114 (Durham, s. xv¹), fols. 153r–159r.

O   Oxford, Bodleian Library, Bodley 596 (Durham, s. xi/xii; later provenance St Augustine's, Canterbury), fols. 203r–206v.

HISTORIA DE SANCTO CUTHBERTO

[a]Incipit historia de sancto Cuthberto et de commemoratione locorum regionumque eius prisce possessionis, a primordio usque nunc temporis.[a]

1. In Nomine Dei summi de sancto Cuthberto, et de commemoratione locorum regionumque eius[a] priscae possessionis, a primordio usque nunc temporis, hoc modo incipit.

2. In prima [a]sua iuuentute,[a] quando sanctus Cuthbertus erat uigilans super pecora domini sui [b]prope aquam quae uocatur Leder,[b] in spiritu orabat ad dominum, sicut ei mos erat semper ab infantia [c]sua et semper ei fuit[c] quam diu uixit cum hominibus. Erat autem[d] etiam sibi mos [e]semper intrare in frigidissimam[e] aquam secreto et [f]suo solo consilio.[f] Et hoc primum fuit miraculum sibi diuinitus ostensum, quod cum dormientibus sociis suis super pecora uigilaret[g] et in modum crucis positus oraret,[h] uidit animam beati Aidani Lindisfarnensis episcopi ab angelis in celis deferri. Et statim mane facto noluit amplius custodire pecora, sed domino suo reddidit et ad monasterium quod [i]Meilros uocatur iuit[i] et ad pedes sancti abbatis[j] Bosili cum magna deuotione cecidit, [k]et ei[k] quicquid uiderat de anima beati[l] episcopi diligenter indicauit, et[m] statim tonso et coronato capite monacus effectus est, et postea theoricam actualemque uitam usque in finem uitae suae bene custodiuit.

3. [a]Tunc sanctus abbas Boisil statim notam fecit regi Osuingio sanctam uisionem beati Cuthberti, et quod plenus esset spiritu sancto.[a] Tunc rex et omnes meliores Angli dederunt sancto Cuthberto omnem hanc terram que iacet iuxta fluuium Bolbenda cum his uillis: Sugariple, et Hesterhoh,[b] et Greatadun,[c] et Pacrestun,[d] et Cliftun, et Scerbædle, et Colwela,[e] et

a–a *rubricated; appears only in C*

1. a ipsius *L*

2. a–a iuuentute sua *L*
    b–b iuxta fluuium quod uocatur Lader *L*
    c–c *om. L*
    d *om. L*
    e–e sepe in frigidam intrare *L*
    f–f sui solius *L*
    g uigilare *L*
    h orare *L*
    i–i uocatur Mailros uenit *L*
    j sacerdotis et monachi *L*
    k–k eique *L*

l sancti Aidani *L*
m et et *L*

3. a–a Deinde sanctus Boisilus supradicte uisionis ordinem regi Oswigio aperuit. Et quia beatus Cuthbertus uere spiritus sancti templum ex sanctissime uite studio declaretur edocuit *L*
    b Hetteshoh *L*
    c Grstatadun *C*
    d Perstun *L*
    e Colpela *L*

THE HISTORY OF ST CUTHBERT

Here begins a history of St Cuthbert and a record of the places and regions of his ancient patrimony, from the beginning up to the present time.

1.   In the name of the highest God: [the history] of St Cuthbert and the record of the places and regions of his ancient patrimony, from the beginning up to the present time, begins in this way.

2.   In his earliest youth, when blessed Cuthbert was watching over his lord's flocks near the river that is called the Leader, he prayed in spirit to the Lord, as was his habit from infancy and continued to be for as long as he remained living among men. Moreover, it was also ever his custom to enter the coldest water in secret and at his own sole discretion. And this was the first miracle divinely granted to him, that while his companions were sleeping and he was watching over the flocks and praying, positioned in the shape of a cross, he saw the soul of St Aidan, bishop of Lindisfarne, being carried off to heaven by angels. As soon as morning had come, no longer wanting to tend the flocks, he returned [them] to his lord and went to the monastery called Melrose and fell with great devotion at the feet of saintly Abbot Boisil and diligently described to him everything he had seen concerning the soul of the saintly bishop, and immediately, with his head crowned in the tonsure, he was made a monk, and thereafter he faithfully observed both the contemplative and active ways of living to the end of his own life.

3.   Then saintly Abbot Boisil immediately made known to King Oswin [d. 651][1] the sacred vision of blessed Cuthbert, explaining that he was filled with the Holy Spirit. Then the King and all the English magnates gave to St Cuthbert all that land that lies near the river Bowmont, with these vills: Sourhope(?), Staerough, Old Graden, Pawston, Clifton, Shereburgh(?), Colewell, Halterburn, Thornington(?), Shotton, Kirk Yetholm and Mindrum.

---

[1]   This reference to King Oswin is clearly ahistorical; according to Bede, Oswin died eleven days before Aidan (*HE* III.14). The author seems to have confused Oswin with King Oswiu [d. 670]; this has been corrected by the scribe of L. For further discussion of this point see below, Commentary, *HSC* 3.

Eltherburna, et Thornburnum, et Sceotadun, et Gathan,[f] et Mynethrim. [g]Et ipse sanctus abbas, sub testimonio ipsius regis, monasterium Melros cum omnibus suis appendentiis, ut haberet illud proprium post diem obitus sui. Quo mortuo, idem sanctus Cuthbertus post eum abbas extitit et diu ibi uixit, uerbum Dei euuangelizans et multitudinem magnam baptizans.[g] Tandem [h]disponens arcius uiuere,[h] [i]inde exiuit et in quandam remotam insulam nomine Pharne[i] se contulit [j]et ibi per[j] nouem annos se quasi in carcere conclusit, pugnans contra[k] humani generis hostem [l]ne mens sua a Deo auerteretur, et ibi erat cum eo spiritus sanctus, sicut nunc est et semper erit.[l] In hac eadem insula [m]diu moratus est[m] sanctus [n]Aidanus episcopus,[n] [o]tempore Pendae regis[o] [p]filii Pybbindti regis,[p] quibus successit rex Osuingius.[q] [r]Eodem tempore defunctus rex Oswegius est, et[r] regnauit pro eo filius eius Egfrith. [s]Quo regnante,[s] Theodorus [t]archiepiscopus Eboracensis[t] et omnis [u]populus, communi consilio et una concordia, sanctam Cuthbertum fieri episcopum apud Hestaldesham acclamauerunt.[u] Ille uero [v]omnibus modis[v] renitebatur se peccatorem et episcopatu indignum asserens, [w]et se[w] in sua insula arcissime concludens [x]exemplo beati Gregorii pape, qui cum peteretur episcopus a Romanis fugit et non nisi per uim rediit, secundum illud euuangelicum, 'Omnis qui se exaltat humiliabitur, et qui se humiliat exaltabitur'.[x] Tunc rex Ecgfrith et [y]archiepiscopus Theodorus[y] [z]et omnis populus[z] congregata sinodo [a]communi consilio[a] decreuerunt, ut eum uellet nollet de[b] insula educerent et in episcopatu subrogarent. [c]Quod et factum est.

[f] Gethan *L*
[g–g] Eodem quoque tempore dederunt ei supradictum monasterium Mailros cum omnibus suis appendiens ut suum semper esset proprium, sed mortuo sancto sacerdote Boisilio, beatus Cuthbertus prepositi officio eidem prefuit monasterio et non solum monachis uiuendi norma extabat, sed et uerbum Dei circumquaque omnibus euangelisans, baptizando et exhortando, uite uias aperuit *L*
[h–h] arcius uiuere disponens *L*
[i–i] in remotam insulam quandam Farne nominatem *L*
[j–j] ibique *L*
[k] cotidie contra *L*
[l–l] ut coronam mereretur perennem *L*
[m–m] moratus est diu *L*
[n–n] presul Aidanus *L*
[o–o] Pende regis tempore *L*
[p–p] qui Pybbindri regis fuit filius *L*
[q] Oswigius *L*

[r–r] quo non multo post tempore defuncto *L*
[s–s] Cuius tempore *L*
[t–t] Eboracensis archiepiscopus *L*
[u–u] clerus cum populo sanctum Cuthbertum apud Hehstaldensem ecclesiam episcopum fieri communi consilio elegerunt *L*
[v–v] modis omnibus *L*
[w–w] seque *L*
[x–x] sicut beatus Gregorius Romanorum ita et ipse recusabat fieri presul Anglorum *L*
[y–y] Theodorus archepiscopus *L*
[z–z] cum populo uniuerso *L*
[a–a] pari consensu *L*
[b] ab *L*
[c–c] Igitur a sede sua et latibulis, multum lacrimans et ipso quoque rege et episcopo pariter plorantibus, detrahitur et ad uillam nomine Alna iuxta Eboracam ciuitatem deducitur *L*

And the saintly abbot himself, under witness of the same king, [gave] the monastery of Melrose with all its dependencies, so that he [i.e. Cuthbert] might have it as his own after the day of his [i.e. Boisil's] death. After he died, St Cuthbert succeeded him as abbot and long lived there, spreading the word of God and baptizing a great multitude. At length, deciding to live more strictly, he departed from there and took himself to a certain remote island called Farne and for nine years enclosed himself there as if in a prison, fighting against the enemy of humankind lest his mind be averted from God, and there the Holy Spirit was with him, as it is now and forever will be. The saintly bishop Aidan long dwelt on this same island in the time of King Penda, son of Pybba, whom King Oswin succeeded.[2] At the same time, King Oswiu died and his son Ecgfrith [r. 670–685] ruled in his place. During his reign, Archbishop Theodore of York and all the people, by common counsel and with one accord, acclaimed St Cuthbert to be bishop of Hexham. He, however, resisted this in every way, asserting himself to be a sinner and unworthy of the bishopric, confining himself most strictly on his island after the example of the saintly Pope Gregory who, when asked [to be] bishop by the Romans, fled and returned only under duress, in accordance with the Gospel passage: 'Everyone that exalteth himself shall be humbled, and he that humbleth himself shall be exalted'. [Luke XIV.11] Then King Ecgfrith and Archbishop Theodore and the whole people gathered in a synod decreed by common counsel that, whether he wished it or not, they would take him from the island and install him in the bishopric.[3] And so it was done. Seized

---

[2] According to Bede, it was Oswiu who defeated and succeeded both Oswin and Penda (*HE* III.14 and III.24), as L correctly states.

[3] Bede states that Cuthbert's election as bishop took place in the last year of King Ecgfrith's reign (*HE* 4, 27), which places it in the year 685.

Raptus enim a populo, iuxta Eboracam ciuitatem ad uillam que uocatur Alna deductus.[c] [d]Vbi accepto ab omnibus fidelitatis sacramento, ad Eboracam ciuitatem honorifice est perductus, et in ecclesia beati Petri apostoli[d] a Theodoro archiepiscopo est ordinatus. In qua ordinatione fuerunt septem episcopi: Ceadde et Cedde et quattuor alii sancti episcopi. [e]Eadem die Eata episcopus Lindisfarnensis et sanctus Cuthbertus,[e] communi consilio Ecgfrith regis et archiepiscopi et illorum septem episcoporum et omnium maiorum, sedes suas commutauerunt. Sicque Eata apud Helstaldesham[f] sedit; sanctus uero Cuthbertus, [g]propter priorem conuersationem,[g] Lindisfarnensem cathedram optinuit.

4. Et hic est Lindisfarnensis terrae terminus: a fluuio Tweoda[a] usque ad Warnedmuthe,[b] et inde superius ad[c] illum locum ubi haec aqua [d]quae uocatur[d] Warned oritur iuxta montem Hybberndune, et ab illo monte usque ad fluuium qui uocatur Bromic, et inde usque ad fluuium [e]qui uocatur[e] Till, et tota terra quae iacet ex utraque parte ipsius fluminis Bromic usque ad illum locum ubi oritur. Et illa terra ultra[f] Tweoda ab illo loco ubi oritur fluuius Edre ab aquilone usque ad illum locum ubi cadit in Tweoda, et tota terra quae iacet inter istum fluuium Edre et alterum fluuium qui uocatur Leder uersus occidentem, et tota terra quae iacet ab orientali parte istius aquae quae uocatur Leder usque ad illum locum ubi cadit in fluuium Tweoda uersus austrum, et tota terra quae pertinet ad monasterium sancti Balthere, quod uocatur Tinningaham,[g] a Lombormore usque ad Esce muthe.

5. Et rex Ecgfrith[a] et Theodorus archiepiscopus dederunt sancto Cuthberto in Eboraca ciuitate totam terram quae iacet a muro aecclesiae sancti Petri usque ad magnam portam uersus occidentem, et a muro aecclesiae sancti Petri usque ad murum ciuitatis uersus austrum. Dederunt etiam ei uillam quae uocatur Creca et tria miliaria in circuitu ipsius uillae, ut ibi [b]mansionem haberet[b] quociens ad Eboracam ciuitatem[c] iret uel inde rediret. Et ibi sanctus Cuthbertus congregationem monachorum posuit et abbatem ordinauit, et quia uidebatur parua terra, adiecit ciuitatem quae uocatur Luel, quae habet in circuitu .XV. miliaria, et in eadem ciuitate posuit congregationem sanctimonialium, et abbatissam ordinauit et scolas[d] constituit.

d–d Tempore transacto ad Eboracensum sancti Petri ecclesiam honorifice perductus et *L*

e–e Ordinatus fuerat multo ante Eata Lindisfernnensi ecclesie episcopus, sed *L*

f Hagestaldesham *L*

g–g quia ibi prius conuersatus era, *L*

4. a *regularly* Tueda *L*
    b Whrnamuthe *C*

c usque *L*

d–d *om. L*

e–e *om. L*

f in fluuium *L*

g Tiningham *L*

5. a *regularly* Ecgfrid *or* Ecgfridus *L*
    b–b haberet mansionem *L*
    c *om. L*
    d scolas ibi *L*

indeed by the people, he was taken to the vill which is called Alne, near the city of York. Having there accepted an oath of fealty from all, he was conducted honorably to York, and in the church of St Peter the apostle, he was ordained by Archbishop Theodore. There were seven bishops at this ordination: Chad and Cedd and four (*sic*) other holy bishops.[4] The same day Eata, bishop of Lindisfarne, and St Cuthbert, in common counsel with King Ecgfrith and the archbishop and those seven bishops and all the magnates, exchanged their sees. Thus Eata sat at Hexham and saintly Cuthbert, on account of his previous monastic life there, obtained the bishop's seat at Lindisfarne.

4.   And this is the boundary of the territory of Lindisfarne: from the river Tweed as far as the mouth of Warren Beck, and from there upwards as far as the place where Warren Beck rises next to Hepburn Hill, and from that hill as far as the river that is called Breamish, and from there as far as the river that is called Till, and all the land that lies on both sides of the same river Breamish up to the place where it rises. And that land beyond the Tweed from the place where the river Blackadder rises in the north as far as the place where it flows into the Tweed, and all the land that lies between that river Blackadder and another that is called the Leader towards the west, and all the land that lies on the east side of that water that is called the Leader as far as the place where it flows into the Tweed toward the south, and all the land that pertains to the monastery of St Balthere, which is called Tynningham, from the Lammermuir Hills as far as the mouth of the Esk.

5.   And King Ecgfrith and Archbishop Theodore gave to St Cuthbert in the city of York all the land that lies from the wall of the church of St Peter as far as the great gate towards the west, and from the wall of the church of St Peter as far as the city wall towards the south. They also gave him the vill that is called Crayke and three miles in circumference around the same vill, so that he might have a stopping-place there whenever he went to or returned from York. And St Cuthbert installed a congregation of monks there and ordained an abbot, and because it seemed a small territory, he added the city that is called Carlisle, which has a circumference of fifteen miles, and in the same city he placed a congregation of nuns, and ordained an abbess and established schools.

---

4   As Colgrave has pointed out, by this date Cedd and Chad would have been dead for twenty-one and fourteen years respectively; see Colgrave, 'Post-Bedan Miracles', p. 307.

6.   Postquam uero sanctus Cuthbertus suscitauit puerum a mortuis in uilla quae uocatur Exanforda,[a] dedit ei rex Ecgfrith terram quae uocatur Cartmel[b] et omnes Brittanni cum eo, et [c]uillam illam[c] quae uocatur Suthgedling[d] et quicquid ad eam pertinet. Hec omnia sibi a sancto Cuthberto commissa, bonus abbas Cineferth filius Cygings[e] sapienter ordinauit, sicut uoluit.

7.   Ea tempestate pugnauit Ecgfrid rex contra regem Merciorum Wulfhere filium Pendici, et ceso exercitu illius ipsum uicit et in fugam [a]uno tantum comitante puerulo conuertit.[a] Et hoc obtinuit per auxilium sancti Wylfridi, qui cum eo fuit, maxime uero per orationes sancti Cuthberti qui absens erat. Post hoc bellum dedit Ecgfrith rex sancto Cuthberto Carrum et quicquid ad eam[b] pertinet, et habuit eum in summa ueneratione quam diu uixit, ipse et tota sua cognatio, donec eo defuncto uenerunt Scaldingi et Eboracam ciuitatem fregerunt et terram uastauerunt.

8.   [a]Post hoc[a] succesit in regnum Ceolwulf filius Cuthwining, qui etiam se[b] sancto Cuthberto subdidit et, dimisso regno cum uxore pro amore Dei, se cum magno thesauro ad [c]monasterium Lindisfarnansem[c] contulit, barbam deposuit, coronam accepit, et sancto Cuthberto uillam nomine Werceworthe[d] cum suis appendiciis[e] [f]dedit. Et hii sunt termini istius uillae: ab aqua quae uocatur Lina usque ad Cocwuda, et inde usque ad ciuitatem que uocatur Brincewele, et a[g] Cocwuda usque ad Hafodscelfe[h] uersus orientem, et ab Alna usque in dimidiam uiam inter Cocwud et Alna.

9.   Hoc tempore obiit sanctus Cuthbertus et successit Ezred[a] episcopus, qui transportauit quondam ecclesiam olim factam a beato Aidano tempore Osuualdi regis [b]de Lindisfarnensi[b] insula ad Northam,[c] ibique eam reedificauit et illuc corpus sancti Cuthberti et Ceolwulfi regis transtulit, ipsamque uillam sancto confessori dedit cum duabus aliis uillis, Gedwearde [d]et altera Gedwearde[d] et quicquid ad eas pertinet, a Duna usque ad Tefegedmuthe, et inde ad Wiltuna, et inde ultra montem uersus austrum. Postea idem sanctus episcopus Ecgred edificauit aecclesiam apud uillam

---

6. [a] Eranforda *L*
    [b] Ceartmel *L*
    [c-c] illam uillam *L*
    [d] Suthgedluit *C*
    [e] Cygincg *L*

7. [a-a] conuertit uno tantum comitante puerulo *L*
    [b] eum *L*

8. [a-a] Cui *L*
    [b] de *L*
    [c-c] Lindisfernensem monasterium *L*

[d] *regularly* Werkeworde *L*
[e] *regularly* appendentiis *C*
[f] *O begins at this point*
[g] ad *C*
[h] Hfodscelfe *C*; Hafodscefe *L*

9. [a] Ecred *corrected to* Eadbertus *L*
    [b-b] Lindisfarnensis *C*
    [c] *regularly* Norcham *corrected to* Norham *L*
    [d-d] *om. L*

48

6.   After St Cuthbert raised a boy from the dead at the vill that is called *Exanforda*, King Ecgfrith and all the Britons with him gave him [i.e. Cuthbert] the territory of Cartmel, and the vill that is called Gilling(?) and whatever pertains to it. The good abbot Cyneferth son of Cygincg wisely governed all of these [places which were] committed to him by St Cuthbert, just as he [i.e. Cuthbert] wished.

7.   In that time King Ecgfrith fought against the king of the Mercians, Wulfhere son of Penda, and having cut down [his] army he vanquished him and put him to flight with only one small boy accompanying [him]. And he [i.e. Ecgfrith] obtained this through the aid of St Wilfrid, who was with him, but especially through the prayers of St Cuthbert, who was absent. After this battle King Ecgfrith gave Carham and whatever pertains to it to St Cuthbert and held him in the highest veneration as long as he lived, himself and all his kindred, until after his death the Scaldings [i.e. Danes] came and crushed York and devastated the land.

8.   After this Ceolwulf son of Cuthwining succeeded to the kingship [729–37], and he also submitted himself to St Cuthbert and, giving up his kingdom and his wife for the love of God, he took himself to the monastery of Lindisfarne with great treasure, shaved off his beard, accepted the crown [of the tonsure], and gave to St Cuthbert the vill named Warkworth with its dependencies. And these are the boundaries of that estate: from the river Line as far as Coquetdale, and from there as far as the town that is called *Brincewele*, and from Coquetdale as far as Hauxley to the east, and from the Aln to the middle of the road between Coquetdale and the Aln.

9.   At this time saintly Cuthbert died and was succeeded by bishop Ecgred [830–45], who transported a certain church, originally built by St Aidan in the time of King Oswald, from the isle of Lindisfarne to Norham and there rebuilt it, and translated to that place the body of St Cuthbert and [that] of King Ceolwulf and gave the vill itself to the holy confessor with two other vills, Jedburgh and Old Jeddart and whatever pertains to them, from Dunion Hill as far as Jedmouth, and from there to Wilton, and from there beyond the hill [Dunion?] towards the south. Afterwards the same saintly

quae uocatur Gegnford[e] et dedit eam sancto Cuthberto et quicquid ad eam pertinet, a flumine Tese[f] usque ad Weor, et a uia que uocatur Deorestrete[g] usque ad montem uersus occidentem, et ultra fluuium Tese tria miliaria uersus austrum et sex uersus occidentem. Et idem episcopus edificauit duas uillas, Ileclif[h] et Wigeclif ultra Tese, et Billingham[i] in Heorternesse,[j] et dedit eas sancto Cuthberto.

10.   Post haec Osbertus rex abstulit sancto Cuthberto duas uillas, Werceworthe et Tyllemuth. Sed post spacium unius anni, eripuit Deus ab eo uitam et regnum. Cui successit rex Ælle, qui bene promisit sancto confessori sed male egit. Nam abstulit ab eo Billingham, et Ileclif, et Wigeclif, et Creca. Et ideo ira Dei et sancti confessoris accensa est super eum. Nam Ubba dux Fresciorum cum magno Danorum exercitu in regnum eius uenit, et in sancto die palmarum apud Eboracam[a] ciuitatem applicuit. Quod cum audisset Ælle, qui[b] tunc propter odium sancti Cuthberti in Creca morabatur, cum magna superbia surrexit,[c] exercitum cum fratre suo Osberto congregauit, in hostem irruit, sed mox ira Dei et sancti confessoris perterritus, ceso exercitu fugit et corruit, uitamque et regnum perdidit, sicut olim contigit Sauli regi filio Cis, qui cum bene promisisset Deo et Samueli prophetae mentitus est et male egit, et iccirco in pugna contra Philisteos cum filio suo Ionathan et melioribus filiorum Israel cecidit. Iccirco caueant reges et principes ne mentiantur et ne quid auferant sancto Cuthberto, nec consentiant auferentibus. Quia, ut ait sanctus Paulus, 'Non solum peccant qui faciunt, sed qui consentiunt'.

11.   Priusquam Scaldingi uenirent in Anglicam terram, dederunt Ceoluulfus rex et episcopus Esdred sancto Cuthberto quattuor uillas:[a] Wudacestre,[b] et Hwitingham,[c] et Eadwulfincham,[d] et Ecgwulfincham,[e] et ecclesias harum uillarum[f] consecrauit[g] idem episcopus.

12.   Occiso igitur[a] Ælle et fratre eius Osberto, nullus de cognatione eorum regnauit,[b] obtinente hoc apud Deum sancto Cuthberto in quem multum peccauerant, quia Scaldingi omnes prope Anglos in meridiana et[c] aquilonari parte occiderunt, ecclesias fregerunt et spoliauerunt. Igitur

[e] Gegnford *corrected to* Geaignford C; Ganford *L*
[f] *regularly* Tesæ *O*
[g] Derestrete *L*
[h] Ileclip *C*
[i] Billigaham *C*
[j] Heorcernetsyre *C*

10. [a] *regularly* Æboracam *O*
    [b] *om.* L
    [c] surrexerunt (*for* surrexerit?) *L*

11. [a] scilicet *inserted after* uillas *O*
    [b] Uudecestre L
    [c] Hwitincham *O*; Bwitingham *L*
    [d] Eadwulfingham *L*
    [e] Ecgwulfingham *C*
    [f] duarum uillarum *L*
    [g] consecrauerunt *L*

12. [a] *om.* C
    [b] remansit *L*
    [c] et in *C*

bishop Ecgred built a church in the vill that is called Gainford and gave it to St Cuthbert with whatever pertains to it, from the river Tees as far as the Wear, and from the road that is called Dere Street as far as the hill toward the west, and beyond the river Tees three miles toward the south and six toward the west. And the same bishop built two vills beyond the Tees, Cliffe and Wycliffe, and Billingham in Hartness, and gave them to St Cuthbert.

10. After this King Osberht [d. 867] stole from St Cuthbert two vills, Warkworth and Tillmouth. But after the space of one year, God took from him [his] life and kingdom. He was succeeded by King Ælle, who made good promises to the holy confessor but acted badly. For he stole from him Billingham and Cliffe and Wycliffe and Crayke. And this ignited the wrath of God and of the holy confessor against him. For Ubba, duke of the Frisians, entered his kingdom with a great army of Danes and approached the city of York on Palm Sunday. When this news reached Ælle who, out of hatred for St Cuthbert, was then staying at Crayke, he rose up with great arrogance, gathered an army with his brother Osberht, and rushed upon the enemy; but soon, terrified by the wrath of God and St Cuthbert, [his] army having been struck down, he fled, and fell, and lost life and kingdom, just as once happened to King Saul the son of Kish who, when he had made good promises to God and the prophet Samuel, lied and acted badly, and in consequence fell in battle against the Philistines with his son Jonathan and the best of the sons of Israel.[5] Therefore let kings and princes beware lest they lie and lest they take anything from St Cuthbert, or consent to [others] taking. For as St Paul says, 'Not only do they sin who act, but they who condone'.[6]

11. Before the Scaldings [i.e. Danes] came to England, King Ceolwulf and Bishop Esred [Ecgred?] gave to St Cuthbert four vills: Woodhorn(?) and Whittingham and Edlingham and Eglingham, and the same bishop consecrated the churches of these vills.

12. So, with Ælle and his brother Osberht slain, none of their kinsmen ruled – this [favour] from God having been obtained by St Cuthbert, against whom they had sinned much – for the Scaldings slew nearly all the English in the southern and the northern part [of England], demolished and despoiled

5 Cf. Sam. I.9–15 and 31.
6 This is a paraphrase of Rom. I.32: '. . . they did not understand that they who do such things are worthy of death, and not only they that do them, but they also that consent to them that do them' ('. . . non intellexerunt quoniam qui talia agunt, digni sunt morte: et non solum qui ea faciunt, sed etiam qui consentiunt facientibus').

Halfdene[d] rex Danorum in Tinam intrauit et usque Wircesforde[e] nauigauit, omnia uastans et contra sanctum Cuthbertum crudeliter peccans. Sed mox ira Dei et sancti confessoris super eum uenit. Nam adeo[f] cepit insanire et[g] foetere, quod totus [h]exercitus suus eum[h] a se expulit, et longe in mare fugauit nec postea comparuit.

13.   Eo tempore sanctus Cuthbertus apparuit in nocte sancto abbati de Luercestre nomine Eaddred, talia ei firmiter iniungens: 'Vade,' inquit, 'super Tinam ad exercitum Danorum, et dic eis ut si uolunt mihi obedientes esse, ostendant tibi emtitium quendam puerum cuiusdam uidue nomine Guthred filium Hardacnut, et[a] summo mane [b]da tu et totus exercitus[b] pro eo precium uidue, et hora tercia super[c] precium, hora uero sexta duc eum ante[d] totam multitudinem ut eum [e]regem eligant,[e] hora uero nona duc eum cum toto exercitu super montem qui uocatur Oswigesdune[f] et ibi pone in brachio eius[g] dextero armillam auream, et sic eum omnes regem constituant. Dic etiam ei postquam rex effectus fuerit, ut det mihi totam terram inter Tinam et Wyrram, et quicumque ad me confugerit, uel pro homicidio uel pro aliqua necessitate, habeat pacem per triginta septem dies et noctes.' Hac uisione certus[h] et rationabili beati confessoris praecepto roboratus, ad barbarum exercitum sanctus ille abbas confidenter properauit, a quo honorifice exceptus eo ordine quo sibi iniunctum fuerat fideliter executus est. Nam et puerum illum inuenit, redemit, et magno tocius multitudinis fauore regem constituit, terram et pacem accepit. Tunc Eardulfus episcopus detulit ad illum exercitum et ad illum montem corpus sancti Cuthberti, super quod iurauit ipse rex et totus exercitus pacem et fidelitatem donec uiuerent, et hoc iusiurandum bene seruauerunt.

14.   Igitur exercitus ille quem Ubba dux Fresonum et Healfdena[a] rex Denorum in Anglicam terram adduxit in tres partes diuisus est; una Eboracam ciuitatem reedificauit, terram in circuitu coluit, et ibi remansit. Alia uero quae terram Merciorum occupauit, et tercia quae terram Australium Saxonum inuasit, per tres annos multa mala egerunt omnesque regii generis interfecerunt, praeter solum Elfredum[b] patrem Eadwardi regis, qui his tribus annis in Glestigiensi palude latuit in magna penuria.

d	Haldane *C*	d	ad *L*
e	Wyrcesforda *C*	e–e	eligant regem *L*
f	a Deo *O*	f	Oswigedune *C*; Oswiesdune *L*
g	ac *C*	g	quo *C*
h–h	eum exercitus suus *O*	h	certificatus *inserted after* certus *L*
13. a	a *L*	14. a	Healdena *C*; Halfdena *L*
b–b	tu da et exercitus totus *C*	b	*regularly* Alfredum *L*
c	legale *C*		

the churches. Then Halfdan, king of the Danes, entered the Tyne and sailed as far as *Wircesforda*, devastating everything and sinning cruelly against St Cuthbert. But soon the wrath of God and of the holy confessor fell upon him. For he began to rave and to reek so badly that his whole army drove him from its midst, and he was chased far across the sea and was never seen again.

13.   At that time St Cuthbert appeared in the night to the holy abbot of Carlisle named Eadred, firmly commanding him as follows: 'Go', he said, 'over the Tyne to the army of the Danes, and tell them that if they wish to be obedient to me, they should show you a certain young man named Guthred son of Hardacnut, the slave of a certain widow. In the early morning you and the whole army should offer the widow the price for him, and at the third hour [take him] in exchange for the price; then at the sixth hour lead him before the whole multitude so that they may elect him king, and at the ninth hour lead him with the whole army upon the hill which is called *Oswigesdune* and there place on his right arm a golden armlet, and thus they shall all constitute him king. Tell him also, after he has been made king, to give me all the land between the Tyne and the Wear and [to grant that] whoever shall flee to me, whether for homicide or for any other necessity, may have peace for thirty-seven days and nights.' Certain of this vision and strengthened by the reasonable command of the holy confessor, that holy abbot confidently hurried to the barbarian host, by which [he was] honorably received, [and] there he faithfully carried out [everything] in the order in which he had been commanded. For he found that boy, redeemed [him], and with the great support of the whole multitude constituted him king, received the land and the peace. Then bishop Eardulf brought to that host and to that hill the body of St Cuthbert, over which the king himself and the whole host swore peace and fidelity as long as they might live, and this oath they faithfully observed.

14.   Then that army which Ubba duke of the Frisians and Halfdan king of the Danes led into England was divided into three parts: one rebuilt York, cultivated the surrounding land and settled there. The second, however, which occupied the land of the Mercians, and the third, which invaded the land of the South Saxons, committed many crimes over the next three years and slew all those of royal stock excepting only Alfred [871–99], the father of King Edward, who for these three years hid in the Glastonbury marsh in great want.

15. Quadam igitur die cum totam familiam suam misisset piscatum, praeter uxorem et unum familiarem ministrum, peregrinus quidam affuit, ad eum intrauit, cibum peciit. Quod cum ex humana condescensione ei caritatiue largiri praecepisset, et nichil ibi esse ad totum diurnum uictum praeter unum panem et parum uini a ministro didicisset, Deo gratias egit et utriusque medietatem ei libenter impertiri iussit. Quod cum minister deuote impleuisset[a] et de gratiarum actione illius[b] domino suo retulisset, illuc[c] citissime reuersus panem quidem [d]et uinum integrum[d] repperit, illum uero non inuenit nec quomodo per paludes illas uenisset uel redisset, maxime cum ibi nauis non esset inuestigare potuit. Super hoc autem non parum admirante Alfredo et cogitante, ecce hora diei nona reuersa est piscatu familia cum tribus nauibus omnino plenis piscibus, asserentes plus illa die cepisse quam tribus annis quibus morati sunt in palude. Letus igitur et de hoc euentu sollicitus, diem illum[e] letius et habundantius solito transegit, factaque nocte cum uxore suo[f] dormitum iuit.

16. Illa uero [a]somno occupata[a] dum Elfredus de diurno euentu sollicitus uigilaret, ecce lumen magnum sicut sol refulsit, et in ipso lumine senex sacerdos infulatus nigris quidem capillis, habens in dextera manu euangelii textum auro gemmisque ornatum apparuit, [b]et sic eum uigilantem cum his uerbis[b] benedixit, et ab eo diligenter inquisitus quis esset et quomodo nominaretur: 'Care,' inquit, 'Elfrede, letus esto, ego sum ille cui hodie cibum praebuisti caritatiue, uocor autem Cuthbertus Christi miles. Esto robustus, et attende diligenter et laeto animo [c]quod tibi dixero.[c] Nam ego deinceps ero scutum tuum et amicus tuus et defensor filiorum tuorum, et nunc dicam [d]quid tibi[d] post hac[e] sit agendum. Surge summo diluculo, sona fortiter cornu tribus uicibus, ut inimici tui audiant et expauescant,[f] et circa horam nonam habebis quingentos[g] armatos, et hoc signo credas quod post septem dies habebis [h]Dei dono et meo auxilio[h] totum huius terrae exercitum apud montem Assandune in auxilio tuo paratum. Sicque contra hostes tuos pugnabis, et sine dubio eos[i] superabis. Post haec [j]esto letus[j] et robustus sine timore, quia Deus tradidit inimicos tuos in manibus tuis, et totam istam terram et regnum hereditarium, tibi et filiis tuis et filiis filiorum tuorum. Esto fidelis mihi et populo meo, quia tibi et filiis tuis data est tota Albion. [k]Esto iustus, quia tu es electus rex totius

---

15. [a]   implesset *C*
   [b]   illius de *L*
   [c]   *om. C*
   [d–d] integrum et uinum *C*
   [e]   istum *C*
   [f]   *om. L*

16. [a–a] occupata somno *L*
   [b–b] uigilantem *C*

[c–c] quam dixero tibi *C*
[d–d] tibi quid *L*
[e]   hoc *C*
[f]   expaliescant *O*
[g]   quingentos uiros *C*
[h–h] dono Dei et auxilio meo *L*
[i]   *om. L*
[j–j] letus esto *L*
[k–k] *om. L*

15. Then, on a certain day when he had sent his whole household fishing, except for [his] wife and one personal servant, a certain stranger appeared, came to him and asked for food. Therefore, out of human consideration, he charitably ordered [food] to be given to him; and [having] learned from the attendant [that] nothing was left there to eat for the whole day except one loaf and a little wine, he gave thanks to God and ordered half of each to be freely shared with him. When the attendant had faithfully done as he was told and had brought back the thanks of that person to his lord, he returned very quickly and discovered the bread and wine in fact whole, but he did not find that person nor could he discover how he might have come or gone through those marshes, particularly since he could see no sign of a boat there. While Alfred was marvelling and pondering not a little over this, behold at the ninth hour of the day his household returned from fishing with three boats completely filled with fish, claiming to have caught more on that day than during the three years they had spent in the marsh. Joyful therefore and moved by this event, he passed that particular day more happily and satisfied than usual, and when night came he went to sleep with his wife.

16. She was in fact occupied with sleep while Alfred remained awake, moved by the day's events, [when] behold, a great light shone like the sun, and within that light appeared an old priest wearing a bishop's insignia and with black hair, holding in his right hand a gospel-book ornamented with gold and gems. He blessed the wakeful one with these [following] words, and, asked by him respectfully who he might be and what his name was, he replied, 'Dear Alfred, be glad: I am the one to whom today you charitably gave food, and I am called Cuthbert, soldier of Christ. Be strong, and attend diligently and with a glad spirit to what I shall say to you. For henceforth I will be your shield and your friend and the defender of your sons, and now I will tell you what is to be done hereafter. Arise at dawn, sound [your] horn loudly three times so that your enemies may hear and be terrified, and by the ninth hour you will have five hundred armed men; by this sign believe that after seven days you will have, by God's gift and with my aid, the whole army of this land prepared to aid you at the hill of *Assandune*.[7] And so you shall fight against your enemies, and without doubt you will overcome them. Afterwards be joyful and strong without fear, since God has delivered your enemies into your hands, and likewise all this land, and [established] hereditary rule for you and your sons and the sons of your sons. Be faithful to me and to my people, for all Albion has been given to you and your sons. Be just,

---

7 There is at present scholarly disagreement over whether this *Assandune* is the modern Ashingdon (the traditional choice) or Ashdon, both in Essex. *Assandun* is given in the *Anglo-Saxon Chronicle* as the location of Cnut's crucial victory over Edmund in 1016 (*ASC* DEF 1016). The author of the *Historia* has confused *Assandun* with *Ethandune* (Edington in Wiltshire), the site of Alfred's victory over Guthrum (*ASC* 878).

Brittanniae.[k] Sit tibi Deus misericors, et ego [l]tibi sic[l] ero amicus,[m] ut nullus
aduersarius aduersum te possit praeualere.'

17.   [a]Et haec omnia acta sunt secundum hoc quod Spiritus Sanctus dixit
per os Dauid prophetae; 'Dominus a dextris tuis confregit in die irae suae
reges.' Et alibi, 'De fructu uentris tui ponam super sedem tuam.' Tunc
Elfredus gratias egit Deo et sancto Cuthberto propter misericordiam eorum et
perpetuam auxilium secundum hoc quod dixit Deus ad Dauid per os Samuelis
prophetae; 'Iurauit Dominus et non penitebit eum.' Et alibi, 'Filii tui et filii
filiorum tuorum sedebunt super sedem tuam.'[a] Sic uisitauit, confortauit,
docuit, iuuit[b] iste sanctus confessor Christi Cuthbertus Elfredum, sicut olim[c]
in Anglica historia legitur sanctus Petrus Eadwino regi pagano crucem
auream dextera gestans apparuit, se Petrum principem esse apostolorum
asseruit, coronam ostendit, et ut paganismum relinqueret praecepit, et sic
eum ubique uictorem futurum praedixit, sicut etiam Samuel Dauid regi fecit.
Deinceps Elfredus rex fuit fortis et letus, quia sciebat se ubique fore uictorem
quam diu uiueret, per donum Dei et auxilium patroni sui sancti Cuthberti.

18.   Itaque [a]facto mane[a] surrexit, ad terram nauigauit, cornu suo tribus
uicibus signum dedit, quo sonitu omnes amici eius sunt exaltati, inimici uero
humiliati. Itaque secundum uerbum Dei circa[b] nonam ipsius diei[c] horam
congregatis ad eum quingentis de melioribus et carioribus amicis suis;
publice narrauit quid praecedenti nocte uidisset et a sancto confessore
audisset et qualiter ab eo confortatus esset. Asseruit etiam illis quod per
[d]donum Dei[d] et auxilium sancti Cuthberti, cui deinceps deberent merito
obedire, hostes uincerent et terram hereditario iure obtinerent. Ammonuit
[e]etiam eos[e] ut secundum doctrinam beati Cuthberti fugerent auariciam,
inuidiam, longam iram, adulteria, periuria, homicidia et omnia mala, et[f] ut
essent Deo fideles, pacientes, humiles, hospitales, elemosinarii, misericordes,
modesti, et ut haberent inter se[g] sanctam fidem, et iusticiam, et ueritatem.
Ammonuit etiam filium suum Eadwardum qui ibi erat, quod si uellet esse
fidelis Deo et sancto Cuthberto, non ei esset timendum de inimicis suis. Tunc
secundum uerbum uiri Dei Elfredus [h]in hostes irruit,[h] eosque[i] superauit, et
regnum Brytanniae accepit, sanctaeque et iuste omnibus in commune bonus,[j]

l–l	sic tibi *C*	c	Dei *L*
m	amicus tuus *C*	d–d	Dei donum *L*
		e–e	eos etiam *C*
17. a–a	*om. L*	f	*om. O*
b	nunc *L*	g	sem *C*
c	olim ut *L*	h–h	irruit in hostes *L*
		i	eos quae *O*
18. a–a	mane facto *L*	j	bonis *C*
b	cura *L*		

for you are chosen King of all Britain. May God be merciful to you, and I shall be your friend so that no adversary may prevail against you'.

17.   And all these things were carried out as the Holy Spirit said through the mouth of the prophet David: 'The Lord at thy right hand hath broken kings in the day of his wrath', [Ps. CIX.5] and elsewhere, 'Of the fruit of thy womb I will set upon thy throne'. [Ps. CXXXI.11] Then Alfred gave thanks to God and St Cuthbert for their mercy and perpetual aid, as God said to David through the mouth of the prophet Samuel: 'The Lord hath sworn, and he will not repent', [Ps. CIX.4] and elsewhere, 'Thy children and their children shall also sit upon thy throne'. [Ps. CXXXII.12][8] Thus that holy confessor of Christ, Cuthbert, visited, comforted, instructed and assisted Alfred, just as once, as can be read in English history, St Peter appeared to Edwin the pagan king bearing a golden cross in his right [hand], asserted himself to be Peter prince of apostles, held forth a crown, commanded that [Edwin] relinquish paganism, and thus predicted that he would be victorious everywhere, just as Samuel did for King David.[9] Henceforth King Alfred was brave and joyful, for he knew he would be victorious everywhere as long as he might live, through the gift of God and the aid of his patron St Cuthbert.

18.   And so when morning came he arose, sailed to land [and] gave a signal on his horn three times, at which sound all his friends were uplifted while his enemies were downcast. Then, in accordance with the word of God, by the ninth hour of the same day five hundred of the best and dearest among his friends gathered around him; he publicly related what he had seen on the preceding night and [what] he had heard from the holy confessor and how he was comforted by him. He also asserted to them that, through the gift of God and the aid of St Cuthbert, whom they henceforth rightfully ought to obey, they would vanquish their enemies and obtain the land by hereditary right. He also admonished them that, according to the doctrine of the blessed Cuthbert, they should flee avarice, envy, enduring wrath, adulteries, perjuries, homicides, and all evils, and that they should be faithful to God, patient, humble, hospitable, generous, merciful, modest, and that they should preserve holy faith, justice and truth between one another. He also advised his son Edward, who was there, that if he wished to be faithful to God and St Cuthbert, he should not be afraid of his enemies. Then, in accordance with the word of the man of God, Alfred rushed upon his enemies and overwhelmed them and took over the rule of Britain [and was] virtuously and

---

8   The text of this psalm has been somewhat compressed; in full, it reads 'If thy children will keep my covenant, and these my testimonies which I shall teach them, their children also for evermore shall sit upon thy throne.' ('Si custodierint filii tui testamentum meum, et testamonia mea hæc quæ docebo eos, et filii eorum usque in sæculum sedebunt super sedem tuam.')

9   Cf. *HE* II.12. There a spirit appears to King Edwin and promises him victory, but is never identified as St Peter.

pauperibus et diuitibus, bonis et malis, amicis et inimicis, secundum euangelicum praeceptum.

19a. His et aliis quam plurimus uirtutibus insignitus, postquam intellexit[a] finem uitae sibi adesse, diu regnans et bona confectus senectute, uocauit [b]hunc eundum[b] filium suum Eadwardum et per eum transmisit sancto Cuthberto duas armillas et auream turibulum, monuitque eum diligenter ut amaret Deum et sanctum Cuthbertum, et speraret in eis sicut[c] ipse semper sperauit, et adhuc maxime sperabat. [19b.] Igitur antequam Deus hunc fidelem sibi regem de hac uita uocaret, addita sunt quaedam praedia aecclesiae sancti confessoris. Nam Ethred[d] supradictus abbas emit a praefato rege Guthred, et a Danorum exercitu qui sibi sub eo terram diuiserant, has uillas: Seletun, Horetun, duas Geodene, Holum, Hotun, Twilingatun, et eas sancto Cuthberto contulit.

20. Eodem quoque tempore bonus episcopus Eardulfus et abbas Eadred tulerunt corpus sancti Cuthberti de Lindisfarnensi insula et cum eo errauerunt in terra, portantes illud de loco in locum per septem annos, et tandem peruenerunt ad fluuium qui uocatur Derunt muthe et illud ibi in naui posuerunt, ut sic per proximum mare in Hiberniam transueherent. Tunc omnis populis eius qui eum diu erat secutus, dolens quod eripiebatur pius eorum patronus, stans in littore[a] flebat et ululabat, eo quod et ipsi relinquebantur captiui et captiuus [b]eorum abducebatur[b] dominus. Tunc Deus magnum miraculum ostendit pro amore dilecti sui confessoris. Horta siquidem in mari horribili tempestate maximae tres undae in nauim ceciderunt et statim, mirabile dictu, aqua illa in sanguinem est conuersa. Quo uiso episcopus et abbas ad pedes sancti uiri ceciderunt, et timore perterriti ad litus quamtocius [c]reuersi sunt,[c] et sanctum illud corpus ad Crecam detulerunt, et ibi a bono abbate nomine Geue caritatiue excepti quattuor mensibus manserunt, et inde sanctum corpus ad Cunceceastre[d] transtulerunt. Eo tempore obiit rex Elfredus et Eardulfus episcopus.

21. Tunc Eadwardus, diu[a] sapienter a patre edoctus, in regnum successit et illud sapienter rexit, et Cutheardus episcopalem cathedram apud Cunceceastre accepit. Eodem tempore Cuthardus episcopus fidelis emit de pecunia sancti Cuthberti uillam que uocatur Ceddesfeld et quicquid ad eam pertinet, praeter quod tenebant tres homines: Aculf, Ethelbyriht,[b] Frithlaf.[c]

19. [a]   intellexerunt (*for* intellexerit?) *L*
    [b–b]   om. *L*
    [c]   sicut et *C*
    [d]   Ethdred *C*; Edred *L*

20. [a]   licore *L*
    [b–b]   aducebatur eorum *C*

[c–c]   sunt reuersi *C*
[d]   Cuncecester *L*

21. [a]   domini *L*
    [b]   Edelbhrich *C*; Ethelbrith *L*
    [c]   Frithlac *L*

justly good to all in common, to poor and rich, good and bad, friends and enemies, according to the evangelical precept.

19a.   Distinguished by these and as many other virtues as possible, after he understood the end of his life to be drawing near, long having ruled and worn out by ripe old age, he summoned this same son Edward and through him conveyed to St Cuthbert two armlets and a golden thurible, and admonished him diligently to love God and St Cuthbert and to trust in them just as he himself had always trusted and very much continued to trust. [19b.] So then, before God called this faithful king to himself from this life, certain estates were added to the church of the holy confessor. For Eadred the above-mentioned abbot bought from the aforesaid King Guthred, and from the Danish host which under him had divided the land among themselves, these vills: Monk Hesleden, Horden Hall, Yoden and Castle Eden, Hulam, Hutton Henry, *Twilingatun*, and conferred them on St Cuthbert.

20.   Also at that time the good bishop Eardulf and abbot Eadred bore the body of St Cuthbert from the isle of Lindisfarne and wandered with it through the land, carrying it from place to place for seven years, and finally they arrived at the mouth of the river that is called Derwent [Derwentmouth], and there they placed it in a boat so that they might thus transport it across the adjoining sea to Ireland. Then all his [i.e. St Cuthbert's] people who had long followed him, mourning that their pious patron was being taken away, wept and wailed as they stood on the shore, because they themselves were captives being left behind and their captive lord was being abducted. Then God manifested a great miracle out of love for his beloved confessor. For a horrible storm arose on the sea, three very great waves fell on the ship and at once, marvellous to say, that water was turned to blood. Having seen this, the bishop and the abbot fell at the feet of the saint and, terrified with fear, they returned to the shore as quickly as possible and carried the holy body to Crayke, and there, having been charitably received by the good abbot named Geve, they remained for four months, and from there they translated the holy body to Chester-le-Street. At this time King Alfred died, as well as bishop Eardulf.

21.   Then Edward [899–924], long wisely taught by his father, succeeded to the kingdom and wisely ruled it, and Cuthheard [901–15?] accepted the episcopal seat at Chester-le-Street. At the same time the faithful bishop Cutheard bought with the money of St Cuthbert the vill which is called Sedgefield and whatever pertains to it, except what three men were holding: Aculf, Æthelbriht, Frithlaf. Over this nevertheless the bishop had sake and

Super hoc tamen habuit episcopus[d] sacam et socnam. Emit etiam idem episcopus de pecunia sancti Cuthberti uillam que uocatur Bedlingtun cum suis appendiciis: Nedertun, Grubbatwisle,[e] Cebbingtun,[f] Sliceburne,[g] Commes.[h] Tempore eiusdem Eadwardi regis Tilred abbas de Hefresham uillam quac uocatur Iodcnc Australcm cmit. Cuius dimidiam partem dedit sancto Cuthberto ut esset frater in eius monasterio, alteram apud Northam ut ibi [j]esset abbas.[j] Eodem tempore Bernardus[k] presbiter dedit uillam suam nomine Twilingatun[l] sancto Cuthberto ut esset frater in eius monasterio.

22.   His diebus Elfred[a] filius Birihtulfinci, fugiens piratas, uenit ultra montes uersus occidentem et quaesiuit misericordiam sancti Cuthberti et episcopi Cutheardi ut praestarent sibi aliquas terras. Tunc episcopus Cutheardus, pro caritate Dei et[b] amore sancti Cuthberti, praestitit illi has uillas: Esingtun, Seletun, Thorep, Horedene, Iodene, duas Sceottun,[c] Iodene Australem, Holum, Hotun,[d] Twilingtun,[e] Billingham cum suis appendiciis, Scurufatun.[f] Has omnes uillas sicut dixi prestitit episcopus Elfredo, ut sibi et congregationi fidelis esset et de his plenum seruicium redderet. Quod et fideliter fecit donec Regenwaldus rex uenit cum magna multitudine nauium, occupauitque[g] terram Aldredi filii Eadulfi, qui erat dilectus regi Eadwardo sicut et pater suus Eadulfus dilectus fuit regi Elfredo; fugatus igitur Aldredus in Scottiam iuit, Constantini regis auxilium quaesiuit, illum[h] contra Regenwaldum regem apud Corebricge in proelium adduxit.[i] In quo proelio, nescio quo peccato agente, paganus rex uicit[j] Constantinum, fugauit Scottos, fudit Elfredum sancti Cuthberti fidelem, et omnes meliores Anglos interfecit praeter Ealdredum et fratrem eius Uhtred.

23.   Quibus fugatis et tota terra superata, diuisit uillas sancti Cuthberti, et alteram partem uersus austrum dedit cuidam potenti militi suo qui uocabatur Scula, a uilla quae uocatur Iodene usque ad Billingham. Alteram uero partem dedit cuidam qui uocabatur[a] Onalafball, a Iodene usque ad fluuium Weorram. Et hic filius diaboli inimicus fuit quibuscunque modis potuit Deo et sancto Cuthberto. Quadam itaque die cum plenus inmundo spiritu, cum furore

[d] episcopus et *C*
[e] Grubba, Twisle *C*; Grubbatwise *L*
[f] Bedlingtun *C*; Cebbengtun *L*
[g] Scliceburn *L*
[h] Commer *C*
[i] Helfresham *L*
[j-j] abbas esset *C*
[k] Berrardus *O*
[l] Twinlingatun *C*; Twilingtun *L*

[b] et pro *C*
[c] Scotun *C*; Sceotton *L*
[d] Hotoun *L*
[e] Twinlingtun *C*
[f] Scrufatun *L*
[g] et occupauit *L*; occupauit *C*
[h] illumque *O*
[i] adduxerunt *L*
[j] uincit *C*

22. [a] *regularly* Alfred *L*   23. [a] uocatur *L*

soke. The same bishop also bought with the money of St Cuthbert the vill which is called Bedlington with its dependencies: Nedderton, Twizell(?), Choppington, West Sleekburn, Cambois. In the time of the same King Edward, Tilred abbot of Heversham bought from King Edward the township which is called Castle Eden. Half of it he gave to St Cuthbert so that he might be a brother in his monastery; the other [half he gave] to Norham, so that he might be abbot there. At the same time Bernard the priest gave his township named *Twilingatun* to St Cuthbert so that he might be a brother in his monastery.

22.   In these days Elfred son of Brihtwulf, fleeing pirates, came over the mountains in the west and sought the mercy of St Cuthbert and Bishop Cutheard so that they might present him with some lands. Then Bishop Cutheard out of devotion to God and out of love for St Cuthbert presented to him these townships: Easington, Monk Hesleden, Little Thorp, Horden Hall, Yoden, the two Shottons, Castle Eden, Hulam, Hutton Henry, *Twilingatun*, Billingham with its dependencies, Sheraton. All these townships, as I said, the bishop presented to Elfred, provided that he be faithful to him and the congregation and render full service for them. This he did faithfully until King Rægnald came with a great multitude of ships and occupied the territory of Ealdred son of Eadwulf [of Bamburgh],[10] who was a favourite of King Edward, just as his father Eadwulf had been a favourite of King Alfred. Ealdred, having been driven off, went therefore to Scotland, sought aid from King Constantine, and brought him into battle against King Rægnald at Corbridge. In this battle, I know not what sin being the cause, the pagan king vanquished Constantine, routed the Scots, put Elfred the faithful [man] of St Cuthbert to flight, and killed all the English magnates except Aeldred and his brother Uhtred.

23.   When they had fled and the whole land was conquered, he [i.e. Rægnald] divided the estates of St Cuthbert, and one part toward the south, from the township which is called Castle Eden as far as Billingham, he gave to a certain powerful warrior of his who was called Scula. The other part, however, from Castle Eden as far as the river Wear, he gave to a certain one who was called Onlafbald. And this son of the devil was an enemy, in whatever ways he was able, of God and St Cuthbert. Thus one day, while filled

---

[10] For the identification of these men as Ealdred and Eadulf of Bamburgh see Wainwright, 'Battles at Corbridge', p. 164.

intrasset ecclesiam beati[b] confessoris, astante episcopo Cutheardo et tota cogregatione: 'Quid,' inquit, 'in me potest homo iste mortuus Cuthbertus cuius [c]minae cotidie opponuntur?[c] Iuro per [d]meos potentes deos[d] Thor et Othan, quod ab hac hora inimicissimus ero omnibus uobis.' Cumque episcopus et tota congregatio genua flecterent ante Deum et sanctum Cuthbertum et harum minarum uindictam, sicut scriptum est, 'Mihi uindictam et ego retribuam;' ab[e] eis expeterent,[f] conuersus ille filius diaboli cum magna superbia et indignatione uoluit egredi. Sed cum alterum pedem posuisset[g] iam extra limen,[h] sensit quasi ferrum in altero pede sibi altius[i] infixum. Quo dolore diabolicum[j] [k]eius cor[k] transfigente corruit, suamque peccatricem animam diabolus in infernum trusit. Sanctus uero Cuthbertus, sicut iustum erat, terram suam recepit.

24. Tempore supradicti [a]Eadwardi regis[a] dedit Wulfheardus[b] filius Hwetreddinci[c] sancto Cuthberto uillam quae uocatur Bynnewalle. Eodem tempore Edred filius [d]Rixinci equitauit[d] uersus occidentem ultra montes et interfecit Eardulfum principem, eiusque uxorem rapuit contra pacem et uoluntatem populi, et ad patrocinium sancti Cuthberti confugit et ibi tribus annis mansit, cum pace colens terram sibi a Cuthardo episcopo et[e] congregatione prestitam, a Cuncaceastre usque ad Dyrwente fluuium, et inde usque ad Werram uersus austrum, et inde usque ad uiam quae uocatur Deorestrete[f] in occidentali et australi parte, et uillam super Tese quae uocatur Geagenforda[g] et quicquid ad eam pertinet. Hanc terram idem Edred cum fidelitate sancti Cuthberti tenuit et censum fideliter reddidit, donec supradictus Regenwaldus rex congregato iterum exercitu apud Corebrygce pugnauit, ipsumque Edred et maximam Anglorum multitudinem interfecit, et uictor effectus totam illam terram quam Edred tenuerat sancto Cuthberto abstulit, et dedit Esbrido[h] filio Edred et fratri suo Elstano[i] comiti, qui in hoc proelio robusti bellatores fuerunt. Tandem [j]ipse maledictus[j] rex cum filiis et amicis suis periit,[k] nichilque[l] de his quae sancto confessori abstulerat secum praeter peccatum tulit.

b	sancti *C*		b	Wulfear *C*
c–c	in me cotidie mine opponuntur *C*;		c	Hwetorddinci *C*; Huecreddinci *L*
	mine cotidie michi apponuntur *L*		d–d	Riuxinci (*or* Rinxinci)
d–d	potentes deos meos *C*			equitauerunt *L*
e	et ab *L*		e	et a *C*
f	expecterent *L*		f	Dorestræte *C*
g	potuisset *O*		g	Genforda *L*
h	lumen *L*		h	Asbrido *L*
i	*om. L*		i	Alstano *L*; Æltano *C*
j	diabolum *L*		j–j	maledictus ipse *C*
k–k	cor eius *C*		k	prout *L*
			l	nichil *C*
24. a–a	regis Edwardi *L*			

with an unclean spirit, he entered the church of the holy confessor in a rage, and with Bishop Cutheard and the whole congregation standing [there] he said, 'What can this dead man Cuthbert, whose threats are mentioned every day, do to me? I swear by my powerful gods Thor and Odin that from this hour I will be the bitterest enemy to you all.' When the bishop and the whole congregation knelt before God and St Cuthbert and begged from them vengeance for these threats, just as it is written 'Vengeance is mine and I shall repay',[11] that son of the devil turned away with great arrogance and disdain, intending to leave. But just when he had placed one foot over the threshold, he felt as if an iron bar was fixed deeply into the other foot. With this pain transfixing his diabolical heart, he fell, and the devil thrust his sinful soul into Hell. St Cuthbert, as was just, regained his land.

24.   In the time of the above-mentioned King Edward, Wulfheard son of Hwetreddinc gave to St Cuthbert the vill which is called Benwell. At the same time Eadred son of Ricsige rode westwards across the mountains and slew Prince Eardwulf, seized his wife, violating the peace and the will of the people, and fled to the protection of St Cuthbert and remained there for three years, peacefully cultivating the land presented to him by Bishop Cutheard and the congregation, from Chester-le-Street as far as the river Derwent, and from there as far as the Wear toward the south, and from there as far as the road which is called Dere Street to the west and south, and (also) the vill upon the Tees which is called Gainford and whatever pertains to it. The same Eadred faithfully held this land in fealty to St Cuthbert and faithfully rendered the assessment for it until the above-mentioned King Rægnald, having again gathered an army, fought at Corbridge and slew this same Eadred and a very great multitude of English, and being victorious seized all that land which Eadred held from St Cuthbert and gave it to Esbrid,[12] the son of Eadred, and to his brother Count Ælstan, who were staunch warriors in this battle. Finally this same accursed king perished with his sons and friends, and of the things that he had stolen from St Cuthbert he took away with him nothing except [his] sin.

---

11 Cf. Deut. XXXII.35: 'Revenge is mine, and I will repay them' ('Mea est ultio et ego retribuam').
12 Craster suggests that this should read 'Egbrid', assuming that the Anglo-Saxon *g* has been misread as *s*; see Craster, 'Patrimony', p. 191, n. 2.

25. Eo tempore Eadwardus rex, plenus dierum et confectus [a]bona senectute,[a] filium suum Æthelstanum[b] uocauit, eique regnum suum tradidit, et ut sanctum Cuthbertum diligeret et supra omnes sanctos honoraret diligenter inculcauit, notificans ei qualiter patri suo regi Elfredo in paupertate et in exilio misericorditer subuenisset et qualiter eum contra omnes hostes uiriliter iuuisset, et quomodo sibimet ipsi in omnibus necessitatibus suis euidentissime promptissimus semper adiutor fuisset. Qua ammonitione facta, feliciter obiit.

26. Igitur Æthestanus rex magnum exercitum de australi parte eduxit et uersus aquilonalem plagam in Scotiam illum secum trahens, ad oratorium sancti Cuthberti diuertit, eique regia munera dedit, et inde hoc [a]subscriptum testamentum[a] composuit et ad caput sancti Cuthberti posuit.

[b]Karta Regis Æthelstani.[b]

[c]In Nomine Domine Nostri Iesu Christi.[c] Ego Æthelstanus rex do sancto Cuthberto hunc textum[d] euangeliorum, ·II· casulas, et ·I· albam et ·I· stolam cum manipulo, et ·I· cingulum, et ·III· altaris cooperimenta, et ·I· calicem argenteum, et ·II· patenas, alteram auro paratam alteram greco opere[e] fabrefactam, et ·I· turibulum argenteum, et ·I· crucem auro et ebore artificiose paratam, et ·I· regium pilleum auro textum, et ·II· tabulas auro et argento fabrefactas, et ·II· candelabra argentea auro parata, et [f]·I· missalem,[f] et ·II· euangeliorum textus auro et argento ornatos, et ·I· sancti Cuthberti uitam metrice et prosaice scriptam, et ·VII· pallia, et ·III· cortinas, et ·III· tapetia, et ·II· coppas argenteas cum cooperculis, et ·IIII· magnas campanas, et ·III· cornua auro et argento fabrefacta, et ·II· uexilla, et ·I· lanceam, et ·II· armillas aureas, et meam uillam dilectam Wiremuthe Australem cum suis appendiciis, id est Westun,[g] Uffertun,[h] Sylceswurthe, duas Reofhoppas,[i] Byrdene, Sæham,[j] Sætun,[k] Daltun, Daldene, Heseldene. Hec omnia do sub Dei et Sancti Cuthberti testimonio, ut si quis inde aliquid abstulerit dampnetur in die iudicii cum Iuda traditore et trudatur in ignem eternum qui paratus[l] est diabolo et angelis eius.

27. Impleuit etiam praedictas coppas pecunia optima, et iussu ipsius obtulit totus exercitus eius sancto Cuthberto ·XII· hundred et eo amplius. Fratrem uero suum Eadmundum, de sanctitate et fideli patrocinio sancti

25. [a–a] senectute bona *L*
  [b] *regularly* Ethelstanum *O; regu-*
    larly Athelstanum *L*

26. [a–a] scriptum testamento *C;*
    testamentum *L*
  [b–b] *rubricated; appears only in C*
  [c–c] *capitalized in O; underlined in L*
  [d] estum *O*

[e] *om. L*
[f–f] missalem ·I· *L*
[g] Wertun *C*
[h] Ussentun *corrected to* Uffentun *C*
[i] Reophoppas *C*
[j] Saham *L*
[k] Setun *O;* Satun *L*
[l] praeparatus *C*

25. At that time King Edward, full of days and worn down by ripe old age, summoned his son Æthelstan, handed his kingdom over to him, and diligently instructed [him] to love St Cuthbert and honour him above all saints, revealing to him how he had mercifully succoured his father King Alfred in poverty and exile and how he had boldly aided him against all enemies, and in what way he had always very clearly come most promptly as his continual helper whenever there was need. After making this admonition, he happily died.

26. Therefore, while King Æthelstan [924–39] was leading a great army from the south to the northern region [of Britain], taking it to Scotland, he made a diversion to the church of St Cuthbert and gave royal gifts to him, and then composed this signed testament and placed it at St Cuthbert's head.

King Æthelstan's Charter

In the name of our Lord Jesus Christ. I, King Æthelstan, give to St Cuthbert this gospel-book,[13] two chasubles, and one alb, and one stole with maniple, and one belt, and three altar-coverings, and one silver chalice, and two patens, one finished with gold, the other of Greek workmanship, and one silver thurible, and one cross skilfully finished with gold and ivory, and one royal headdress woven with gold, and two tablets crafted of silver and gold, and two silver candelabra finished with gold, and one missal, and two gospel-books ornamented with gold and silver, and one life of St Cuthbert written in verse and in prose,[14] and seven palls, and three curtains, and three tapestries, and two silver cups with covers, and four large bells, and three horns crafted of gold and silver, and two banners, and one lance, and two golden armlets, and my beloved vill of Bishop Wearmouth with its dependencies, namely *Westun*, Offerton, Silksworth, the two Ryhopes, Burdon, Seaham, Seaton, Dalton-le-Dale, Dawdon, Cold Hesledon. All these I give under witness of God and St Cuthbert, so that if anyone steals anything there, let him be damned on the Day of Judgement with the traitor Judas and be thrust 'into everlasting fire which was prepared for the devil and his angels'. [Matt. XXV.41]

27. He also filled the afore-mentioned cups with the best coin, and at his order his whole army offered St Cuthbert twelve hundred [shillings?] and more. Then he fraternally instructed his brother Edmund, who had already

---

13 'This book' is generally assumed to be London, British Library, Cotton Otho B.ix, a gospel book which contained a donor-portrait apparently showing King Æthelstan presenting a book to St Cuthbert, as well as two Old English inscriptions describing the King's gifts to the saint. For further discussion, see below, Commentary, *HSC* 26.

14 The 'life of St Cuthbert written in verse and prose' listed here has been identified as Cambridge, Corpus Christi College 183. For a complete discussion of this volume see Rollason, 'St Cuthbert and Wessex'.

confessoris diligenter prius[a] edoctum, fraterne commonuit[b] ut si quid sinistri sibi in hac expeditione eueniret, corpus suum sancto Cuthberto referret et ei illud in die iudicii [c]Deo repraesentandum[c] commendaret. Post haec abiit, feliciter pugnauit, prospere rediit, sapienter[d] multis annis postea regnauit, [e]tandem feliciter obiit.[e]

28.   Eo[a] defuncto, [b]Eadmundus frater eius[b] in regnum successit, magnum [c]rursus exercitum[c] congregauit et in Scotiam properauit. In eundo tamen ad oratorium sancti Cuthberti diuertit, ante sepulchrum eius genua flexit, preces fudit, se et suos Deo et sancto confessori commendauit, exercitus sexaginta libras obtulit, ipse uero manu propria ·II· armillas aureas et ·II· pallia greca supra sanctum corpus posuit, pacem uero et legem quam unquam [d]habuit meliorem[d] omni terrae sancti Cuthberti dedit, datam confirmauit,[e] [f]et factus quasi alter Abraham, qui properans in hostes panem et uinum Melchisedeh obtulit;[f] finita oratione, multociens se et totum exercitum beato confessori commendans, abiit.[g]

29.   [a]IN NOMINE Dei summi et indiuidue Trinitatis.[a] Ego Styr filius Ulfi impetraui a domino meo Ethelredo[b] rege ut daret sancto Cuthberto uillam quae uocatur Dearthingtun[c] cum saca et socna,[d] et ego emi propria pecunia et dedi sancto Cuthberto[e] ·IIII· carrucatas[e] terrae in Cingresclife,[f] et ·IIII· in Cocertune, et ·IIII· in Halhtune, et ·IIII· in Northmannabi, et ·II· in Ceattune cum saca et socna, et ·II· in Lummalea, sub testimonio Ethelredi regis, [g]et Elfrici[g] archiepiscopi Eboracensis, et Alduni episcopi Lindispharnensis, et Alfwoldi abbatis qui sub episcopo erat, et illorum omnium principum qui ea die in Eboraca ciuitate cum rege fuerunt.[h] Quod si quis de his aliquid sancti confessoris abstulerit, recipiat hanc maledictionem in die iudicii: 'Discedite a me maledicti in ignem aeternum.'

30.   Item Snaculf filius Cytel dedit hanc terram sancto Cuthberto: Brydbyrig, Mordun, et Socceburg, et Grisebi, cum saca et socna.

31.   Hae sunt terrae quas Aldhun episcopus et tota congregatio sancti Cuthberti prestitit his tribus, [a]Ethred eorle,[a] et Northman eorle, et Uhtred

27. [a]   proprius *C*
    [b]   communuit *O*
    [c–c] de praesentandum *C*
    [d]   *om. L*
    [e–e] *om. L*

28. [a]   Quo *C*
    [b–b] frater eius Eadmundus *L*
    [c–c] exercitum rursus *C*
    [d–d] meliorem habuit *C*
    [e]   confirmabit *C*
    [f–f] *om. L*

[g]   *C ends at this point*

29. [a–a] *om. L*
    [b]   *regularly* Adelredo *L*
    [c]   Dearningtun *L*
    [d]   *regularly* socne *L*
    [e–e] ·III· carrucas *L*
    [f]   Cingcesclife *O*
    [g–g] Wlstani *L*
    [h]   fuerant *L*

31. [a–a] Edred corle *L*

been informed of the sanctity and faithful patronage of the holy confessor, that if anything sinister should befall him on this expedition to return his body to St Cuthbert and commend it to him for presentation to God on the Day of Judgement. After this he departed, fought happily, returned success-fully, ruled wisely for many years afterwards [and] at last died happily.

28.   When he died his brother Edmund [939–46] succeeded to the kingdom, again gathered a great army and hastened to Scotland. On the way, however, he made a diversion to the church of St Cuthbert, knelt before his tomb, poured out prayers, and commended himself and his [men] to God and the holy confessor; the army offered sixty pounds, while he himself with his own hand placed two golden armlets and two Greek palls upon the holy body, granted peace and law better than any it ever had to the whole territory of St Cuthbert, confirmed the grant, and became like another Abraham, who as he hastened toward the enemy offered to Melchisedek bread and wine.[15] When he finished [his] prayer, having commended himself and his whole army many times to the holy confessor, he departed.

29.   IN THE NAME of God most high and the indivisible Trinity. I, Styr son of Ulf, have obtained from my lord King Æthelred [978–1016] that he should give to St Cuthbert the vill which is called Darlington, with sake and soke, and I have bought with my own money and given to St Cuthbert four carucates of land at High Coniscliffe, and four at Cockerton, and four at Haughton-le-Skerne, and four at *Northmannabi*, and two at Ketton with sake and soke, and two at Great Lumley, under witness of King Æthelred and Ælfric archbishop of York, and Aldhun bishop of Lindisfarne, and Abbot Ælfwold who was under the bishop, and all their magnates who were there that day in York with the King. If anyone seizes any of these [lands] of the holy confessor, may he receive this curse on the Day of Judgement: 'Depart from me, ye cursed, into everlasting fire'. [Matt. XXV.41]

30.   Snaculf son of Cytel likewise gave this land to St Cuthbert: Bradbury, Mordon, Sockburn, and Girsby, with sake and soke.

31.   These are the lands which Bishop Aldhun [990–1018] and the whole congregation of St Cuthbert presented to these three, Earl Ethred, Earl

---

15 Cf. Gen. XIV.18–19, although in fact it is Melchizedek who offers bread and wine to Abraham.

eorle: Gegenford, Queorningtun, Sliddewesse, Bereford, Stretford,[b] Lyrtingtun, Marawuda, Stantun, Stretlea,[c] Cletlinga,[d] Langadun, Mortun, Persebrigce, Alclit ·II·, Copland, Weardseatle,[e] Bynceastre,[f] Cuthbertestun, Thiccelea,[g] Ediscum, Wudutun,[h] Hunewic, Neowatun, Healme.[i] Quicumque de his aliquid abstulerit sancto Cuthberto pereat in dic iudicii.

32.   Item Cnut rex dedit sancto Cuthberto tempore Eadmundi episcopi, sicut ipsemet[a] tenuit cum saca et socna, uillam quae uocatur Standropa[b] cum suis appendiciis: Cnapatun, Scottun, Raby, Wacarfeld, Efenwuda, Alclit, Luteringtun, Elledun, Ingeltun, Thiccelea,[c] et Middeltun. Quisquis aliquid de his a sancto Cuthberto auerterit, auertatur Deus ab illo. Item Cnut rex dedit sancto Cuthberto tempore Eadmundi[d] episcopi Bromtun cum saca et socna.

33.   Hoc est Dei et sancti Cuthberti miraculum ualde animaduertendum[a] et magnificandum, quod aliquando Scotti cum innumerabili multitudine Tuidam fluuium transierunt et terram sancti Cuthberti uastauerunt, et Lindisfarnense monasterium nunquam prius[b] uiolatum spoliauerunt. Quo audito Guthred[c] rex, pro uindicta sancti confessoris illuc parua admodum manu properauit, eisque iam extrema parte diei in loco qui dicitur Mundingedene occurrit. Et ideo bellum non est inceptum. Nocte uero subsecuta cum rex Guthred multum perterritus et anxiatus, eo quod ipse paruissimum hostes uero qui iam in manibus erant maximum haberent[d] exercitum, et sic nec pugnare nec posset[e] fugere, prae nimia et uaria cura obdormisset, ecce miles Christi Cuthbertus ei manifeste apparuit et nimis exanimatum his uerbis animauit. 'Ne timeas,' inquit, 'quia ego tecum sum neque difidas paucitati militum, quia hostes mei adhuc uiui iam coram Deo sunt mortui, nec poterunt tibi resistere qui pacem Dei et meam non timuerunt uiolare. Facto mane surge uelociter, irrue in eos confidenter, quia mox in primo conflictu terra aperietur et uiuos in infernum demittet.' His dictis abscessit, rex uero euigilauit. Exiliens itaque exercitum conuocauit, omnia haec omnibus[f] puplice narrauit, moxque facto mane in hostes irruit, sed[g] secundum uiri Dei uerbum eos mox in primo conflictu uiuos terra dehiscente,

[b] Strecforde *L*
[c] Streclea *L*
[d] Cleclinga *L*
[e] Weardsecle *L*
[f] Bincestre *L*
[g] Ticcelea *L*
[h] Wudetun *L*
[i] Helme *L*

32. [a] ipse emit *L*
[b] Standrope *L*

[c] Ticcelea *L*
[d] prefati *L*

33. [a] anima aduertendum *L*
[b] *om. L*
[c] Guthreth *O*
[d] habent *L*
[e] *om. L*
[f] *om. L*
[g] et *inserted after* sed *L*

Northman and Earl Uhtred: Gainford, Whorlton, Sledwich, Barforth, Startforth, Lartington, Marwood Green, Stainton, Streatlam, Cleatlam, Langton, Morton Tinmouth, Piercebridge, Bishop Auckland and West Auckland, Copeland, *Weardseatle*, Binchester, St Andrew Aucklad (?), Thickley, Escombe, Witton-le-Wear, Hunwick, Newton Cap, Helme Park. Whoever seizes from St Cuthbert any part of these, may he perish on the Day of Judgement.

32.   King Cnut [1017–35] likewise gave to St Cuthbert in the time of Bishop Edmund, just as he himself had held it, with sake and soke, the vill that is called Staindrop with its dependencies: *Cnapatun*, Shotton, Raby, Wackerfield, Evenwood, West Auckland, Lutterington Hall, Old Eldon, Ingleton, Thickley and Middleton House (?). Whoever diverts any part of these from St Cuthbert, may God be averted from him. In the time of Bishop Edmund, King Cnut also gave to St Cuthbert Brompton with sake and soke.

33.   This is a miracle of God and St Cuthbert greatly to be heeded and praised, [namely] that once the Scots crossed the Tweed with an innumerable multitude and devastated the land of St Cuthbert and despoiled the monastery of Lindisfarne, which had never before been violated. When King Guthred heard of this, in order to avenge the holy confessor he hastened thither with just a small company and encountered them at the end of the day at the place that is called *Mundingedene*. And thus [because of darkness] the battle was not begun. But during the night which followed, King Guthred was much terrified and anxious because he had a very small army while his enemies, who were at close quarters, had a very large one, and thus he could neither fight nor flee: when he fell asleep in the face of many and various cares, behold Cuthbert the soldier of Christ plainly appeared to him and cheered the greatly despairing king with these words. 'Do not fear', he said, 'for I am with you, nor despair at the fewness of [your] soldiers, for my enemies, [although] still alive, are already dead in the eyes of God, nor will they, who did not fear to violate God's peace and mine, be able to resist you. When morning comes, arise quickly and rush upon them confidently, for then at the first clash the earth will be opened up and will let them drop alive into Hell'. Having said these [words], he departed and the king awoke. And so, springing up, he summoned the army, described all this openly to everyone, and as soon as morning came rushed upon the enemy, but in accordance with the word of the man of God he did not come upon them, [for they were] swallowed alive by the gaping earth in the first clash; the ancient miracle, when

absortos non inuenit, renouato ibi mirabiliter antiquo miraculo quando aperta est terra et deglutiuit Dathan et operuit super congregationem Abyron.[h]

34. Prouide rex tantis Dei magnaliis exhilaratus exercitu suo collaudante, hanc sancto legem constituit confcssori Cuthberto ut si quis ei terram daret, uel si pecunia ipsius aliqua terra emeretur, nullus ius aliquod super eam haberent preter eum, sed cum saca et socna cuiuscunque prius esset sua postmodum perpetuo foret. Et siquis quoquomodo infringere moliretur, eterno anathemate damnaretur.

[h]   *O ends at this point*

'the earth opened and swallowed up Dathan, and covered the congregation of Abiron', [Ps. CVI.17] was wonderfully repeated there.

34.   The king, encouraged by such great deeds of God, with his army joining in praise, circumspectly established this law for the holy confessor Cuthbert: that if anyone should give land to him, or if any land should be bought with his own money, no one should have any right over it except him, but it should be his forever afterward, with sake and soke, whosoever's it may have been before. And if anyone were to attempt in any way to infringe [on this], he would be damned with eternal anathema.

COMMENTARY

HSC 1 *Introduction*

This single-sentence introduction, which places at least as much emphasis on St Cuthbert's patrimony as on the saint himself, accurately sets the tone for the *Historia* as a whole. As Gransden has observed, such a concern for the rights and possessions of a saint's see or monastery is particularly typical of saints' lives written in the late eleventh century.[1]

HSC 2 *Cuthbert's Entry into Monasticism*

Cuthbert's vision of Aidan's death is described in both the anonymous *Vita Cuthberti* (*VCA* I.5) and in Bede's (*VCB* 4). The *VCA* places the event in the hills near the river Leader, while Bede simply places it in the distant mountains. Both sources depict Cuthbert as a pious youth and describe how, after he became a monk, Cuthbert would spend nights praying in the cold sea (*VCA* II.3; *VCB* 10); neither mentions a habit of cruciform prayer. Cuthbert's entry into monastic life is described in *VCA* II.1–2, where he apparently enters Ripon, and *VCB* 6, where he enters Melrose. Bede explains that some years after his entry into Melrose, Cuthbert was appointed guestmaster at the newly founded monastery of Ripon (*VCB* 7); this would seem to explain the discrepancy in the *Anonymous Life*. Bede dates Aidan's death, and thus Cuthbert's entry into the monastic life, to 651 (*HE* III.14). According to Bede, Boisil was actually prior of Melrose under Abbot Eata (*HE* IV.27); *HSC* L follows Bede at this point by describing Boisil as 'sacerdos et monachus' rather than 'abbas' (*VCB* 6).

HSC 3 *King Oswin*

Oswin, king of Deira, is described by Bede as a devout ruler and friend of St Aidan. He was betrayed and put to death by Oswiu, king of Bernicia, in 651; Aidan himself died eleven days later (*HE* III.14). Oswiu thereby became king of all Northumbria, and further consolidated his rule by defeating Penda, king of Mercia, in 655 (*HE* III.24); he ruled until 670. The *Historia*'s description of a meeting between Boisil and Oswin to discuss Cuthbert's vision of St Aidan's ascent into heaven, and Oswin's subsequent grant of land to Cuthbert, is thus clearly ahistorical, since Oswin predeceased Aidan. Further-

---

[1] See Gransden, *Historical Writing*, p. 69; Gransden herself nevertheless accepts the traditional tenth-century date for the *Historia*. For further discussion of related texts, see above, pp. 12–14.

more, the lands given to Cuthbert in this episode lay along the Bowmont Water, deep within Bernicia and outside of King Oswin's territory. It thus seems clear that there has been some confusion between King Oswin and King Oswiu; it is Oswiu who was alive at the time, and the Bowmont Water lands lay within his kingdom. Furthermore, the late eleventh-century *Cronica monasterii Dunelmensis* states that King Ecgred 'confirmed by royal authority what his father Oswiu had given [to St Cuthbert], namely that [land] which lies along the Bowmont Water' (*CMD*, lines 2–4). Finally, manuscript L of the *Historia* makes no mention of Oswin, and instead refers to King Oswiu throughout.[2]

It is therefore tempting to assume that the scribe of C simply mistook *Osuigius* for *Osuingius* in *HSC* 3. I am, however, reluctant to do this. First, such an error would have had to take place not once but twice, since Oswin is metioned twice in C, once at the beginning of *HSC* 3 and once near the middle. The second *Osuingius* occurs only one line above an *Oswegius* ('Oswiu'), which would suggest that our scribe knew how to distinguish between the two names. The inclusion of Oswin in *HSC* 3[C] also makes sense from a textual point of view. The second mention of Oswin occurs just before a reference to the death of King Oswiu, and the transitional phrase between them is *eodem tempore*, 'at the same time'. This would only make sense if the names refered to two different kings. Finally, from a strictly narrative point of view, it makes sense that our author would choose Oswin, who had a close relationship with St Aidan, to be the king in this episode. The point of the story, here as throughout the *Historia*, is to link a miracle of St Cuthbert (in this case, his miraculous vision of St Aidan) with a grant of land to his community, and chronological accuracy is secondary to this goal.

The Bowmont Water Grant

Craster, who followed manuscript L and ascribed this grant to King Oswiu, observed that 'the tale [in the *HSC*] is quite unhistorical, but the list of vills which formed the gift does read like a mutilated version of a genuine land-boc . . . Accepting the reality of the gift, one is left to guess at the real recipient.'[3] If the Bowmont Water grant is as early as the seventh century, it must, as Craster assumed, have originated with Oswiu rather than Oswin, since the latter never controlled Bernicia, where the Bowmont Water estate lies. However, as shown above, it seems likely the original text of the *Historia* mistakenly ascribed this grant to Oswin, which calls its authenticity into

---

2 For a discussion of the divergence between C and L in *HSC* 3 and the relative trustworthiness of C, see above, pp. 24–5.

3 Craster, 'Patrimony', p. 180. Craster's association of this grant in the *Historia* with King Oswiu has influenced subsequent scholars; both Barrow and Kapelle, for example, cite the *Historia* as recording that Oswiu granted the Bowmont water vills to the community of Lindisfarne. See Barrow, *History of the Scots*, p. 32, and Kapelle, *Norman Conquest*, p. 79.

question. Our author may well have misread or misrepresented an authentic charter of King Oswiu; confusion may have been caused by the fact that Oswiu's name can occur as the patronymic *Osuing*.[4] It does seem likely that this passage preserves a description of a relatively early composite estate; however, whether that estate was ever actually granted to the community of St Cuthbert, and if so by whom, cannot be determined.

The identifiable vills listed in this grant all lie within a few miles of one another along the Bowmont Water from where it rises near Sourhope to where it joins College Burn to become the river Glen (see map, fig. 2). When these vills are mapped using surviving township boundaries they form a discrete block of territory containing roughly 7,600 hectares of usable agricultural land below 200m in altitude, as well as a considerable amount of grazing land above that altitude. It seems very likely that what is being described here is a single composite estate consisting of a group of adjacent vills administered from a single estate centre; this is the first of eight such estates to be described in the *Historia*.[5] Unlike the other composite estates described later in the *Historia*, the vills in this list do not seem to be in any kind of geographic order. The vills occupy the early parish of Yetholm and much of the parish of Morebattle, both in Scotland, as well as the northwestern corner of Kirknewton parish in Northumberland. Since the estate centres of the *Historia*'s other composite estates all became early parish centres, this suggests that Kirk Yetholm may have been the original estate centre for the Bowmont Water lands.

The Grant of Melrose

Boisil's grant of Melrose would have been flatly impossible according to Bede, since Cuthbert succeeded Boisil as prior of Melrose under Abbot Eata rather than becoming abbot himself (*VCB* 9; *HE* IV.27), and Boisil would therefore have lacked authority to give the monastery to anyone. In addition, the image of an abbot disposing of a monastery as if it were his personal property seems, at best, anachronistic. Melrose is, however, also claimed for the community of St Cuthbert in a description of the property of Lindisfarne given in the *Historia regum* (*HR*iii 89). This entry, which otherwise reproduces information given in the *HSC*, includes a unique list of northern 'manors' (*mansiones*) belonging to Lindisfarne.[6] The list includes a number of monastic houses, namely Melrose, Abercorn, Coldingham, Norham, Tyningham, and Tillmouth. This has been interpreted to suggest that the community at some point exercised jurisdiction over a cluster of northern monasteries that included Melrose. Whether this jurisdiction was simply

---

4 Thus Oswiu's son Ecgfrith is listed as Ecgfrith Osuing in the earliest surviving version of the Anglian collection of royal genealogies: see D. Dumville, 'The Anglian Collection of Royal Genealogies and Regnal Lists', *Anglo-Saxon England* 5 (1976), 30. I am endebted to Alex Woolf for bringing this evidence to my attention.
5 For a discussion of these eight composite estates, see Appendix II.
6 For the text of this entry see below, Appendix I.1.

administrative, making Lindisfarne the mother-house of a 'paruchia' of daughter-monasteries from an early date, as Craster suggests, or whether these lands were acquired outright by the community, probably in the aftermath of the Danish raids of the ninth century, as Hall claims, remains uncertain.[7]

Whatever the reality, the author of the *Historia* certainly believed that the monastic lands of Melrose (*HSC* 3), Tyningham (*HSC* 4) and Norham (*HSC* 9) had become the direct property of the community. In the case of Melrose, the phrase 'with its dependencies' used to describe this grant has a particular meaning in the *Historia*; as becomes clear later in the text, it is used specifically to refer to composite estates consisting of an estate centre and a number of dependent vills.[8]

Cuthbert's Religious Life

As all three early sources make clear, Cuthbert never actually served as abbot of Melrose. Instead, he was made prior of Melrose upon Boisil's death and was later transferred to Lindisfarne by Abbot Eata (*VCA* III.1, *VCB* 9 and *HE* IV.27). The statement that Cuthbert lived as a hermit for nine years is also unique to the *Historia*; Bede simply states that he lived in solitude for many years.

Although it does not add anything of importance to the story of St Cuthbert's life, the *Historia* does, by compressing and selectively editing out most of the detail from the early Lives, significantly alter the saint's character. The early Lives present Cuthbert's life as a progression through four distinct stages: child, monk, hermit, bishop.[9] As a youth, Cuthbert was already chosen by God, marked by sanctity and aided by miracles. As a monk he distinguished himself, eventually becoming prior of Melrose and then of Lindisfarne. Here the *Anonymous Life* concentrates on Cuthbert's asceticism with its long fasts and vigils, while Bede also emphasises his zeal in helping those around him to lead a more godly life, outside as well as within the monastery.[10] As a hermit on the island of Farne, Cuthbert devoted himself

---

7   See Craster, 'Patrimony', pp. 179–80, and Hall, *Community of St Cuthbert*, p. 67.

8   For further discussion of these composite estates see below, Appendix II.

9   This structure is established most explicitly in the *Anonymous Life*, which is divided into four books corresponding to the four stages of Cuthbert's life. Bede's *Prose Life* reflects this same structure, and even in the *Historia ecclesiastica* Bede, while ignoring Cuthbert's childhood, gives separate descriptions of his life as prior, as a hermit, and finally as bishop.

10 Compare *VCA* II.1 with *VCB* 9 and *HE* IV.27. Bede particularly emphasises Cuthbert's preaching, which is mentioned only in passing in the *Anonymous Life*: 'He used mainly to visit and preach in the villages that lay far distant among high and inaccessible mountains, which others feared to visit and whose barbarity and squalor daunted other teachers. Cuthbert, however, gladly undertook this pious task, and taught with such patience and skill that when he left the monastery, it would sometimes be a week, sometimes two or three, and occasionally an entire month before he returned home, after staying in the mountains to guide the peasants heavenward by his teachings and virtuous example' (*HE* IV.27).

entirely to the contemplative life, and it was only with great difficulty that King Ecgfrith and Archbishop Theodore were able to convince him to withdraw from his island and accept the bishopric. As bishop, he preserved his own ascetic lifestyle and paid particular attention to the poor and defenseless within his bishopric.[11] Finally, after two years as bishop, Cuthbert returned again to Farne to live in solitude and prepare for death.[12] This is a fitting conclusion to his story; throughout the early Lives, St Cuthbert emerges as a model of Christian humility and ascetic life who turns his back on temporal riches and earthly glory, at last fleeing his cathedral to return to a life of holy contemplation.

Miracles play an important role in defining St Cuthbert's character in the early Lives, and their use follows a similar pattern in both the *Anonymous Life* and the *Prose Life*.[13] Chapters concerning Cuthbert's life as a monk and a hermit are dominated by nature-miracles in which the elements themselves, as well as the birds of the air and the fish of the sea, do the saint's bidding or act in accordance with his prophecies. When Cuthbert becomes bishop of Lindisfarne, these nature-miracles are replaced by a series of healing miracles, in which men, women and children suffering from various illnesses are brought back from the point of death. Throughout his life Cuthbert is also gifted with visions; the most important of these are his visions of St Aidan's soul being carried off to heaven and of the Northumbrian king Ecgfrith's death in battle against the Picts. Finally, the early Lives conclude with a number of posthumous miracles in which supplicants who come to the saint's tomb are cured of demonic possession, illness and paralysis.

The author of the *Historia de sancto Cuthberto* compresses all of St Cuthbert's life into his first pages; the rest of the work is dominated by later grants of property to the saint and by posthumous miracles. In this process of compression, descriptions of the saint at each of the four stages in his life are reduced to a single sentence or less.[14] Only two incidents from Cuthbert's

---

11 See *VCA* IV.2, *VCB* 26 and *HE* IV.28. This passage from the *Prose Life* is typical: 'Gladly and diligently he practiced his wonted frugality and, amid the thronging crowds, rejoiced to preserve the rigours of monastic life. He gave food to the hungry, clothing to the suffering, and he was duly adorned with all else that should mark the life of a bishop' (*VCB* 26).

12 See *VCA* IV.11, *VCB* 37 and *HE* IV.29. 'So after two years he resigned of his own will the worldly honours of his bishopric, for being filled with the prophetic spirit of God, he foresaw his death and, being attracted by the love of his former solitary way of life, he returned to the island from which he had formerly been withdrawn by compulsion' (*VCA* IV.11).

13 The account of Cuthbert's life in the *Historia ecclesiastica*, being much briefer, limits itself to two nature-miracles on Farne (*HE* IV.28) and the saint's prophecy of his own death (*HE* IV.29).

14 As a young man Cuthbert 'prayed in spirit to the Lord, as was his habit from infancy' (*HSC* 2); as a monk he 'faithfully observed both the contemplative and the active ways of living to the end of his own life' (*HSC* 3); as abbot (*sic*) of Melrose he 'spread the

lifetime are preserved in any detail; these are the miraculous vision of St Aidan being carried up to heaven which prompted Cuthbert to become a monk, and the sequence of events which led to Cuthbert's consecration as bishop of Lindisfarne. Finally, miracle-stories from Cuthbert's lifetime are also scarce. Apart from Cuthbert's vision of Aidan, there is only one oblique reference to the time when he 'revived a boy from the dead at the vill which is called *Exanforda*' (*HSC* 6).

As we can see, our author ignores the vast majority of the information in his three sources. What remains highlighted are the two key events which best serve as credentials of Cuthbert's sainthood. The first of these, Cuthbert's vision of St Aidan, is the miracle by which God first marks Cuthbert's holiness. The second is the episcopal consecration with which that holiness was acknowledged by the temporal authorities, namely King Ecgfrith and Archbishop Theodore.[15] The character of Cuthbert's spiritual life, and the many miracles which help define that spirituality, remain secondary to these demonstrations of his authority. Beyond establishing Cuthbert's sainthood, the events of the saint's life are used primarily to provide an historical explanation of certain properties held by the church of Lindisfarne; Cuthbert's vision of Aidan's death, for example, is used to explain the community's acquisition of a group of vills along the Bowmont Water. This linking of property grants with specific historical events establishes a pattern that continues throughout the *Historia*.

While the events of the saint's lifetime receive short shrift in the *Historia*, his posthumous miracles are given considerably more attention. These miracles include: (1) the destruction of kings Osberht and Ælle (*HSC* 10); (2) the destruction of King Halfdane (*HSC* 12); (3) King Guthred's election (*HSC* 13); (4) King Alfred's dream and subsequent victory (*HSC* 15–18); (5) the waves of blood (*HSC* 20); (6) the destruction of Onlafbald (*HSC* 23); and (7) King Guthred's dream and subsequent victory (*HSC* 33). Three of these seven miracles describe the bad ends of kings and magnates who steal or destroy the property of St Cuthbert, while three more describe how the saint helps kings whom he favors gain control of their kingdoms and/or defeat opposing armies. The *Historia* contains only single examples of St Cuthbert's visionary gifts (*HSC* 2) and his healing powers (*HSC* 6), and there are no longer any nature-miracles at all; instead, the emphasis in miracles has shifted toward the saint's ability to help his friends and destroy his enemies.

---

word of God and baptized a great multitude' (*HSC* 3); and as a hermit he 'took himself to a certain remote island called Farne, and for nine years enclosed himself there as in a prison, fighting against the enemy of humankind' (*HSC* 3).

15 The version of Cuthbert's consecration given in the *Historia* is closest to Bede's description in the *Historia ecclesiastica* (*HE* IV.27); the only real changes are the extended comparison between Cuthbert and Gregory the Great, the anachronistic reference to Chad and Cedd, and the substitution of a vill named Alne for Bede's site of *Adtuifyrdi* on the River Aln.

Furthermore, while the early Lives portray the saint as turning his back upon the temporal life and political entanglements, the posthumous Cuthbert of the *HSC* is quite active politically, acting as king-maker on behalf of Alfred and Guthred.[16]

In fact, St Cuthbert as portrayed in the *Historia de sancto Cuthberto* has been transformed from an unworldly hermit into a powerful temporal patron capable of protecting the rights of his community, both by threatening potential transgressors with violent retribution and by securing political protection in the form of royal patronage.[17] As D. P. Kirby has recently noted, 'A saint's Life was a meditative reflection on the spiritual experiences of the community, designed not only to commemorate the saint but to serve the interests of the community and meet its needs.'[18] In other words, the historical context that shaped the experience of a particular monastic community at a particular time will be reflected in that community's image of its patron saint. Thus, the early Lives of St Cuthbert were influenced by Lindisfarne's struggle to survive as an independent see, and reflected both the community's need for a respected patron saint and its desire to rehabilitate their Irish-influenced anchoritic tradition in the wake of the synod of Whitby.[19] In the same way,

---

[16] As several authors have pointed out, the starkly spiritual and apolitical image of Cuthbert presented in the early lives is itself somewhat misleading; for example, the saint is known to have had contact with abbess Ælflæd, sister of King Ecgfrith (*VCA* III.6 and *VCB* 23–4), and to have advised the king himself concerning his planned invasion of the Picts (*HE* IV.26).

[17] This transformation from a spiritual recluse into a powerful patron who regularly wields temporal power on behalf of his community is not unique to St Cuthbert, but is part of a pattern which has been observed in numerous saints' lives and which seems to have reached its height in the eleventh and twelfth centuries: see, for example, E. G. Whatley, *The Saint of London: The Life and Miracles of Saint Erkenwald* (Binghamton, NY, 1989), especially pp. 82–3; Ward, *Miracles*, ch. 3; and Sigal, 'Le châtiment divin'. The traditional explanation, recently expressed by Sigal, has been that the decline of royal authority in the ninth and tenth centuries forced churches and monasteries to replace royal protection with the threat of divine retribution by powerful patron saints; see Sigal, 'Le châtiment divin', p. 52. While this explanation seems workable for Carolingian Europe, it provides only part of the answer for Anglo-Saxon England, since English kings had never achieved such complete control over the Church as their Carolingian counterparts, and since even great kings like Alfred were sometimes known to confiscate Church lands rather than protect them; see e.g. Nelson, 'A King Across the Sea', pp. 58–61 and 65–6. In the *Historia*, kings represent potential threats to the community who must either be won over by saintly aid (as with Guthred and Alfred) or destroyed (as with Osberht and Ælle).

[18] Kirby, 'Genesis of a Cult', p. 385.

[19] Probably the most significant factor affecting the community of Lindisfarne in the late seventh and early eighth centuries, as Kirby has pointed out, was the struggle with Bishop Wilfrid of York and his followers over control of the bishopric. Scholars have long remarked on the striking contrast between the characters of Cuthbert and Wilfrid; it may be that one purpose of the early Lives was to establish Cuthbert as the spiritual antithesis of the worldly and political Wilfrid. Furthermore, Lindisfarne had been a key

the character of St Cuthbert in the *Historia de sancto Cuthberto* had come to reflect the values and needs of a powerful and well-established late-Saxon monastic community concerned with preserving its lands in the face of a series of political upheavals.

HSC 4 *The Bounds of Lindisfarne*

Hart dates this section of the *Historia* c. 756 x 875, observing that 'it is difficult to regard this archaic description of the bounds of Lindisfarne territory as being other than authentic'.[20] I am less optimistic, and believe that this description can be best analysed by breaking it down into three separate components (see map, fig. 2). First, this passage claims lands on the south bank of the Tweed between the river Till and Warren Beck, which flows into the sea just south of Lindisfarne. This large swathe of territory thus occupies the coast between Lindisfarne and Berwick, extending inland as far as the Till and its tributary, the river Breamish. It includes two estates claimed for the community in later sections of the *Historia*; Norham (*HSC* 9) lies near the confluence of the Till and the Tweed, while Eglingham (*HSC* 11) lies between Warren Burn and the Breamish. The history of Eglingham is obscure, but if it ever belonged to the community it had been lost by the time of the Conquest. Norham, on the other hand, long remained in the hands of the community; however, according to a later section of the *Historia* (*HSC* 9), it was only acquired in the time of Bishop Ecgred (830–45). Norhamshire and the adjacent territory of Islandshire (named after the holy island of Lindisfarne) were still associated with St Cuthbert after the Conquest and are described in both *Boldon Book* and the *Liber feodorum*; interestingly, both of these shires seem to have contained on the order of a dozen vills apiece.[21] Together Norhamshire and Islandshire describe an arc of territory which follows the south bank of the Tweed from Norham to Tweedmouth and

centre of Irish monasticism in England, held in disfavour after the synod of Whitby. Cuthbert as portrayed in the early Lives was the heroic embodiment of the Irish ascetic tradition and yet at the same time was fully Catholic in his habits and beliefs, thus helping to rehabilitate the Irish tradition and Lindisfarne's own reputation. For a complete discussion see Kirby, 'Genesis of a Cult', pp. 388–97.

20 Hart, *Early Charters*, p. 137.

21 Norhamshire in *Boldon Book* consists of the vills of Norham, Cornhill (in manuscript B only), Tillmouth, Heaton, Twizel, Ord, Grindon, Newbiggen (*Neuburga*, which Austin takes as Newburn, but which I think is identical with *Neubiging* in the *Liber feodorum*), Upsetlington, Thornton, and Horncliffe (*BB*, pp. 33–5). This is identical with the list in the *Liber feodorum* except for the omission of Norham (*LF* omits the heads of both shires, but I have included them in my counts) and Horncliffe, and the addition of Tweedmouth, Duddo and Felkington (*LF*, pp. 26–7). For Islandshire, *LF* lists Ancroft, Allerdean, Ross, Scremerston, Chesewick, Beal, Goswick, Haggerston, Kyloe, Berrington, Low Lynn, and Buckton; Fenwick, the head of the shire, is omitted (*LF*, pp. 27–8).

extends south along the coast as far as Lindisfarne. If any lands to the south of this, between Warren Beck and the Breamish, ever belonged to the community, there is no record of it outside of the *Historia* itself.

Second, the *Historia* claims lands on the north bank of the Tweed between the rivers Blackadder and Leader. It seems likely that the community did indeed hold some property in this area, since the large early parish of Eccles, which lies between the Tweed and the Blackadder and may well preserve the core of a larger early estate, was dedicated to St Cuthbert.[22] There are, however, no other documentary references to Cuthbertine holdings in this region, and any property the community may have held must have been lost by the end of the tenth century as the Scots gained control of all territory north of the Tweed.

Finally, the passage claims the lands of Tyningham, which lie along the Firth of Forth to the east of Edinburgh. Tyningham, like Melrose, is included in the list of Lindisfarne's property recorded in the *Historia regum* (*HR*iii 89).[23] This list also includes Pefferham and Aldham, both of which are located in the parish of Tyningham. The monastery of Tyningham could hardly have been among the early properties of Lindisfarne, since it only came into existence in the eighth century; its founder St Balthere was not even born until after St Cuthbert's death. St Balthere's might have been a daughter house administered by Lindisfarne, and/or its lands could conceivably have passed directly to St Cuthbert after St Balthere's was destroyed by Anlaf the Dane in 941, but they would have been lost again to the Scots by the end of the tenth century. The lands of Tyningham were purportedly restored to the monks of Durham by King Duncan of Scotland in 1094 in a charter Craster describes as being 'of doubtful authenticity'.[24]

HSC 5 *Grants at York and Crayke*

Hall suggests that the territory granted to St Cuthbert in York can be identified with the parish of All Saints, Pavement.[25] The church of All Saints was still claimed by the Bishop of Durham in *Domesday Book*, which also records that St Cuthbert had a home in York which claimed to be exempt from all customary dues (*DBY* C.2). *Yorkshire Domesday* also lists Crayke and its church, dedicated to St Cuthbert, among the property of the Bishop of Durham (*DBY* 3Y.10). Although the *Historia* states that King Ælle confiscated Crayke (*HSC* 10), the fact that *HSC* 20 states that the community spent four months there in the course of the seven years' wandering supports the claim that it was affiliated with the community at that time, and a vernacular

---

[22] See Barrow, *Kingdom of the Scots*, p. 30.
[23] For the text of this list, see below, Appendix I.1.
[24] Craster, 'Patrimony', p. 179; see also Lawrie, *Early Scottish Charters*, pp. 10 and 241.
[25] See Hall, *Community of St Cuthbert*, p. 54.

note in the *Liber uitæ Dunelmensis* records that Earl Thured gave the community two additional hides there in the late tenth century (*LVD* 43v).

Grant of Carlisle

All three early sources associate Cuthbert with Carlisle (*VCA* IV.8; *VCB* 27; *HE* IV.29), and there was later a parish of St Cuthbert Without in that city. Carlisle also contained a nunnery, but according to Bede this already existed when Cuthbert visited the city in 685 (*VCB* 27). As Craster notes, Carlisle would have been lost when Cumberland fell to Norse invaders in the early tenth century, but when William Rufus reconquered the territory in 1092 Carlisle was placed under the spiritual jurisdiction of the church of Durham.[26] The continuation of the *Libellus de exordio* lists both Teviotdale (*HSC* 9) and Carlisle among the appendages of the diocese of Durham, and states that both were lost to the community during Bishop Flambard's exile in 1101 (*LDE continuatio*, § 1).

HSC 6 *Grants of Cartmel and Gilling*

Exanforda has never been identified and is not mentioned in any other source, but this episode may well have grown out of a miracle in the early Lives (*VCA* IV.6; *VCB* 33). In both the *Anonymous Life* and the *Prose Life* Cuthbert visits a certain village (unnamed in the *VCB* but called *Medilwong* in the *VCA*) during a widespread plague and assures a weeping mother that her young son, already at the point of death, will live. There is no mention in any other early source of a Cuthbertine claim to Cartmel. If this estate ever did belong to the community it had been lost by the time of Edward the Confessor, at which point it belonged to Tostig, earl of Northumberland.[27]

The identification of Gilling, while possible, is far from certain. It was first proposed by Craster, who identified *Suthgedling* in *HSC* L with Bede's *Ingetlingum* (*HE* III.14).[28] The difficulties with this identification are that it is based solely on text L (the least reliable of the three surviving texts), that it has no geographic relationship to Cartmel, as we might expect from their association in the text, and that Gilling is not associated with the community of St Cuthbert in any other early source, but is instead associated with Ripon.[29] Gilling is not mentioned in either of the other early lists of community holdings in Yorkshire which are recorded in the *Liber uitæ Dunelmensis* (*LVD*, pp. 76–7) and the *Cronica monasterii Dunelmensis* (*CMD*, pp. 527–8). It is included in the Yorkshire Domesday survey, which states that it was held by Earl Edwin of Mercia before the Conquest and which describes it as a substantial estate with nine berwicks and twenty-one sokelands (*DBY* 6N.1). Craster identifies 'Cineferth filius Cygincg' as Abbot Cynefrid of Gilling,

---

[26] See Craster, 'Patrimony', p. 181.

[27] *Ibid.*, p. 181.

[28] *Ibid.*, p. 182.

[29] For a brief summary of this problem see Morris, 'Northumbria and the Viking Settlement', p. 91, n. 97.

who died in a widespread plague according to the anonymous *Historia abbatum*; he suggests that this was the great epidemic of 664, and thus 'it follows that [Cynefrid] was already dead when Cuthbert became bishop, and cannot have owed his ordination to that saint'.[30]

HSC 7 *Grant of Carham*

No battles between kings Ecgfrith and Wulfhere are mentioned in the *Anglo-Saxon Chronicle*, but in the *Historia ecclesiastica* Bede notes that Ecgfrith defeated Wulfhere, drove him out of Lindsey and installed a bishop there; this battle must have taken place between Ecgfrith's accession in 670 and Wulfhere's death in 675 (*HE* IV.12). As Craster points out, this places the battle several years before Cuthbert became a bishop, thus weakening the credibility of the *HSC*'s story.[31] Although the *Historia* states that St Wilfrid was with the king at this battle, the *Vita sancti Wilfridi*, while describing Ecgfrith's victory over Wulfhere (VW 20), makes no mention of Wilfrid's presence, nor does it give him, still less St Cuthbert, any credit for the victory.

The reference to Carham 'and whatever pertains to it', together with the fact that Carham became the head of a medieval parish, suggests that this was a substantial estate rather than a single vill.[32] This estate would have been adjacent to Norhamshire on the east and the Bowmont Water estate to the south, and thus would have linked that estate to the main body of community holdongs on the south bank of the Tweed (see map, fig. 2). Although Carham would thus have been a valuable estate for the community, the grant of Carham to St Cuthbert is not recorded in any other early source. However, a writ of Queen Maud (r. 1106–16) confirms the rights of Durham to the church of Carham, which was dedicated to St Cuthbert, and whatsoever belongs to it.[33]

HSC 8 *Grant of Warkworth*

King Ceolwulf's abdication is described and dated in several sources including the *Anglo-Saxon Chronicle* (*ASC* 737 E); however, there is no mention of the grant of Warkworth in any other early source. *Brincewele* ('Brynca's spring' or 'Brynca's pool') is a lost site which presumably lay near Brinkburn ('Brynca's stream') on the river Coquet. Watts has noted that there is a promontory fort near Brinkburn and suggested that this may have been the 'civitas' of *Brincewele*.[34] A Roman road known as the Devil's Causeway crosses the Coquet less than a mile east of Brinkburn and proceeds

---

30 Craster, 'Patrimony', p. 182.
31 See Craster, 'Patrimony', p. 184.
32 For a discussion of the potential link between early estates and later parishes in the *Historia*, see below, Appendix II.
33 See Raine, *North Durham*, appendix, dcclxxxv.
34 Victor Watts, pers. comm. (30 September 1997).

north past Edlingham to cross the Aln near Whittingham. If this is the *uiam* referred to, the *Historia* is laying claim to a huge territory which includes virtually all the viable farmland (i.e. land below 200m) between the rivers Aln and Coquet and extends south of the Coquet as far as the Line (see map, fig. 2). According to a later chapter of the *Historia*, this territory was lost to the community in the mid-ninth century when it was confiscated by King Osberht (*HSC* 10) and seems never to have been recovered.

A somewhat different version of this grant is recorded in the *Cronica monasterii Dunelmensis*, which states that King Ceolwulf took the monastic habit, 'handing over royal treasures and the lands of *Breiesne* and Warkworth with their appurtenances, and the church which he had built there, and the four vills *Wudecester*, *Witingham*, *Eaduluingham* and *Egguluingham* like-wise to St Cuthbert' (*CMD*, lines 7–10). This passage is repeated word for word in the *Libellus de exordio* with *Breiesne* rendered as *Bregesne* (*LDE* II.1). In these later sources, all of King Ceolwulf's gifts are presented together (rather than being broken up between *HSC* 8 and *HSC* 11), place-name spellings ending in '-incham' are corrected to '-ingham', and the description of the Warkworth estate is limited to '*Breiesne/Bregesne* and Warkworth with their appurtenances'. The place name *Breisne/Bregesne* is problematic but has generally been identified as Brainshaugh, which also lies on the Coquet but is much nearer to Warkworth than Brinkburn, and is in fact adjacent to the early parish of Warkworth.

The territory described in the *CMD* and *LDE* was thus greatly reduced from that claimed in the *HSC*, and may well have consisted of a composite estate similar to others described in the *Historia*, with its estate centre at Warkworth. The ancient parish of Warkworth, together with the adjacent extraparochial of Guizance which contains Brainshaugh, occupied roughly 7,200 hectares, which is a typical size for the twelve-vill composite estates described in the *HSC*. Furthermore, the phrase used to describe Warkworth in the *HSC* is 'vill with its dependencies', which seems to be used specifically to refer to composite estates throughout the text.

HSC 9 *Bishop Ecgred and his Grants*

Bishop Ecgred of Lindisfarne is described in both the *Libellus de exordio* and the *Annales Lindisfarnenses*; both sources date his episcopate to the years 830–45. The *Annales* simply state that Ecgred served as bishop for sixteen years, transferred the body of King Ceolwulf to Norham, and founded churches at Gainford and Jedburgh (*AL* 830). The *LDE* is more detailed, embellishing its description of Ecgred and mentioning in order all the vills described in *HSC* 9 (Norham, the two Jedburghs, Gainford, Cliffe, Wycliffe and Billingham) without adding significant details (*LDE* II.5). Like the *Annales*, however, the *LDE* states only that Ceolwulf's body was translated to Norham, making no mention of St Cuthbert in this regard.

The territory of the two Jedburghs described here corresponds to the northern half of the medieval parish of Jedburgh, and its size (approximately 7,000 hectares) is similar to those of the twelve-vill composite estates described elsewhere in the *Historia*.[35] The continuation of the *Libellus de exordio* states that the lands of Teviotdale, which would have included the Jedburgh estate, were lost to the community along with Carlisle during Bishop Flambard's exile in 1101 (*LDE continuatio*, § 1).

The vills of Cliffe and Wycliffe, although listed separately, actually fall within the described bounds of the Gainford estate (see map, fig. 3), suggesting that this portion of the text may be based on two separate records. The *Historia regum* refers to an Abbot Edwine, also called Eda, who was buried in the church of Gainford in 801 (*HRi* 63), and Craster notes that both Billingham and Gainford contain sculptural remains which predate Ecgred's episcopate.[36] Both of these facts contradict the *Historia*'s claim that Ecgred founded these churches. Austin suggests that the designation *in Heorternesse* indicates that Billingham was originally part of the territory belonging to Abbess Hild's foundation at Hartlepool.[37] The *Libellus de exordio* states that after being confiscated by King Rægnald (cf. *HSC* 23), Billingham was finally restored to the monks of Durham by William the Conqueror (*LDE* III.20).

The Translation to Norham

Although the fact is ignored later in the *Historia* (*HSC* 20) as well as in the authoritative twelfth-century histories of the community, *HSC* 9 actually claims that St Cuthbert's body, and hence presumably the see itself, was translated to Norham in the first half of the ninth century. Interestingly, the *Historia* is not alone in describing such a move; the story of the translation of St Cuthbert's body to Norham is supported in two apparently independent sources. The first is *Secgan be þam Godes sanctum þe on Engla lande ærost reston*, an eleventh-century list of the burial places of English saints with earlier material embedded in it. One of these records, which Rollason dates to the mid-ninth century, states that St Cuthbert rests in the place called *Ubbanford* next to the river Tweed.[38] The *Historia regum* explains that *Ubbenford* is now called Norham (*HRiii* 89); the shift in name seems to have taken place in the tenth or eleventh century.

The second source to mention Norham is the twelfth-century *Gesta pontificum* (*GPA* III.129). In his discussion of the see of Lindisfarne, William of Malmesbury quotes Alcuin's letter to King Æthelred describing the Viking raid of 793 and explains that because of this, it was determined to remove the saint's body from the island. As in *HSC* 20, an attempt was made to flee to

---

35 For the characteristic traits of the composite estates described in the *Historia* see below, Appendix II.
36 See Craster, 'Patrimony', p. 187.
37 See Austin, 'Fieldwork and Excavation at Hart', pp. 72–5.
38 See Rollason, 'Lists of Saint's Resting Places', p. 68. For the complete text see Liebermann, *Die Heiligen Englands*, pp. 9–19.

Ireland, although according to William its failure was due to contrary winds rather than waves of blood. Following this, the holy body was placed in *Ubbanford* beside the river Tweed with all the honour it deserved, and there it lay for many years until the time of King Æthelred.[39]

HSC 10 *Osberht and Ælle*

The defeat of kings Osberht and Ælle is described in the *Anglo-Saxon Chronicle* (*ASC* 867); essentially the same story is repeated in the *Gesta Alfredi* (*GA* 27), the *Historia regum* (*HR*i 70 and *HR*iii 92), and the *Libellus de exordio* (*LDE* II.6). In this version of events, the Northumbrian people repudiate King Osberht and elect Ælle, who is not of royal blood. When the Danes arrive and capture York, the two settle their differences and attack York with a combined force; their army gets within the walls of York but is then routed, and both kings are slain. The date given for this battle in both the *HR* and *LDE* is the twelfth kalends of April, which would have been the Friday before Palm Sunday. The *Annales Lindisfarnenses*, like the *HSC*, have the Danes attacking York rather than defending it, name Ubba as their leader, and date the battle to Palm Sunday; they do not, however, describe Osberht and Ælle as brothers (*AL* 868). The *Annales* also manage to reconcile the most important difference between the *ASC* and the *HSC* by explaining that the Danes had initially taken York, but were then driven out by Osberht and Ælle before Ubba's attack.[40]

HSC 11 *Grant of Four Vills*

This grant by King Ceolwulf should logically follow *HSC* 8; instead, it intrudes awkwardly between two sections describing the Danish invasion. The *Cronica monasterii Dunelmensis* also describes this grant, combining it with Ceolwulf's grant of Warkworth in a single entry (*CMD*, lines 7–10). Craster has observed that 'There is no supporting evidence to show that the vills were ever made over to Lindisfarne, but one may accept the tradition that the churches [of all four estates] were of early date, going back to a period before the Danish invasions.'[41] There is no Esred listed among the bishops of Lindisfarne, and no room for one; both Craster and Hart assume that the bishop in question is in fact Ecgred, who lived a hundred years later than Ceolwulf.[42] It should be noted that all four of these vills (assuming that Woodhorn is the correct identification of *Wudacestre*) were the centres of substantial early parishes, which raises the possibility that they originated as

---

39 For the full text of this passage see below, Appendix I.4.
40 For a recent analysis of the Viking capture of York, see Smyth, *Scandinavian Kings*, pp. 178–88.
41 Craster, 'Patrimony', p. 186.
42 Craster, 'Patrimony', p. 186; Hart, *Early Charters*, p. 136. Craster notes that 'it was not uncommon for scribes to mistake the Anglo-Saxon *g* for *s*'.

the centres of composite estates.[43] Furthermore, the parishes of Whittingham, Edlingham and Eglingham are all adjacent to one another, forming one large block of territory. This territory would have been adjacent both to the lands of Lindisfarne (*HSC* 4) to the north, and to the lands of Warkworth (*HSC* 8) to the south (see map, fig. 2).

HSC 12 *King Halfdan*

Halfdan, a son of Ragnar Lothbrok, occurs in the *Anglo-Saxon Chronicle* as one of the leaders of the Danish great host. The fact that Halfdan's army wintered on the Tyne in 874–5, overran Northumbria and made frequent attacks on the Picts and Strathclyde Britons is mentioned in *ASC* 875; this is repeated in the *Gesta Alfredi* (*GA* 47) and the *Historia regum* (*HRi* 75). A later chapter of the *Historia regum* repeats this and adds that Halfdan destroyed all the monasteries (*HRiii* 96), while the *Annales Lindisfarnenses* state that Halfdan sailed up the Tyne and that all Northumbria, with its monasteries and churches, was depopulated (*AL* 875). The same theme is developed in more detail in the *Libellus de exordio* (*LDE* II.6); in all three sources this passage is used to introduce the story of the seven years' wandering. A similar description of Halfdan's expedition also occurs in the *Cronica monasterii Dunelmensis* (*CMD*, lines 17–20); as in the *HSC*, it omits specific mention of the destruction of monasteries and is used instead to introduce the story of King Guthred's election.

The extent of the destruction that accompanied Halfdan's expedition up the Tyne, and thus its impact upon Lindisfarne, remains unclear. Smyth, for one, assumes that the destruction was widespread: 'This new Danish activity in northern Britain not only uprooted the community of Lindisfarne; it also had repercussions among the monasteries of Scotland'.[44] As evidence he cites the translation of the relics of St Columba from Dunkeld to Ireland in 878 (*AU* 878). However, it should be remembered that Lindisfarne lies a good fifty miles north of the Tweed, and that Symeon of Durham, the first author to explicitly link Halfdan's raid with the abandonment of Lindisfarne, may have had particular motives for doing so.[45]

The only sources to mention anything of Halfdan's later history are the *Chronicon monasterii Dunelmensis* and the *Libellus de exordio*, both of which give the same passage:

> For as insanity afflicted his mind, so the direst torment afflicted his body, from which there arose such an intolerable stench that he was rendered odius to his whole army. Thus despised and rejected by all persons, he fled

---

[43] For the potential link between composite estates and parish structure in the *Historia*, see below, pp. 127–8.

[44] Smyth, *Scandinavian Kings*, p. 257.

[45] See below, pp. 98–9.

away from the Tyne with only three ships and was never seen again. (*CMD*, lines 21–4)

The *LDE* repeats this, but finishes by saying that he fled away from the Tyne with only three ships 'and shortly afterwards he and all his followers perished' (*LDE* II.13). In fact, Halfdan does seem to have perished shortly after 875; there is now general agreement that Halfdan is identical with Albann, king of the dark heathens (i.e. Danes), whom the *Annals of Ulster* record as falling in battle against the fair heathens (i.e. Norse) at Strangford Lough in 877 (*AU* 877.5). Concerning the version of Halfdan's death given in the *HSC* and subsequent sources, Smyth observes that 'Halfdan's madness and body-odour problem need not concern us further. At the back of this lurid picture of divine vengeance lies the more sober tradition that he was deserted by his warriors and fled from the Tyne with only three ships'.[46] Smyth goes on to suggest that the bulk of Halfdan's warriors, recently settled in Yorkshire, refused to follow their king in his attempt to recover his brother Ivarr's kingdom of Dublin.

HSC 13 *The Election of King Guthred*

A Guthred is mentioned in several sources as king of York in the early 880s; however, with one exception all of those sources could easily derive from the *HSC* itself. The *Historia regum* states that in 883 'Guthred from being a servant was made king' (*HR*i 78), while the *Annales Lindisfarnenses* record that in 881 'Guthred from being a servant was created king through the aid of St Cuthbert' (*AL* 881); however, both statements are interlinear additions to their texts. Both of these sources also record Guthred's death, the *AL* in 883 and the *HR* in 884 (*AL* 883, *HR*ii 81 and *HR*iii 102). Guthred is also included in the *De primo Saxonum aduentu*, a twelfth-century Durham compilation of Anglo-Saxon regnal lists; this source gives Guthred a considerably longer reign. 'Then Guthred [ruled], the son of Hardecnut, a royal youth sold into slavery by the Danes, but St Cuthbert raised him from slavery to kingship. He reigned for fourteen years.'[47]

The only early source independent of the *Historia* which seems to refer to Guthred at all is the *Chronicon Æthelweardi*, which states 'When the course of one year was at an end, Guthfrid, king of the Northumbrians, died on the nativity of St Bartholomew the apostle of Christ [24 August] and his body is entombed in the city of York in the high church' (*CÆ* 895). Scholars have traditionally accepted the identification of the *HSC*'s Guthred with Aethelweard's Guthfrid; Smyth suggests that the monks of St Cuthbert would have arranged the election of this king, whom he calls Guthfrith and identi-

---

46 Smyth, *Scandinavian Kings*, p. 260. For a complete biography of Halfdan, see *ibid.*, pp. 255–66.
47 *Symeonis opera*, ed. Arnold, II, 377.

fies as a Christian Dane, shortly after their arrival at Chester-le-Street around 883, and that he died in 895 and was succeeded by King Sigfrid.[48] It should be noted that there is no numismatic evidence for Guthred/Guthfrith, since the earliest coinage from Danish York is from the reign of Sigfrid.[49]

The *Historia* is one of two relatively early sources to give the complete story of Guthred's rise from slave to king. The other is the *Cronica monasterii Dunelmensis* (*CMD*, lines 24–44), which gives a version of the story that adheres to the plot given in the *HSC* but adds several details. In the *CMD* Guthred's father Hardecnut is a king, Guthred is captured and sold by the Vikings to a widow in *Huityngham*, he is acclaimed king by Angles and Danes together, his grant to St Cuthbert includes the stipulation that anyone violating the saint's peace must pay a fine of 1,200 gold *ore*, and the grant is supported and confirmed by Alfred, king of the South Angles.[50] The inclusion of King Alfred would certainly seem to be a later addition to the story, but other details such as the identification of *Huityngham* and the fine of 1,200 *ore* are more specific than the usual embellishments. One possibility is that both the *HSC* and the *CMD* may have based their stories on an earlier source describing the deeds of Halfdan and Guthred, with the *CMD* utilizing this source in somewhat greater detail.[51]

Whatever the case, later versions of the story which blend details from the *HSC* and *CMD* occur in a late portion of the *Historia regum* (HRiii 98) as well as the *Libellus de exordio* (*LDE* II.13). The *HR* follows the *CMD* fairly closely but omits any mention of King Alfred's involvement. The story in the *LDE* is closer to the *HSC* but breaks Abbot Eadred's vision of St Cuthbert into two distinct halves. Cuthbert first appears to the abbot while the community is staying at Crayke and arranges the election of King Guthred; after the see has been translated to Chester-le-Street, the saint appears to Eadred a second time and dictates the terms of Guthred's grant. The *LDE* repeats the *CMD* in noting that Guthred was acclaimed by Angles and Danes together and that Guthred's grant was confirmed by Alfred. The episode concludes with a very detailed description of that grant, including a fine of ninety-six pounds for violation of the saint's sanctuary.[52]

---

[48] See Smyth, *Scandinavian York* I, 42–6; for an earlier discussion of Guthred and the *HSC*, see Mawer, 'Scandinavian Kingdom of Northumbria', pp. 43–8.

[49] See e.g. Dolley, *Viking Coins*, pp. 19–20.

[50] For the complete text of this episode see below, Appendix I.2.

[51] The mythical overtones of the Guthred story are certainly striking, and several nineteenth-century historians pointed out the parallels between the story of Guthred and the Scandinavian *Thraelaknutr*, a slave-boy who eventually becomes king in *Jómsvíkinga Saga* and *Olaf Tryggvason's Saga*; see e.g. Mawer, 'Scandinavian Kingdom of Northumbria', pp. 44–8. However, no earlier versions of the Guthred story which might establish a link between it and the Scandinavian myths have yet been discovered.

[52] For the full text of this passage see below, Appendix I.3.

Commentary

The Tyne–Wear Grant

King Guthred's grant of all the land between the Tyne and the Wear is repeated in the *Cronica monasterii Dunelmensis* (*CMD*, lines 39–44) and the *Libellus de exordio* (*LDE* II.13). This grant would have included the estate of Chester-le-Street on the north bank of the Wear, to which the community shortly relocated (*HSC* 20). The eastern portion of the grant would also have included the lands of Monkwearmouth and Jarrow; if this portion of the *Historia* is accurate, it suggests that the monks of Wearmouth-Jarrow had fled the Vikings and abandoned their monasteries by the third quarter of the ninth century. According to a later section of the *Historia*, the western half of Guthred's grant was leased out to Eadred son of Ricsige a few decades later (*HSC* 24). The *Libellus de exordio* describes Guthred's grant as extending inland only as far as Dere Street (*LDE* II.13), and the lease to Eadred also stopped at this point. Craster suggests that the lands beyond this remained undeveloped forest;[53] this does indeed seem likely, since the land west of Dere Street is generally above 200m in altitude, while all of the vills mentioned in the *Historia* are located below that altitude (see map, fig. 3).

HSC 14 *The Danish Settlement*

This sections marks a transition from the northern material of the *Historia's* earlier chapters to the lengthy episode concerning St Cuthbert and King Alfred which occupies *HSC* 15–18. That episode clearly stands out from the rest of the *Historia* and has long been assumed to be a later interpolation to the text, though in fact it may simply be the most obvious example of our author's habit of borrowing from pre-existing sources.[54]

The *HSC* is unique in describing a tripartite division of the Danish host, but the concept seems to derive directly from the *Anglo-Saxon Chronicle*, which in three successive entries describes how Halfdan's Danes shared out Northumbria and 'proceeded to plow and to support themselves' (*ASC* 876), how the rest of the host went into Mercia (*ASC* 877), and how they 'occupied the land of the West Saxons and settled there, and drove a great part of the people across the sea, and conquered most of the others; and the people submitted to them, except King Alfred. He journeyed in difficulties through the woods and fen-fastnesses with a small force' (*ASC* 878). In the *ASC* Alfred builds a small fort in the marshes at Athelney to serve as his base of operations, while Asser simply states that Alfred sought refuge in the forests and swamps of Somerset (*GA* 53). The *Historia* is in fact the first source to mention Glastonbury as Alfred's place of refuge. As Simpson notes, this suggests that this portion of the text cannot have been composed before the

---

[53] See Craster, 'Patrimony', p. 189.
[54] For our author's use of existing sources, see above, p. 8.

mid-tenth century, since it was only with the reign of Edmund and the abbacy of St Dunstan that Glastonbury became widely known.[55]

HSC 15–18 King Alfred's Dream

The story of King Alfred's vision of St Cuthbert does not occur in the two earliest descriptions of Alfred's reign, the *Anglo-Saxon Chronicle* and Asser's *De gestis Alfredi*, although the background of the story – the fact that Alfred took refuge in the Somerset marshes and that from there he managed to gather together the local armies and so defeat the Vikings – occurs in both.[56] In fact, the *Historia* itself seems to be the earliest surviving source to link St Cuthbert with Alfred's victory over the Vikings.[57] Versions of the same story also occur in later Durham sources, particularly the *Miracula sancti Cuthberti* (*MSC* 1) and the *Libellus de exordio* (*LDE* II.10); however, the episodes in both of these sources seem to be based directly on the *HSC* itself.[58] The *Miracula* embellishes the narrative given in the *HSC* without adding significant details, while the *LDE* discusses it more briefly, first observing that 'it is unnecessary here to repeat – for it is fully recorded elsewhere – how St Cuthbert appeared to [King Alfred] in a manifest vision, and how, by the assistance of his merits, the king defeated his enemies and regained possession of his kingdom' (*LDE* II.10). Both of these later episodes are also linked to the *HSC* in their placement of Alfred's victory over the Danes at *Assandun* rather than *Ethandune*.

King Alfred's vision of St Cuthbert is also mentioned twice in brief passages in the *Historia regum*. The wording of both passages is identical: 'King Alfred, suitably comforted by St Cuthbert in a vision, fought against the Danes at the time and place the saint commanded, gained the victory, and thereafter was always terrible and invincible before his enemies, and held St Cuthbert in the highest honor. How he defeated these enemies can be read shortly hereafter' (*HRi* 76 and *HRiii* 96). In both cases this passage occurs in a description of King Alfred's life otherwise derived from Asser; since the text reverts to Asser for its description of Alfred's battles, the climactic victory takes place at *Edderandun* (Edington) rather than the *HSC*'s anachro-

---

55 See Simpson, 'King Alfred/St Cuthbert Episode', p. 406.

56 These events are described in *ASC* 878 and *GA* 53–6. In both sources Alfred's climactic victory over the Vikings takes place at *Ethandune* (Edington in Wiltshire).

57 A fragmentary text identified by Macray as belonging to a 'shorter and earlier' version of the Cuthbert/Alfred story is preserved on a single folio of an eleventh-century miscellany now at Oxford (Bodleian Library, Digby 175, fol. 24); see W. D. Macray, *Catalogi codicum manuscriptorum bibliotecæ Bodlianæ* IX (Oxford, 1883), entry 175. In fact, however, this fragment proves to contain the opening paragraphs of the first miracle in the twelfth-century *Miracula sancti Cuthberti*.

58 For a comparison of the Alfred's Dream episodes in the *HSC*, *MSC* and *LDE*, see Colgrave, 'Post-Bedan Miracles', pp. 321–2. Colgrave observes that Symeon must have had both previous versions before him when he wrote the *LDE*.

nistic *Assandune*. Although the first occurrence of this passage occurs in a portion of the *HR* which may have been written as early as the tenth century, quite possibly by Byrhtferth of Ramsey, it may be that it actually derives from the *HSC* and was not interpolated into the *HR* until the twelfth century.[59] This passage, like the reference to the nine years' wandering in *HR*i 75, seems intrusive in a section of the text which otherwise shows little northern interest;[60] it would seem to be more at home when it occurs in *HR*iii, which demonstrates a strong northern interest and was probably produced at Durham.[61]

William of Malmesbury also twice refers to a variant version of the story of King Alfred and St Cuthbert in his *Gesta pontificum Anglorum*. The first reference occurs in his description of the monastery of Athelney, which he explains is where King Alfred was driven by the Danes and where St Cuthbert appeared to the King in a dream and foretold the recovery of his kingdom, and that for this reason Alfred subsequently founded a monastery there (*GPA* III.92). The second telling is more detailed, and occurs in William's description of the see of Lindisfarne (*GPA* III.130). Again Cuthbert appears to Alfred at Athelney and foretells the recovery of his kingdom, although the threat which Alfred must overcome is no longer the army of the Danes, but the sins of the English; as a sign of this, Cuthbert tells Alfred that his men will return with a great catch of fish, although the marsh is frozen over. Both prophecies are subsequently fulfilled.[62] Although this version never quotes the *HSC* directly and contains variant details such as the setting at Athelney rather than Glastonbury, the similarity of features in both stories (especially the miraculous haul of fish) certainly suggests that they derive from a common source.

Interestingly, a similar story is also told about a Cornish saint, Neot. This

---

59 For a discussion of the chronological divisions within the *Historia regum*, see p. 10 above. For the attribution of *HR*i to Byrhtferth, see Lapidge, 'Byrhtferth and the *Historia Regum*', p. 118 and *passim*.

60 Blair notes that 'In the whole section [*HR* 69–90] there are only three entries which are of particularly Northumbrian interest and which are not dependent in some way upon Asser' (Blair, 'Observations', p. 103); these are two of those three passages. If Alfred Smyth's controversial assertion that Asser's *Gesta Alfredi* was actually written by Byrhtferth is correct (see Smyth, *Alfred the Great*, p. 300), then it becomes virtually certain that these passages are later interpolations, since it is difficult to imagine why Byrhtferth (the presumed author of *HR*i) would choose to insert this material into his own work without better integrating it.

61 Blair suggests that the original portions of *HR* iii were written in Durham in the twelfth century, quite possibly by Symeon of Durham himself; see Blair, 'Observations', p. 117. It is clear from other passages that this twelfth-century author was aware of and drew upon the *HSC*; it seems plausible that the description of Alfred's vision originated with him, and that he then inserted a repetition of his passage into *HR*i 76 in order to retain textual continuity.

62 For the full text of this passage see below, Appendix I.4.

story first occurs in the anonymous *Vita prima sancti Neoti*, probably written at St Neot's in Huntingdonshire in the mid-eleventh century. Neot, a Cornish hermit, is twice visited by King Alfred, and chastises the king for his evil ways, lectures him on Christian behaviour, and promises him God's mercy if he should change his ways (*VPN* 7–8). Shortly after Neot's death, the Vikings invade England and Alfred seeks refuge in a swineherd's cottage in the swamps of Athelney. Bearing in mind Neot's words, Alfred emulates Job throughout this period of poverty and suffering, and when the swineherd's wife scolds him for letting her cakes burn, he meekly accepts her insults (*VPN* 12). One night soon after, Neot appears to Alfred in a dream, congratulates him on his behaviour, and promises him help against the Vikings (*VPN* 13). The next morning, forces gather around Alfred from throughout the land, and Alfred leads this new army to meet the enemy at *Ethandun* (*VPN* 14). On the eve of battle, Neot appears to him again and promises to lead his army to victory. Alfred relates this vision to his men, and the next day they are victorious in battle (*VPN* 16).[63]

The similarities shared by these stories about Neot and Cuthbert are striking, and they become more so when we consider that, at first glance, these two saints had very little in common. They lived in different centuries in different kingdoms, and there is no evidence that their cults had any contact with one another. Nevertheless, the cults of St Neot and St Cuthbert did share one common feature. Although neither cult was West Saxon in origin, both came under the influence of the West Saxon royal house during the course of the tenth century. As Eric John has pointed out, monastic patronage served to increase both the political and the ideological strength of the tenth-century kings as they worked to extend their authority throughout England.[64] In the case of St Neot, this royal patronage took the form of the forcible translation of the saint's relics from Cornwall to East Anglia against the wishes of the saint's Cornish community. This resulted in the transformation of an independent Cornish cult into a docile member of a family of reformed fenland abbeys under strong royal influence.[65] In the case of St Cuthbert, the kings through their patronage gained a powerful ally in Northumbria, a region where the extension of West Saxon hegemony was meeting considerable resistance. Here the establishment of royal patronage by Athelstan and Edmund would have also served the community's interests, and presumably took place under their instigation or approval. In both cases, however, the story of an encounter between the community's patron saint and King Alfred, in which the saint aids the king and the king repays the saint

---

63 For full discussions see Appendix I, 'Alfred and the Cakes', in Keynes and Lapidge, eds., *Alfred the Great*, pp. 197–202, and *Annals of St Neots*, ed. Lapidge, pp. cxi–cxxiv.

64 See John, *Orbis Brittaniæ*, pp. 177–80.

65 See Rollason, *Saints and Relics*, p. 155.

with a promise of royal support, neatly provides an 'historical precedent' for what was in fact a novel change in patronage.

At first glance, both of these stories would seem to have monastic origins. Certainly the character of Alfred in both reflects the monastic conception of a good king. In the *Vita Neoti* he is presented as a sinner whose spiritual reform is rewarded with an earthly throne. In the *Historia* he is a Christian king whose charity is rewarded, and who lectures his troops on the seven sins and seven virtues before leading them into battle. This marks a change from Asser's Alfred, who seems more preoccupied with the intellectual than the spiritual life, although he does pray privately.[66] The new Alfred's image as an ardent monastic patron also contradicts historical evidence, which suggests that Alfred's extension of West Saxon power into Kent and Mercia involved large-scale confiscation of ecclesiastical estates.[67]

On the other hand, there is also evidence that the original impetus behind the stories of Alfred and the saints may have lain not in the monasteries, but in the royal court. First, the occurrence of the same basic story in works produced at opposite ends of the country at roughly the same time is most easily explained by transmission through the royal court. Second, we have seen that the tenth-century kings gained substantially from closer links with the communities of both Neot and Cuthbert, and it would therefore have been in their interest to promulgate stories which explained and justified this new royal patronage. Third, as Luisella Simpson points out, the Alfred episode in the *HSC* contains a number of formulæ which fit the pattern of royal propaganda produced at the West Saxon court in the mid-tenth century.[68] Chief among these is Cuthbert's promise to Alfred: 'tu es electus rex totius Britanniæ'. This *rex totius Britanniæ* formula occurs widely in charters beginning with the reign of Æthelstan, and reflects the growing dynastic claims of the West Saxon kings.

It can also be shown that, in the case of St Cuthbert at least, royal interest in the saint was being expressed during the same period. Besides the *Historia* itself, which describes pilgrimages to Chester-le-Street by kings Æthelstan (*HSC* 26) and Edmund (*HSC* 28), there is the evidence of London, British Library, Cotton Otho B.ix, a gospel book bearing the Latin inscription 'Æthelstan, the pious king of the English, gives this Gospel book to St Cuthbert the bishop.'[69] Another of Æthelstan's books, Cambridge, Corpus Christi College 183, contains a wealth of Cuthbertine material including a mass, a rhymed office and a hymn to St Cuthbert, all probably composed in

---

66 See, for example, *GA* 74.
67 See Nelson, 'A King Across the Sea', pp. 58–61.
68 See Simpson, 'The King Alfred/St Cuthbert Episode', pp. 400–4.
69 See Keynes, 'Æthelstan's Books', p. 174. Cotton Otho B.ix was nearly completely destroyed in the Cottonian fire of 1731; the inscription was recorded in Wanley's catalogue of Anglo-Saxon manuscripts (1705).

the south of England in the early tenth century; the rhyming office, at least, was most likely written under royal patronage and intended for the court chapel.[70] As Rollason notes, 'The evidence of CCCC 183 . . . suggests that Æthelstan was instrumental in spreading and developing the saint's cult and associated himself closely with it.'[71]

It seems clear from the awkward way it is incorporated into the rest of the *Historia de sancto Cuthberto* that the Alfred/Cuthbert episode originally existed as an independent story. The evidence we have seen suggests that this story may have been composed during the first half of the tenth century, perhaps in the reign of Æthelstan, a king who seems to have demonstrated a genuine interest in St Cuthbert. It is even possible that this particular episode in the *Historia de sancto Cuthberto* was originally composed not at Durham, but in Wessex.[72] Given the evidence of interest in the cult of Cuthbert in the south of England, where kings like Æthelstan were working to establish a link between themselves and the saint, and given the odd occurrence of similar stories at two widely separated monasteries whose only shared trait was recent royal patronage, the royal court should be considered as a potential point of origin for this story.

HSC 19a *Alfred and Edward*

Like *HSC* 14, this brief passage serves as a rather awkward transition between the St Cuthbert / King Alfred episode and the rest of the text. More importantly, it establishes a pattern in which reverence for St Cuthbert is passed down from one king to the next. This pattern will be repeated with similar scenes between Edward and Æthelstan in *HSC* 25 and between Æthelstan and Edmund in *HSC* 27. In fact, this tradition of reverence forms a dominant theme through the second half of the *Historia*, introducing the lavish gifts given to St Cuthbert by kings Æthelstan (*HSC* 26) and Edmund (*HSC* 28). This pattern originates with King Alfred and the story of Alfred's

---

70 See Rollason, 'St Cuthbert and Wessex', pp. 414–19. There is no evidence that either the hymn or the rhyming office were known in the north before the late eleventh century, while the mass never appears to have been used in the north at all (p. 416). Since the rhyming office is a rare English example of a recent continental development, and since it was intended for a secular rather than a monastic church, it is likely that it originated in court circles and was intended for the royal chapel (p. 417).

71 Rollason, 'St Cuthbert and Wessex', p. 423. Rollason argues that CCCC 183 was not originally produced as a gift for the saint, as has traditionally been assumed, but was instead intended as a private devotional book for the king which only later found its way to Durham (pp. 420–2). However, even if this were not the case, the book's contents clearly suggest strong royal interest in the saint and his cult.

72 Simpson argues that the King Alfred episode was written in the north, since it refers to the south of England as *terram Australium Saxonum*; see Simpson, 'The King Alfred/St Cuthbert Episode', p. 407. However, this error, which occurs in the introduction to the episode (*HSC* 14), could easily have been the work of the *HSC*'s Northumbrian author/compiler rather than the original author of the story.

dream, which may imply that the story is not simply a later insertion but an integral part of one of the *Historia*'s main themes.

HSC 19b *The Monk Hesleden Grant*

This episode returns abruptly to the subject of Abbot Eadred and King Guthred, last mentioned in *HSC* 13. The six identifiable vills in this grant all lie near one another and form a compact block of territory on the coast of County Durham just south of Easington (see map, fig. 3). The vills are listed in geographic order from north to south; the only exception to this is Monk Hesleden itself, which heads the list even though this places it out of order. Monk Helseden also stands out by virtue of being the head of an ancient parish. When the vills in this list are mapped according to surviving township boundaries they describe a discrete block of territory which corresponds precisely with the early parishes of Monk Hesleden and Castle Eden and is roughly 3,500 hectares in size. In fact, these vills seem to form a half-size version of the twelve-vill composite estates found elsewhere in the *Historia*, consisting of an estate centre at Monk Hesleden and six dependent vills.[73]

Although the purchase of Monk Hesleden is not verified in any other early source, its constituent vills do make up part of the twelve-vill estate leased by the community to Elfred son of Brihtwulf in the early tenth century (*HSC* 22); these vills continued to be held by the church of Durham after the Conquest.

HSC 20 *The Waves of Blood*

This episode reintroduces the figure of Abbot Eadred, the man through whom St Cuthbert arranged the election of King Guthred.[74] It represents the earliest surviving version of the story of the attempt to move St Cuthbert's body to Ireland and the saint's miraculous intervention. The story was subsequently repeated in the *Miracula sancti Cuthberti* and the *Libellus de exordio*. The episode in the *Miracula* (*MSC* 2) embellishes on the story given in the *Historia* without adding any significant details and seems to be based entirely on the *HSC*.[75] Interestingly, however, the *MSC* does not mention seven years of wandering, instead describing the monks as 'longo tempore

---

[73] For complete discussion of these composite estates and of the use of later township and parish boundaries in reconstructing them, see below, Appendix II.

[74] Abbot Eadred is in fact a rather puzzling character. The *HSC* identifies him as 'Eadred, abbot of Carlisle'; if this is true, it raises the possibility that Eadred was not involved in the actual departure from Lindisfarne, but instead joined the saint's body during its wanderings. If *HSC* 20 is correct in describing an attempted flight to Ireland via the Derwent, then it would make sense if the monks had taken refuge in their daughter-house at Carlisle along the way, and Abbot Eadred could have most logically joined them at that point.

[75] See Colgrave, 'Post-Bedan Miracles', p. 322.

migrantes'. The seven years of wandering are, however, described explicitly in the *Libellus de exordio* (*LDE* II.10–12); the *LDE* not only describes the miracle of the waves of blood but gives a specific date for the years of wandering (875–83) and adds several details which are not in the *HSC*.[76]

Another attempt to translate the body of a northern saint to Ireland, this one successful, took place in Scotland at about the same time. According to the *Annals of Ulster*, in 878 the relics of St Columba (which had been moved from Iona to Dunkeld shortly after 800) were translated to Ireland (*AU* 878.9). Smyth suggests that this event may have prompted the attempt to move St Cuthbert to Ireland.[77]

The Seven Years' Wandering

The move from Northumberland to Durham is one of the most crucial events in the whole history of the community of St Cuthbert, and also one of the most obscure. The *Historia* is the earliest surviving source to describe this move; *HSC* 20 states that Bishop Eardulf and Abbot Eadred left Lindisfarne and wandered with the saint's body for seven years before settling at Chester-le-Street, but gives no dates for these events.[78] Another relatively early source, the *Chronicon monasterii Dunelmensis*, gives a detailed description of Abbot Eadred's involvement in the election of King Guthred but makes no mention at all of the seven years' wandering. It is only in the twelfth century that more details emerge. Both Symeon's *Libellus de exordio* (*LDE* II.6) and the *Annales Lindisfarnenses* (*AL* 875) state that the community departed Lindisfarne in 875 in the wake of Halfdan's expedition up the Tyne. Both sources also repeat the *HSC*'s reference to seven years of wandering; the *LDE* does not specifically date the community's arrival at Chester-le-Street, while the *Annales* date the establishment of the see at Chester-le-Street to 883 (*AL* 883). The same dates of 875–83 are also given in the *Historia regum*; however, these dates are most likely to have originated only with the twelfth-century portions of the text.[79]

---

[76] See below, p. 98.

[77] See Smyth, *Scandinavian Kings*, pp. 257–8.

[78] The chronology of the *Historia* at this point is particularly vague. *HSC* 12 (Halfdan's departure, c. 876) and *HSC* 13 (the election of Guthred) are linked by the phrase 'at that time' (*eo tempore*). This is followed (*igitur*) by *HSC* 14–19 (King Alfred's dream, c. 878), which is linked to *HSC* 20 (the seven years' wandering) by another 'at the same time' (*eodem tempore*).

[79] All three divisions of the *Historia regum* contain references to the seven years' wandering. (For the three divisions within the *HR* see Blair, 'Observations', p. 117; see also p. 10 above.) The tenth-century portion of the text follows its description of Halfdan's expedition in 875 by stating that Bishop Eardulf and Abbot Eadred left Lindisfarne with St Cuthbert's body, fleeing before the barbarians from place to place with that treasure for nine years (*HR*i 75). It later states that in 883 Guthred was made from slave to king and an episcopal see was established at Chester-le-Street (*HR*i 78); however, this entry is an interlinear addition to the text. The eleventh-century portion of the *Historia regum* notes the death of Bishop Eardulf in 899, stating that he was the

How trustworthy are the dates 875–83? All three twelfth-century sources make an explicit link between Halfdan's expedition up the Tyne in 875 and the community's departure from Lindisfarne, although no such connection is established in the *HSC*.[80] Since the *HSC* gives no motive for the move from Lindisfarne, it would be logical enough for a twelfth-century author to find that motive in the recent raid by Halfdan, who had 'sinned cruelly against St Cuthbert' (*HSC* 12). This link provides a starting date of 875; adding precisely seven years to this brings us to 882, while allowing for four additional months at Crayke places the arrival in Chester-le-Street in 883. In this way a twelfth-century author armed with nothing more than the *HSC* itself might logically arrive at the dates 875–83. However, beyond taking the reference to seven years more literally than it may have originally been intended (seven was, after all, a mystical number, and it occurs here in the context of a miracle-story), these dates may be no more than a logical guess based on a source (the *HSC*) whose chronological organization of its various sources, as we have seen, is often less than logical.

In fact, it seems that the author of the *Historia* had actually brought together material from three different and potentially contradictory sources, each of which contains a different perspective on the move from Lindisfarne. These are: (1) the translation of the bodies of King Ceolwulf and St Cuthbert, and presumably the see itself, from Lindisfarne to Norham by Bishop Ecgred (*HSC* 9); (2) the election of King Guthred and his subsequent gift to St Cuthbert of all the land between Tyne and Wear, set shortly after Halfdan's

man who had translated the body of St Cuthbert to Chester-le-Street after having 'fled from the pagan army with great labour and poverty for nine years' (*HR*ii 82). The twelfth-century portion of the text also follows its description of Halfdan's expedition in 875 with a reference to the wandering, noting that Bishop Eardulf and Abbot Eadred bore the body of St Cuthbert from Lindisfarne and 'wandered here and there for seven years' (*HR*iii 96). An entry for 883 then gives a full description of King Guthred's election and explains that Guthred re-established the former episcopal see of Lindisfarne at Chester-le-Street 'after a seven-year-long transmigration from the isle of Lindisfarne' (*HR*iii 98).

What can we make of all this? First, it seems likely that the two references in *HR*i are later interpolations and do not actually date from the tenth century; one of these is an interlinear addition while the other is one of three Northumbrian intrusions in a portion of the text which is otherwise based on Asser. (See Blair, 'Observations', p. 103.) Furthermore, both of these entries closely mirror passages in later portions of the *Historia regum*; since both *HR*ii and *HR*iii show clear signs of Northumbrian origins while *HR*i does not, it seems most likely that they originated in the Northumbrian portions of the text and were inserted into *HR*i by a later compiler. Second, it is worth noting that *HR*ii, while it agrees with the *HSC* in associating the translation with Bishop Eardulf, refers to nine years of wandering rather than seven and fails to give specific dates. It is only with *HR*iii that we find seven years of wandering and the dates 875–83, the same information given in the *Libellus de exordio* and the *Annales Lindisfarnenses*.

80 Recent scholars continue to accept this connection; see e.g. Smyth, *Scandinavian Kings*, p. 257.

raid on the Tyne and his subsequent destruction (*HSC* 12–13); and (3) an attempt to flee to Ireland, set during an unspecified time when Bishop Eardulf and Abbot Eadred wandered from Lindisfarne with the body of St Cuthbert for seven years and eventually settled at Chester-le-Street (*HSC* 20). Twelfth-century historians dealt with these three different episodes by changing the first into a translation of Ceolwulf alone and by integrating the second and third episodes, placing the election of King Guthred and subsequent acquisition of Chester-le-Street at the culmination of the seven years' wandering.[81] It was the integration of these two episodes that in turn allowed the dating of the seven years' wandering to 875–83.

The evidence of the *Historia* thus suggests that St Cuthbert's wanderings may have been more complex than the twelfth-century sources allow, that they may have included a protracted stay at Norham and thus lasted longer than a literal seven years, and that we have no sure way of knowing when they began or ended.[82] Nevertheless, by the time of Symeon of Durham this equivocal and potentially contradictory evidence had been hammered into a uniform narrative that has been generally accepted ever since.[83] Symeon also added a number of new details, including two additional miracles (the saint's provision of a horse to pull the cart containing his body, and the loss and recovery of the Lindisfarne Gospels during the abortive voyage to Ireland) and a description of St Cuthbert's seven bearers.[84] By far the most significant addition to the *LDE*, however, was the fact that the monks' departure from Lindisfarne was linked to the earlier destruction of the monastery by Vikings, a point never mentioned in the *HSC*:

> they left that noble church, the first in the nation of the Bernicians and in which so many saints had lived their lives. They left it, I say, to flee from the barbarians, it being the year of the Incarnation of Our Lord 875, the two-hundredth and forty-first since King Oswald and Bishop Aidan had

---

[81] The best example of this integration occurs in the *Libellus de exordio* (*LDE* II.6 and II.13). The sequence begins with Halfdan's expedition (from *HSC* 12), which leads to the seven years' wandering (from *HSC* 20), ending when God's judgement falls on Halfdan (from *HSC* 12), allowing the community to settle at Crayke (from *HSC* 20), at which point Abbot Eadred arranges the election of King Guthred and the see is transferred to Chester-le-Street (from *HSC* 13).

[82] These conclusions are supported in part by the evidence of the *Secgan be þam Godes sanctum þe on Engla lande ærost reston* and the *Historia pontificum*; see above, Commentary, *HSC* 9.

[83] Symeon interweaves elements from *HSC* 12–13 and *HSC* 20 as well as the story of King Alfred's dream (*HSC* 15–18) and three miracles concerning St Cuthbert's punishment of disobedient women into a prolonged narrative which occupies *LDE* II.6–13.

[84] See *LDE* II.10–12. No earlier written sources for this additional material survive, which suggests that Symeon may have drawn it from local oral tradition. If so, this in turn suggests that, by the twelfth century at least, the seven years' wandering had become a traditional part of the lore surrounding St Cuthbert.

founded that same church and placed in it an episcopal see with a congregation of monks, the one hundredth and eighty-ninth from the passing of father Cuthbert, the twenty-second of the episcopate of Eardwulf. That is the eighty-third year since that church (as was said above) was sacked in the time of Bishop Higbald, and almost all the monks, apart from a very few who somehow escaped, perished by various deaths. With the coming of this new devastation of which we are now speaking, these survivors also dispersed . . . (*LDE* II.6)

In the introductory summary to the *LDE*, probably composed after the main text,[85] this linkage becomes much more explicit and the distinction between the events of 793 and 875 virtually disappears.

a cruel force of barbarians crossed to England in innumerable ships and devastated everything everywhere, even killing kings (of which the English had many at that time) – amongst them the glorious martyr Edmund. Indeed, they devastated the provinces of the Northumbrians so atrociously and destroyed all the churches and monasteries with fire and sword, that when they departed they left behind them hardly a sign of Christianity. The bishop of the aforesaid church, Eardwulf, barely escaped death when with a few companions he fled with the undecayed body of the holy confessor Cuthbert. Moreover, the monks who had placed their trust in the holy character of the place and had remained were dragged from the church [and tortured in various ways] . . . all perished forthwith. In this way the monastic congregation around the body of St Cuthbert came to an end. (*LDE summary*, pp. 259–61)

By linking the events of 793 and 875 in this way, the *Libellus* creates the image of a monastic community that barely escaped complete destruction by the Vikings and fled in great disarray, losing its monastic character and never recovering its former greatness.[86] This image, which served to justify the Norman restructuring of the community, has been generally accepted down to the present day.[87]

---

85 Rollason suggests that it was composed 'in or shortly after the first quarter of the twelfth century', while also observing that 'Symeon would still have been alive at the time of composition and may even have been its author'; Rollason, *Symeon of Durham*, p. lxvi and n. 274.

86 I have suggested elsewhere that by the standards of Symeon and his fellow Norman monks, the late-Saxon community of St Cuthbert did not appear to have been monastic at all, and that Symeon saw the Vikings as the logical cause of this perceived collapse in monastic discipline; see South, 'Norman Conquest of Durham'.

87 This can be seen, for example, in the writing of Edmund Craster: 'It is evident that in the course of time the congregation of St Cuthbert changed its character. The main cause of the change may be found in the wholesale massacre of monks at Lindisfarne by Danish pirates in 793. That terrible diminution of their number was never made good, and, from then on to Bishop Carilef's introduction of Benedictine monks into Durham, history records the names of no more than two abbots . . . the community came to be almost wholly secular' (Craster, 'Patrimony', pp. 197–8).

The evidence of the *Historia de sancto Cuthberto* and other early sources calls this image of wholesale destruction and willy-nilly flight into question in several important ways. First, the *Historia* never mentions the Viking raid of 793 at all,[88] and its description of Halfdan's expedition up the Tyne in 875 (a good fifty miles from Lindisfarne itself) makes no mention of attacks on the monks. Second, as we have seen, the community may well have begun the process of relocation before Halfdane's invasion in 875 with a move to Norham. This suggests that the monks were not caught completely unprepared in 875, as Symeon claims. Furthermore, as Rollason has pointed out, St Cuthbert's wanderings show signs of being an orderly relocation designed to keep the community's power intact, rather than being the disorganized flight described in the *LDE*.[89] The monks did not wander randomly across the face of northern England; whenever we can localize them (at Norham, Derwentmouth, and Crayke) they are at or near places where the community is known to have possessed property. This impression of an organized, large-scale relocation is also supported by the *HSC*'s statement that Bishop Eardulf and Abbot Eadred were long accompanied by 'all the saint's people' (*HSC* 20), which flatly contradicts Symeon.

There is also a ninth-century source which, if it was in fact produced at Lindisfarne (or Norham) as has traditionally been believed, also supports the conclusion that the community retained its strength and influence after the Viking raid.[90] The original portion of this text, the *Liber uitæ Dunelmensis*, which probably dates from shortly before 840, contains the names of some 2,500 nobles, monks and clerics who desired the community's prayers on their behalf.[91] The *Liber uitæ* thus implies that the community was still a respected religious centre at the very time that Symeon claims it was in complete disarray, and that it was in active contact with other religious houses throughout England, with which it must have traded lists of names. It also demonstrates that the community was stable and wealthy enough during

---

[88] In fact, as Peter Sawyer has noted, the story of the attack in 793 seems to have grown in the telling: 'Alcuin's letters show that although the community of St Cuthbert on Lindisfarne was disrupted by the attack of 793 it survived, together with many of its treasures and manuscripts (ten of which, including the Lindisfarne Gospels, still exist) and the church, built in the seventh century by St Aidan, was not destroyed.' (Sawyer, *Kings and Vikings*, p. 94.)

[89] See Rollason, *Saints and Relics*, pp. 211–12.

[90] Gerchow has recently suggested that the ninth-century portion of the *LVD* may have actually been produced at Monkwearmouth-Jarrow rather than Lindisfarne, and that the book only came into the possession of the monks of St Cuthbert as the result of a tenth-century gift by King Athelstan; see Gerchow, *Gedenküberlieferung*, pp. 121–3. If this is correct, then obviously the *LVD* can tell us nothing about the state of the community of St Cuthbert during the ninth century.

[91] For a discussion of the date of production of the earliest portion of the *LVD* see Gerchow, *Gedenküberlieferung*, pp. 130–1.

this period to produce a deluxe manuscript extensively decorated with gold and silver lettering.

Finally, the land holdings recorded in the *HSC* show no evidence of the community's collapse, either after 793 or after 875. Instead, they show the community continuing to control a substantial patrimony throughout this period, though the focus of this patrimony naturally shifted from Lindisfarne to between the rivers Tyne and Tees. The monks of St Cuthbert continued to be among the greatest land-holders in Northumbria, and the fact that they were able to keep their landed wealth intact suggests that the move was deliberate and well-organized. The *Historia* explains the community's new lands as a gift from King Guthred in return for securing his election (*HSC* 13) and gives credit to Abbot Eadred, who also helped to lead the seven years' wandering. Whether we trust this explanation or not, evidence elsewhere in the *Historia* suggests that by the early tenth century the community did control a large block of territory between the Tyne and Wear;[92] the acquisition of this territory suggests the exercise of considerable political and economic power.

HSC 21 *Bishop Cuthheard*

King Alfred's death and Edward's succession are described in *ASC* 899. The successions of Edward and Bishop Cuthheard are also linked together in the *Historia regum* (*HR*ii 82) and the *Annales Lindisfarnenses* (*AL* 899) and are likewise dated to 899. The *HR* does not mention Cuthheard's death, while the *Annales* date it to 913. The *Libellus de exordio* states that Cuthheard became bishop in the nineteenth year after the community's arrival in Chester-le-Street (*LDE* II.16) and that he died in the fifteenth year of his episcopate (*LDE* II.17); since the *LDE* places the community's arrival at Chester-le-Street in 883, this would date Cuthheard's episcopate to 901–15.

None of Bishop Cuthheard's acquisitions is recorded in any other early source. Sedgefield is listed among the estates belonging to the bishop of Durham in the twelfth-century *Boldon Book* (*BB*, pp. 23–5), as is Bedlington (*BB*, pp. 29–33). Tilred's grant is somewhat confusing; according to *HSC* 19b, Castle Eden had already been purchased for the community by Abbot Eadred. Furthermore, it is difficult to see how this grant could have been split between the community and Norham, since according to *HSC* 9 Norham also belonged to the community by this time. Bernard's grant of *Twilingatun* also conflicts with the statement in *HSC* 21 that this vill had been purchased for the community by Abbot Eadred. The grants of Castle Eden and *Twilingatun*, if accurate, show the high price of admission into the community at this time,

---

[92] Part of this block of territory is described in *HSC* 24, which states that Bishop Cuthheard and the congregation leased to Eadred son of Ricsige all the land between by the Derwent, the Wear, and Dere Street.

suggesting again that the monks of St Cuthbert in the early ninth century were a powerful and prestigious body.

Grant of Sedgefield

Several facts suggest that Sedgefield constituted a substantial estate rather than a single vill. First there is the phrase 'and whatever pertains to it', which suggests additional holdings. Second, Sedgefield eventually became the head of a large early parish, and we find that the estate centres of composite estates listed in the *Historia* almost invariably went on to become the heads of medieval parishes.[93] Third, Sedgefield is listed in *Boldon Book* at the head of a group of six vills clustered together in what would become the medieval parishes of Sedgefield and Bishop Middleham (*BB*, pp. 23–7); one of these, Butterwick, still owed certain services at Sedgefield.[94] Presumably the vills of Bradbury and Morden granted to the community by Snaculf son of Cytel (*HSC* 30), which lay in the same area, would also have been associated with Sedgefield. Together, this evidence strongly suggests that Sedgefield once served as the centre of a composite estate.

Sedgefield is the first of several estates in the *Historia* to be granted 'with sake and soke'. This phrase first appears in the mid-tenth century and is most commonly associated with the obligations owed by the dependent vills of a composite estate or *scir*.[95] The precise meaning of 'sake and soke' continues to be debated and may well vary over time; it is often translated in terms of jurisdiction, as 'cause and suit', although it can sometimes have the broader (and possibly earlier) meaning of all the renders and services owed to the lord of a *scir* (originally the king) and rendered at the estate centre.[96] In the present context, it seems to refer to the rights which the lord of what was or had been a composite estate (in this case, the bishop) continued to hold over a

---

93 For further discussion of this point see below, Appendix II.

94 The vills associated with Sedgefield in *Boldon Book* are Bishop Middleham, Cornforth, Garmondsway, Mainsforth and Butterwick. The villeins of Butterwick plowed and harrowed two acres at Sedgefield and carted a stone to the Sedgefield mill (*BB*, p. 27); similar obligations can be found among the dependent vills of the composite estate of Bedlingtonshire (*BB*, pp. 29–31).

95 The two earliest examples of the phrase 'with sake and soke' occur in a charter of 956 by which King Eadwig granted Southwell in Nottinghamshire to Archbishop Osketel of York (*Cartularium Saxonicum*, ed. Birch, 1029), and a charter of 959 by which King Edgar granted Howden in Yorkshire to the matron Quen (*Cartularium Saxonicum*, ed. Birch, 1052); see Stenton, *Anglo-Saxon England*, pp. 494–5. Both of these use the term to describe the relationship of a number of dependent vills to their estate centre; the Southwell charter lists eleven vills which 'birad in to Sudwellan mid sacce et mid sacne', while the Howden charter lists eight vills which 'hærath to Heofoddene mid sace et mid socne'.

96 The most prominent proponent of the 'cause and suit' intrepretation is Stenton; see Stenton, *Anglo-Saxon England*, p. 498. The broader interpretation was first proposed by Davis; see Davis, *Kalendar of Abbot Samson*, p. xl. For recent summaries of the problem see Kapelle, *Norman Conquest*, pp. 62–5, and Faith, *English Peasantry*, p. 90.

dependent vill or lesser holding which was now in the hands of a sub-tenant. Judging from the evidence of *Boldon Book*, which frequently shows the bishop continuing to receive food renders and labour obligations from vills held by sub-tenants, the broader interpretation of 'customs owed to the estate centre' seems more likely to be correct in the particular context of the *Historia*.[97]

Grant of Bedlington

The vills of 'Bedlington and its dependencies', with the exception of Twizell (if that is the correct identification of *Grubbatwisle*), lie adjacent to one another near the Northumberland coast between the rivers Wansbeck and Blyth; Twizell lies between these same two rivers some five miles further inland. When mapped according to surviving township boundaries, the outline of the five adjacent vills matches precisely with the bounds of the early parish of Bedlington, describing a territory some 3,500 hectares in size. These same five vills are also recorded in *Boldon Book*, where they are collectively referred to as 'Bedelyngton'shir'.[98] In fact, Bedlington (along with Monk Hesleden, *HSC* 19b) appears to be a half-size version of the twelve-vill composite estates found elsewhere in the *Historia*, consisting of an estate centre at Bedlington and four (or five, if one includes *Grubbatwisle*) dependent vills.[99] However, if the identification of Twizell is correct then Bedlingtonshire may have originated as a full-size composite estate, and the *Historia* may show us one estate in the process of shrinking just as it shows another (Easington, *HSC* 22) in the process of growing.[100] If Bedlingtonshire originally consisted of a block of adjacent vills like all the other composite estates in the *Historia*, then this block must have once included several more

---

97 A good example of this kind of sub-tenant in *Boldon Book* is Thomas of Sheraton. 'Thomas holds half of Sheraton and pays 30s for cornage, and half of a cow for metreth, and half of a man for castle-guard, and four scot-chalders of malt, and the same of flour and the same of oats, and each plow of his villeins plows and harrows two acres and each of them does three obligatory days in the autumn with one man and the cart half a cask of wine and mill-stones to Durham' (*BB*, pp. 53–5). I would suggest that these customs represent half of the soke originally rendered by the dependent vill of Sheraton to its estate centre at Easington; the bishop continues to collect this soke even though Sheraton is now held by Thomas and another man, John.

98 'Bedlingtonshire' in *Boldon Book* actually consists of six vills, since Sleekburn is now listed as two vills, East and West Sleekburn. The vills of Bedlingtonshire are distinguished by the fact that they all rendered a series of annual labour obligations together at Bedlington, the estate centre. '[The] townships of Bedlingtonshire [all help to] cart timber and mill-stones, and they similarly make the mill-pond, and they similarly enclose the court, and the similarly cover the hall, and they similarly prepare the fishery, and they similarly carry loads as far as Newcastle and as far as Fenwick and no further' (*BB*, p. 29).

99 For complete discussion of these composite estates and of the use of later township and parish boundaries in reconstructing them, see below, Appendix II.

100 See *HSC* 19a and 22, in which the seven-vill estate of Monk Hesleden expands northwards to become the twelve-vill estate of Easington.

vills which would have lain between Twizell and Bedlington. If this is so, then these vills had somehow been lost by the time the community acquired this estate; by the time of *Boldon Book*, Twizell too would disappear, leaving a only a core of coastal vills.

HSC 22 *Lease of Easington*

Nothing is known of Elfred Brihtwulfing, and this lease is not recorded in any other early source. If we ignore 'Billingham and its dependencies', the other twelve vills in this lease all lie near one another along the coast between Bishop Wearmouth and Hartlepool (see map, fig. 3). When mapped according to surviving township boundaries, these vills define a territory roughly 6,900 hectares in size that corresponds closely to the outlines of the early parishes of Easington, Monk Hesleden and Castle Eden.[101] It seems clear that what is listed here are the constituent parts of a twelve-vill composite estate like those described elsewhere in the *Historia*, this one with its centre at Easington.[102] As for Billingham, the use of the phrase 'and its dependencies' suggests that this was the centre of a second composite estate located near the mouth of the Tees.

It is not known how or when Easington, Little Thorp, the Shottons and Sheraton had been acquired by the community. The purchase of Monk Hesleden and its six associated vills by Abbot Eadred is described in *HSC* 19b. The supposed founding of Billingham is described in *HSC* 9, but this estate is subsequently listed among those confiscated from the community by King Ælle (*HSC* 10); it is not known how it was reacquired. The lease lists its vills in geographic order from north to south; the one exception to this (aside from Billingham) is Monk Hesleden, which is listed second following Easington itself. This may be because Monk Hesleden continued to function as an estate centre or sub-centre, and therefore belonged at the head of the list along with Easington.

According to the *Historia*, both the Easington and Billingham estates were lost to King Rægnald (*HSC* 23); the northern half of the Easington estate would have gone to Onlafbald and been recovered after his death, while the southern half of that estate (centred on Monk Hesleden) and Billingham were

---

[101] The match between parish and township boundaries is exact except for two townships in Easington parish (Hawthorn and Haswell) which are not among the vills listed in *HSC* 22. Both vills lie adjacent to Easington and are first mentioned in the twelfth century, at which time both belonged to the monks and prior of Durham. It is thus conceivable that the parish bounds actually preserve something closer to the original outlines of the Easington estate, and that one or both of these vills was founded after the time of the *Historia* on land which had originally been part of the vill of Easington. For further discussion of the composite estates in the *Historia* and the use of later township and parish boundaries in reconstructing them, see below, Appendix II.

[102] For a complete discussion of the composite estates in the *Historia*, see below, Appendix II.

given to Scula and lost to the community for some time. According to the *Liber uitæ Dunelmensis*, Monk Hesleden had been recovered by the late eleventh century, since Bishop William of St Calais was able to grant it to the monks and prior for their upkeep. At the same time, William the Conqueror restored Billingham 'with all its dependencies' to the monks (*LVD* 49v).

King Rægnald and the 'First Battle of Corbridge'

A King Rægnald is mentioned in the *Anglo-Saxon Chronicle* as capturing York in 923 (*ASC* 923 DE) and later accepting King Edward as father and lord, as did the sons of Eadwulf and all the inhabitants of Northumbria (*ASC* 924 AF). This Rægnald is now identified with Ragnall, king of the Dubhgall and grandson of Ivarr the Boneless, who is mentioned in the *Annals of Ulster* and other Irish sources.[103]

The battle at Corbridge described in this section of the *Historia* has long been a thorny issue. There is evidence in three different sources that a battle between King Rægnald and the Scots took place at Corbridge around 918; this battle is referred to in *HSC* 24.[104] However, the majority of scholars have long believed that this cannot be the same battle described here in *HSC* 22 because the *Historia* links this battle with the subsequent confiscation of community lands by the Viking Onlafbald in defiance of Bishop Cuthheard (*HSC* 23). Since Cuthheard seems to have died in 915 at the latest,[105] it has been widely concluded that there must have been two battles at Corbridge: the first battle, described only in *HSC* 22, would have taken place around 914, while the second battle, described in the *Annals of Ulster*, the *Pictish Chronicle* and *HSC* 24, involved all the same participants but took place around 918.[106]

Given the abundant evidence that the author of the *Historia* often worked by piecing together pre-existing texts, and given that his grasp of chronology in general and the episcopal succession in particular is less than perfect (he has Cuthbert succeeded by Ecgred, a bishop of the mid-eighth century), it seems more reasonable to assume that there was a single battle at Corbridge around 918, that our author was dealing with references to the same battle in two different sources, and that he was mistaken in placing the incident with Onlafbald during Cuthheard's episcopate. This argument becomes even more convincing if we also accept the possibility that our author was actually

---

103 See Wainwright, 'Battles at Corbridge', p. 166, and Smyth, *Scandinavian York* I, 93–6.
104 For a complete discussion of the evidence for this battle, see below, Commentary, *HSC* 24.
105 See above, Commentary, *HSC* 21.
106 See e.g. Mawer, 'Scandinavian Kingdom of Northumbria', pp. 51–3; Wainwright, 'Battles at Corbridge', pp. 163–9; and Smyth, *Scandinavian York* I, 97–9. The only scholar in recent memory to suggest that there was only one battle at Corbridge has been Craster, 'Patrimony', p. 191, n. 1.

working in the mid- or late eleventh century, more than a century after the events he was describing.

HSC 23 *The Story of Onlafbald*

The *Annales Lindisfarnenses* state that in 899 'King Reingauld, landing with a large fleet, divided the land of St Cuthbert between two of his generals, Scula and Onhlafball' (*AL* 899). The *Miracula sancti Cuthberti* (*MSC* 3) and the *Libellus de exordio* (*LDE* II.16) give more elaborate versions of the story of Onlafbald's destruction without adding significant details.[107] None of these twelfth-century texts shows any signs of reliance on earlier sources other than the *HSC* itself.

The vills from Castle Eden Burn to the Wear which the *Historia* claims were lost to Onlafbald and subsequently recovered would have comprised the northern half of the composite estate of Easington; this territory subsequently evolved into the medieval parish of Easington. The rest of the land between Castle Eden Burn and the Wear would have been occupied by the composite estate of Bishop Wearmouth, which according to a later section of the *Historia* was only acquired by the community in the reign of Æthelstan (*HSC* 26). The vills confiscated by Onlafbald do seem to have been recovered at some point; Easington, Little Thorp and Shotton all belonged to the bishop of Durham in the twelfth century and were listed among his holdings in *Boldon Book* (*BB*, p. 21).

HSC 24 *Lease of Chester-le-Street and Gainford*

Nothing is known of Eadred son of Ricsige; Robertson has suggested that his father was King Ricsig of Northumbria.[108] The parallels between this episode and *HSC* 22 – both Elfred and Eadred travel across the mountains, lease land from St Cuthbert and die in battle at Corbridge – must arouse some curiosity concerning our author's sources for these episodes. The meaning of the text is also somewhat confusing: is Ælstan the brother of Eadred or of Esbrid? Was Rægnald so impressed by the bravery of Esbrid and Ælstan that he allowed his enemies to inherit Eadred's land, or did they earn their reward by fighting on Rægnald's side against their kinsman?

It is unclear whether 'Gainford and whatever pertains to it' refers to the same large territory on the Tees described in *HSC* 9, or to the smaller thirteen-vill estate centred on Gainford described in *HSC* 31. The large territory here associated with Chester-le-Street represents the lion's share of the land between Tyne and Wear purportedly granted to the community by King Guthred. It seems likely that this territory represented the community's home estate during the tenth century; if so, it is surprising that monks would have leased out these lands unless they were under duress. In any event, Esbrid and

---

107 See Colgrave, 'Post-Bedan Miracles', pp. 323–4.
108 See E. W. Robertson, *Scotland under her Early Kings* (Edinburgh, 1862) I, 58.

Ælstan apparently kept fealty to St Cuthbert like Eadred before them, since this territory seems to have remained in the hands of the community; Gainford and its dependent vills were included among the lands leased out by Bishop Aldhun in the late tenth or early eleventh century (*HSC* 31), while Chester-le-Street itself is listed among the bishop of Durham's holdings in *Boldon Book* (*BB*, p. 13). On the other hand, the composite estate of Staindrop, which falls within the bounds of the original Gainford grant described in *HSC* 9, was lost at some point, since *HSC* 32 records the grant in which Cnut returned this estate to the community.

The 'Second Battle of Corbridge'

There is general agreement that the battle at Corbridge described in this section of the Historia took place around 918. It is assumed that Cuthheard's episcopate lasted until 915 and that he made the grant to Eadred son of Ricsige in that year; since the *HSC* states that Eadred cultivated his lands in peace for three years, this brings us down to 918. Smyth has argued persuasively that this battle at Corbridge is identical with ones described in the *Annals of Ulster* and the *Pictish Chronicle* which took place in the same year. The *Annals* describe a battle in 918 between King Ragnall and the Scots on the banks of the Tyne (*AU* 917.4); the battle seems to have been inconclusive, with the Scots defeating the majority of the Viking army but then suffering a destructive counterattack led by Ragnall himself. The *Chronicle* states that a battle it calls 'bellum Tinemore' took place between Constantine and Ragnall in the eighteenth year of Constantine's reign (918), and that the Scots were victorious.[109] Given the different points of view represented by these three sources, it is indeed plausible that all three are referring to the same battle, particularly if the battle itself was inconclusive.

It has traditionally been assumed that this battle is different from and later than the battle of Corbridge described separately in *HSC* 22. However, since there is no evidence in any other source referring to an earlier battle at the same site, I find it more likely that the author of the *Historia*, working with two separate references to the same battle (which actually took place around 918), mistakenly created two battles of Corbridge.[110]

King Rægnald's Death

The death of King Rægnald is noted in the *Annals of Ulster* under the year 921, where he is called 'Ragnall grandson of Imar, king of the fair foreigners [i.e. Norse] and the dark foreigners [i.e. Danes]' (*AU* 921.4); no details concerning his death are given.[111] Although the *HSC* states that Rægnald died

---

109 See *Chronicles of the Picts*, ed. Skene, p. 9. For a recent discussion, see Smyth, *Scandinavian York* I, 93–9; for earlier interpretations, see Wainwright, 'Battles at Corbridge', and Mawer, 'Scandinavian Kingdom of Northumbria', pp. 51–2.

110 See above, Commentary, *HSC* 22.

111 For a complete reconstruction of Rægnald's career, see Smyth, *Scandinavian York* I, ch. 6.

'taking nothing with him of what he had stolen from St Cuthbert except his sin', it should be noted that a number of vills along the north bank of the Tees display notable Scandinavian influence in their place-names.[112] Furthermore, the estate of Staindrop, which lies in this region, was somwhow lost to the community and only recovered in the reign of Cnut (*HSC* 32). Both of these facts suggest that the real situation was not as simple as the *HSC* would have it seem, and that portions at least of the community's holdings near the Tees were claimed by Rægnald's followers and only regained by the community with some difficulty.

HSC 25 *Edward and Æthelstan*

This transitional section, like *HSC* 19a above and *HSC* 27 below, uses a death-bed conversation to make the shift from the period of one king to that of his successor. Like the other two transitions, it also takes pains to establish that a special reverence for St Cuthbert was handed down from one king to the next.

HSC 26 *King Æthelstan's Visit*

Æthelstan's campaign against the Scots is described in the *Anglo-Saxon Chronicle* (*ASC* 933 A / *ASC* 934 DEF), although no mention of a diversion to St Cuthbert's church is made. The *Annales Lindisfarnenses* do not mention Æthelstan's visit either, and they date the Scottish campaign a decade early (*AL* 924). The *Historia regum* twice makes brief mention of Æthelstan's visit, noting that he gave lands and other royal gifts and consigned any potential thieves to eternal flame (*HR*ii 83 and *HR*iii 107), while the *Libellus de exordio* gives the same information a more elaborate presentation, adding that the gifts were recorded in a cartulary which still survived and that they included twelve vills (*LDE* II.18); both sources date the king's visit to 934. The only source that adds anything to the information given in the *HSC* is the *Cronica monasterii Dunelmensis*, which dates Æthelstan's visit to 935. The *CMD* states that the king gave 'regal gifts in gold and silver, palls and curtains and great bells and many other precious ornaments' (*CMD*, lines 88–90) and it names the twelve vills of the Bishop Wearmouth estate. It concludes with the following passage:

> and finally he [i.e. Æthelstan] gave two armlets which he bore on his arms, saying 'I intend that these be a sign for all who shall come after me that I have established, with most devout heart and under threat of anathema, firm laws and perpetual liberty for the church of my dearest patron, the holy confessor Cuthbert, and of most holy Mary mother of God, as did my predecessors'. (*CMD*, lines 94–8)

---

112 See Watts, 'Place-names', pp. 259–61.

Such a grant of royal privilege is not mentioned in any other account of Æthelstan's visit, but it may be related to the *Historia*'s description of his brother Edmund, who a decade later 'placed with his own hand two golden armlets and two Greek palls upon the holy body, and granted peace and law, better than any it had ever had, to the whole territory of St Cuthbert' (*HSC* 28).

'King Æthelstan's Charter'

The original 'Charter of Æthelstan' was apparently inscribed in a book, since its text opens with the words 'I, King Æthelstan, give to St Cuthbert this gospel-book'. This book has traditionally been identified as London, British Library, Cotton Otho B. ix, which was almost completely destroyed in the Cotton Library fire of 1731. Keynes has suggested that the *HSC*'s charter is in fact based on two Old English records inserted into a blank space preceding the Gospel of St John in Otho B. ix. The text of the first record is preserved in a catalogue of 1705; it is a formal inscription recording the gift of *King Æthelstan's Gospel* to St Cuthbert, written in the language of a royal charter. The second record is described in the same catalogue as an Old English note listing Æthelstan's gifts to St Cuthbert. Keynes suggests that 'the Latin *testamentum* [recorded in the *HSC*] is a conflation of both the Old English records, taking its beginning and its end from the inscription and its central part from the note'.[113] He also notes that both texts were later insertions into the gospel book and suggests that the form and style of the inscription is most compatible with a date in the second half of the tenth century.[114]

The Bishop Wearmouth Grant

When mapped, the twelve vills of 'Bishop Wearmouth and its dependencies' all lie near one another in a compact block of territory extending south along the coast from the mouth of the Wear (see map, fig. 3); this fact, together with the 'and its dependencies' formula, suggests that together these vills constituted a single composite estate with its administrative centre at Bishop Wearmouth. When mapped according to the earliest surviving township boundaries, this estate occupies a territory of roughly 6,600 hectares which corresponds quite closely with the early parishes of Bishop Wearmouth, Seaham and Dalton-le-Dale.[115] Several scholars have noted that

---

113 Keynes, 'King Æthelstan's Books', p. 178.
114 See Keynes, 'King Æthelstan's Books', pp. 175–6.
115 There are only two points at which the outline of the Bishop Wearmouth estate fails to correspond with the later parish structure. First, the estate includes the vill of Offerton, which became part of the parish of Houghton-le-Spring. Second, the parish of Dalton-le-Dale includes one vill, Murton, which is not among the vills listed in *HSC* 26. This vill is first recorded in the twelfth century, at which time it belonged to the monks and prior of Durham. It is thus conceivable that the parish here preserves the original outline of the estate, and that Murton was founded later on land which had originally been part of the vill of Dalton-le-Dale. For further discussion of the composite estates in the *Historia* and the use of later township and parish boundaries in reconstructing them, see below, Appendix II.

this estate, which lies just opposite Monkwearmouth, must have originally been held by the monastic community of Monkwearmouth-Jarrow, and have concluded that this community did not survive the Viking raids earlier in the century and that its lands had therefore reverted to the crown.[116] The vills of this estate remained in the hands of the community after the Conquest and were apparently divided between the bishop and the monks when Bishop William of St Calais reformed the monastery; Bishop Wearmouth, Ryhope and Little Burdon are listed among the bishop's holdings in *Boldon Book* (*BB*, pp. 15–17), while Silksworth (*FPD*, p. 18), Burdon (*FPD*, p. 45) and Dalton-le-Dale (*LVD* 49v) were held by the prior and monks.

HSC 27 Æthelstan and Edmund

This is the last of the three transitional sections (the others are *HSC* 19a and *HSC* 25) which explain how a special reverence for St Cuthbert was handed down through the generations from King Alfred to his successors.

HSC 28 Edmund's Visit

King Edmund's expedition to the North is described in the *Anglo-Saxon Chronicle*, which states that he brought all Northumbria under his sway (*ASC* 944) and ravaged Strathclyde (*ASC* 945). It is presumably on the evidence of this expedition that Craster dates Edmund's visit to 'about the year 945'.[117] Interestingly, neither Edmund's expedition to Scotland or his visit to Chester-le-Street is mentioned at all in either the *Historia regum* or the *Annales Lindisfarnenses*, although both refer to Æthelstan's expedition in the previous decade. The *Libellus de exordio* does mention this visit but seems to rely entirely on the *HSC*, briefly stating that Edmund visited St Cuthbert's shrine while on his way to Scotland, prayed for his assistance, gave gold and precious vestments, and confirmed the laws of the saint (*LDE* II.18).

As was the case with King Æthelstan's visit (*HSC* 26), the only source which adds anything to the information given in the *HSC* concerning Edmund's visit is the *Cronica monasterii Dunelmensis*. The *CMD* states that while on his way to restrain the Scots, Edmund came to Durham (*sic*) bearing many and precious kingly gifts,

> humbly knelt before the saint's tomb, removing two armlets from his own arm, and confirmed [the saint's privileges] before the shrine with full *indome* and wreck and writ, utter and inner, and sake and soke (as it is said in the common tongue), that is with full law and peace, inflicting a terrible malediction on all those who might presume in any way to violate the privileges conferred on this church by himself or his predecessors.
>
> (*CMD*, lines 104–9)

---

[116] See, for example, Craster, 'Patrimony', p. 189, and Hart, *Early Charters*, p. 139.
[117] See Craster, 'Patrimony', p. 192.

The reference to Durham presumably dates the composition of this entry to the eleventh century, but the use of an Old English formula leaves open the possibility that the author was working from an earlier source of some kind; this hypothetical Old English record, if it existed, might also have provided the basis for the description of Edmund's visit in the *Historia*.

HSC 29 *The Darlington Grant*

Styr son of Ulf is mentioned briefly in the late eleventh-century *De obsessione Dunelmi*, which identifies him as a wealthy citizen of York whose daughter became the second wife of Earl Uhtred (see *HSC* 31). Craster interprets King Æthelred's role in this grant as implying that Darlington was bookland which was held by Styr but which could not be alienated without royal licence.[118] Of the six places listed after Darlington in this grant, Great Lumley is located northeast of Durham while the five preceding sites (with the possible exception of *Northmannabi*, which remains unlocated) all lie in close proximity to Darlington. It should be noted that although Styr appears to be granting parcels of land within particular vills, his blocks of carucates are in fact large enough to have been entire vills.[119] The details of Styr's grant are also recorded in the *Cronica monasterii Dunelmensis* (*CMD*, lines 129–34), which states that it was the church of Darlington 'cum omnibus suis appendiciis' which was given to St Cuthbert by King Æthelred; the six properties given by Styr are listed just as they are in the *HSC*, though the phrase 'cum sacna et socna' now occurs at the end of the list rather than separating Lumley from the other vills. The *Libellus de exordio* simply states that Styr gave Darlington 'cum suis appendiciis' to St Cuthbert with the permission of the king (*LDE* III.4).

The occurrence of the 'cum suis appendiciis' formula in these later sources may suggest that Darlington once served as the centre of a composite estate similar to those described elsewhere in the *Historia*.[120] What is described in *HSC* 29, however, is not a complete composite estate. The five identifiable vills (not including Lumley) are not all adjacent to one another, and they are scattered through an area roughly twice the size of the two other estates in the *Historia* which contain a similar number of vills (see map, fig. 3).[121] Four of these five vills (the exception is Coniscliffe) were held by

---

[118] See Craster, 'Patrimony', p. 193.

[119] Our best comparative source is *Boldon Book*, a twelfth-century survey of the bishop of Durham's lands, which assesses each vill in bovates and carucates. Most ordinary vills in the Boldon survey were assessed at between two and six carucates, with the average being somewhere in the neighborhood of four carucates. Unfortunately, the only one of Styr's vills to be fully assessed in *Boldon Book* is Cockerton, which was at that time six carucates in size. Coniscliffe, *Northmannabi* and Lumley are not mentioned in *Boldon Book*, while Ketton and most of Haughton-le-Skerne had been leased out and were not given full assessments.

[120] For a discussion of these composite estates, see below, Appendix II.

[121] These two estates are Monk Hesleden (*HSC* 19a) and Bedlington (*HSC* 21). In fact,

the bishop of Durham at the time of *Boldon Book*, as were three other vills associated with Darlington (Blackwell, Oxon-le-Flatts and Whessoe). Together, the vills listed in *HSC* 29 and *Boldon Book* do occupy a contiguous block of townships, while the tenants of three of the vills in *Boldon Book* (Darlington, Cockerton and Blackwell) still owe shared obligations of a kind typical of composite estates.[122] The evidence thus suggests that these vills may be the surviving fragments of a twelve-vill composite estate similar to those recorded elsewhere in the *Historia*, and that what we are seeing in *HSC* 29 is an attempt to construct or reconstruct such an estate.

HSC 30 *Grants by Snaculf*

Nothing is known of Snaculf son of Cytel. These grants are also mentioned briefly in the *Cronica monasterii Dunelmensis* (*CMD*, lines 134–6) and the *Libellus de exordio* (*LDE* III.4); no further details are given in either source. The vills of Bradbury and Mordon lie within the early parish of Sedgefield; the estate of Sedgefield belonged to the community (*HSC* 21) and these two vills may well have been associated with it. Sockburn and Girsby lie opposite one another on either side of the Tees; they formed a single parish throughout the Middle Ages in spite of the fact that Girsby actually lay in Yorkshire.

HSC 31 *Lease of Gainford and Auckland*

Nothing is known of Earl Ethred. Northman, a lesser earl, attested a charter of King Æthelred in 994; he also occurs in the *Liber uitæ Dunelmensis*, which records the text of an Old English charter in which Northman gives Escomb and all that belongs to it to St Cuthbert (*LVD*, p. 57). Uhtred, the son of Waltheof, was earl of Northumbria and York from 1006 to 1016, and his first marriage was to Bishop Aldhun's daughter.[123] This lease is also recorded in the *Cronica monasterii Dunelmensis* (*CMD*, lines 137–47) and the *Libellus de exordio* (*LDE* III.4). Both of these sources contain an identical introductory passage which explains that, compelled by necessity,

---

Monk Hesleden contained either six or seven vills while Bedlington contained five or six, but each had a similar overall size of roughly 3,500 hectares. For further details, see above, Commentary, *HSC* 19a and *HSC* 21.

122 The villeins of Darlington, Blackwell and Cockerton all help harvest the bishop's meadow, enclose the copse and the court and repair the mill at Darlington, and cart loads for the bishop beyond the estate (*BB*, pp. 57–9). For similar communal obligations on the composite estate of Bedlingtonshire, see above, note 98.

123 The main source for the life of Earl Uhtred is the late eleventh-century Durham tract *De obsessione Dunelmi* (ed. Arnold, *Symeonis Opera* I, 215–20), which describes how Uhtred raised the siege of Durham by King Malcolm II of Scotland in 1006. For a brief biography of Uhtred, see Kapelle, *Conquest*, pp. 14–26.

Bishop Aldhun temporarily conveyed these lands to the earls, but that subsequent earls had permanently seized nearly all of them.

Craster argues that the three earls are not be understood as co-partners in these lands, and that what we have instead is a compressed account of three separate leases.[124] In fact, these lands seem to divide into two distinct parts rather than three. All twenty-five of the vills listed in this lease fall within territory of 'Gainford and whatever pertains to it' described in *HSC* 9. When mapped, however, they form two distinct blocks of territory. The first thirteen vills in the list, beginning with Gainford itself, all lie near the river Tees and fall within or on the borders of the early parish of Gainford. However, the final twelve vills, beginning with Bishop Auckland, lie further north on the river Wear and all lie in or adjacent to the early parish of Bishop Auckland (see map, fig. 3).[125] It seems likely that what we are seeing in this list are two distinct composite estates, one with its estate centre at Gainford and the other at Bishop Auckland. When mapped according to the earliest surviving township boundaries, each of these estates occupies a discrete block of adjacent townships; reconstructed in this way the Gainford estate occupies roughly 8,000 hectares of useful farmland below 200m in altitude, while the Bishop Auckland estate is some 7,500 hectares in size. The remains of the Bishop Auckland estate were still in the bishop's hands at the time of *Boldon Book*, while the Gainford vills were given to the Baliol family by William the Conqueror and were eventually recovered by Bishop Hugh Puiset.[126]

124 See Craster, 'Patrimony', pp. 194–5. Craster speculates that Earl Northman received back on loan the vill of Escomb which he had granted to St Cuthbert, and that Earl Ethred was a descendant of Eadred son of Ricsige who was taking up the lease of Gainford and its surrounding vills that had originally been granted to his ancestor in *HSC* 24. The remaining vills would have gone to Uhtred.

125 The Gainford estate includes three vills that fall outside the later parish of Gainford. All three of these – Barforth, Startforth and Lartington – lie on the south bank of the Tees in what would become Yorkshire. The medieval parish of Gainford, perhaps to compensate for this loss, extends east beyond Dere Street and contains the additional vills of Bolam and Denton. The Bishop Auckland estate includes Witton-le-Wear, which now constitutes a separate parish, and Thickley, which was also claimed as part of the composite estate of Staindrop (*HSC* 32) and eventually became part of Heighington parish. The parish of Bishop Auckland extends west beyond the vills listed in *HSC* 31 to include the chapelry of Hamsterly, which lies above the 200m contour and is most likely a post-Conquest settlement. It also extends further to the south and east, incorporating the vills of Evenwood, Lutterington and Eldon (all listed among Staindrop's vills in *HSC* 32) and Coundon.

126 Bishop Auckland, West Auckland, Binchester, Thickley, Escomb, Hunwick, Newton Cap and Helmington are all listed among the bishop's holdings in *Boldon Book*. Of these, the two Aucklands, Escomb and Newton Cap owe shared obligations and are collectively referred to as Aucklandshire, while Thickley is actually grouped with the vills of Heighingtonshire; see *BB*, pp. 37 and 69. For the loss and recovery of Gainford see Craster, 'Patrimony', p. 195.

HSC 32 *Cnut's Pilgrimage*

Cnut's visit and a description of his gifts are also recorded in the *Cronica monasterii Dunelmensis* (*CMD*, lines 148–57) and the *Libellus de exordio* (*LDE* III.8). Both of these sources introduce Cnut's grant of Staindrop by explaining that the king demonstrated his love for St Cuthbert by walking barefoot from Garmondsway to Durham, a distance of nearly five miles, and both add a royal immunity clause to the grant. The *LDE*, like the *HSC*, concludes by noting that Cnut also gave to St Cuthbert the vill of Brompton, while the *CMD* goes further and appends a list of all the saint's property in Yorkshire, discussed below.

Craster has dated this grant c. 1031, observing that the only likely time for Cnut to have made a pilgrimage to Durham would have been during an expedition to Scotland when he accepted submission from three Scottish kings, as recorded in the *Anglo-Saxon Chronicle* (*ASC* DE 1031).[127] There is, however, some question about this date in the *ASC*. The entry states that in this year Cnut went to Rome and then to Scotland; as Lawson points out, Cnut is known to have been in Rome in 1027, and a second visit so shortly thereafter would have been unusual. Lawson suggests that 1031 might possibly be a scribal error for 1026 (MXXVI being misread as MXXXI); he also points out that another likely time for Cnut to have been in the North would have been c. 1016–18, at the time of the battle of Carham.[128] Hudson, on the other hand, identifies one of the three Scottish kings as Macbeth, who did not take his throne until 1029; he suggests that Cnut went to Rome in 1027 but did not formally return home until 1031, at which time he did indeed go to Scotland.[129]

Grant of Staindrop

The 'vill of Staindrop with its dependencies' clearly seems to have constituted a twelve-vill composite estate with its administrative centre at Staindrop. When mapped according to surviving township boundaries the twelve vills in this grant describe a contiguous block of territory containing some 7,500 hectares of useful agricultural land below 200m in altitude (see map, fig. 3). The outlines of this territory generally correspond to those of the medieval parish of Staindrop, although the parish has been truncated in the northeast by the expansion of Bishop Auckland parish.[130] It is noteworthy

---

127 See Craster, 'Patrimony', p. 195.

128 See Lawson, *Cnut*, pp. 102–5.

129 See Hudson, 'Cnut and the Scottish Kings', pp. 356–8.

130 The vills of Evenwood, Lutterington and Eldon all fall within the parish of Bishop Auckland, while Thickley bcame part of Heighington parish. It seems clear that these vills were lost to the estate before the medieval parish boundaries coalesced. This might have happened when Bishop William of St Calais reformed the community and reorganized its lands in 1083, granting Staindropshire to the prior and monks (*FPD*, p. 56), since he seems to have kept at least one vill, Lutterington, for himself when he did this; see *BB*, p. 39.

that there is some overlap between the estates of Staindrop and Auckland, since both include the vills of West Auckland and Thickley. The most likely explanation is that the composite estates recorded in the *Historia* retained a degree of flexibility, and that the borders of the Auckland and Staindrop estates had shifted slightly in the decades between Aldhun's lease and Cnut's grant. However, this evidence of change must be balanced against the fact that the *Historia*'s composite estates demonstrate remarkable uniformity of size; any shifts seem to have been calculated to retain a dozen vills in each estate.

Like the estates of Gainford and Auckland between which it lies, Staindrop falls within the territory of 'Gainford and whatever pertains to it' supposedly granted to the community by Bishop Ecgred (*HSC* 9). If this grant did take place, Staindrop must have been lost to the community at some point thereafter, possibly in the aftermath of Rægnald's victory at Corbridge.[131] After being returned by Cnut, Staindrop remained in the hands of the community until being leased to Dolfin son of Uhtred by Prior Algar in 1131 (*FPD*, p. 56).[132]

Grant of Brompton

Brompton is included among the Bishop of Durham's holdings in the Yorkshire Domesday survey (*DBY* 1Y2 and 3Y15). The *Cronica monasterii Dunelmensis* states that Cnut confirmed St Cuthbert's possession of lands in Yorkshire given to him by kings and princes in times past (twenty individual vills and churches are named) and himself gave to the saint the vill of Brompton, comprising twenty-four carucates of land (*CMD*, lines 157–68). Brompton is also included in a list of the community's pre-Conquest holdings in Yorkshire entered in the *Liber uitae Dunelmensis*, where it is described as comprising twenty-three carucates (*LVD* 50v). This is considerably more than the average size of a single vill, which suggests that Brompton in the eleventh century may have been the surviving fragment of a once larger estate. Interestingly, eleven of the vills claimed for the community in both the *CMD* and *LVD*, including Brompton, lie adjacent to one another in the wapentake of Allerton on the south bank of the Tees; the other vills are Girsby, Hornby, Deighton, Harlsey, Osmotherley, Ellerbeck, Winton, Sigston, Knayton, and Foxton. If one includes Sockburn in this list, which also belonged to the community and was closely associated with Girsby (see *HSC* 30), this becomes a list of a dozen adjacent vills. It is therefore within the realm of possibility that these vills originally made up a twelve-vill composite estate of the kind that occurs elsewhere in the *Historia*, with Brompton as the estate centre.

131 See above, Commentary, *HSC* 24.
132 Under Dolphin's descendants, the Nevilles, the estate became the lordship of Raby; see Craster, 'Patrimony', p. 196.

HSC 33 *King Guthred's Dream*

There are several historical difficulties with this episode. First, although the Vikings did attack Lindisfarne in 793, there is no record of any attack on the island by the Scots. Second, this episode is set during the time of King Guthred, nearly a century after the Viking attack, which contradicts the statement that Lindisfarne had never before been violated. Finally, according to the chronology given elsewhere in the *Historia,* the community of St Cuthbert had already moved to Chester-le-Street by Guthred's time; there would no longer have been any monastery at Lindisfarne.

Although the battle of *Mundingedene* is not mentioned in sources independent of the *Historia*, Mawer speculated that this might be identical to a battle described in the *War of the Gaedhil with the Gaill* (§25). In this battle the Danes sailed from Ireland to Scotland just after the death of Halfdan (c. 877) and slew Constantine, King of Alba, and the earth burst open beneath the men of Alba.[133] The chief difficulties with this identification are that in the Irish source the Scots seem to be defending rather than attacking, and the battle is set in Scotland rather than northern England.

An amplified version of this episode, out of chronological order in the same way as in the *HSC* and including the same erroneous statement that Lindisfarne had never before been attacked, is presented in the *Miracula sancti Cuthberti* (*MSC* 4). Symeon of Durham, however, is notably cautious about this episode; although he does make brief mention of the story (now in its proper chronological place) in the *Libellus de exordio* (*LDE* II.13), he gives it none of the elaboration he accords to the other miracles from the *HSC*, instead simply noting that the full story is recorded elsewhere.

A similar story of a Northumbrian saint protecting his church from a Scottish invasion occurs in the *Historia regum* (*HR*i 39), in a subsection on St Acca of Hexham which has been inserted into earlier material. In this story, the Scottish king Malcolm invades Northumbria. The people take refuge in the church at Hexham, but the church appears doomed and its priest gives up hope. In the night, a venerable man appears to the priest, inquires as to the cause of his sadness and tells him not to fear. In the morning comes a storm that floods the Tyne and renders it impassable. Throughout the next night and day, a heavy fog descends; the invaders become lost and dispersed, and retire in confusion. The plot of this story clearly parallels that of *HSC* 33: a protagonist piously commits himself to defending (or avenging) the saint's church and people, but finds himself vastly outnumbered and loses hope; the saint appears to him and promises a miracle, and in the morning the enemy army is overcome by the forces of nature. In the *HSC* the earth swallows the enemy, while in the *HR* the river threatens to swallow them while storm and fog disperse them. It is clear from internal evidence that the Acca material in the

Historia regum dates from the later eleventh century (it refers to the translation of Acca's relics, which took place after 1050), and King Malcolm has been generally identified as Malcolm Canmore, who reigned from 1058 to 1093.[134] In his introduction to this episode, however, the author of the *Historia regum* claims to be preserving a long oral tradition which is in danger of being lost, and it seems possible that this episode and *HSC* 33 might have common roots.

This episode is seriously out of chronological order within the *Historia*, since it is set in the late ninth century and logically belongs with the other Guthred episode (*HSC* 13). Although the author of the *Historia* is often clumsy in organizing episodes that took place near the same time (as with the awkward placement of *HSC* 11 and 14–19a), this is the only case in which an episode is completely misplaced chronologically, and Craster may well have been correct when he suggested that *HSC* 33 is a later interpolation to the text.[135] The conclusion that this episode originated independently of the rest of the *Historia* may also be supported by the fact that an identical version of Guthred's dream occurs as a self-contained text in a manuscript in Paris, Bibliothèque Nationale, Fonds Latin 5362. On the other hand, what seems to be the earliest recorded copy of the *Historia*, which existed in the lost Prior's Book, already contained *HSC* 33–4. It therefore seems that if this final portion of the text was was not part of the *Historia* as initially compiled by our author, it must have been appended shortly afterwards.[136]

HSC 34 *King Guthred's Law*

This colophon, which occurs only in manuscript L, is very similar to a brief record in the *Cronica monasterii Dunelmensis* and to a more elaborate passage in the *Libellus de exordio*.[137] The record in the *Cronica* follows King Oswiu's Bowmont Water grant (cf. *HSC* 3), and states that the king 'with the consent of all men decreed for all time that whichever of his successors or anyone else gave land to St Cuthbert thereafter, they [i.e. the monastic community] would possess it with all honour and peace and liberty in perpetuity' (*CMD*, lines 4–7). The passage in the *Libellus de exordio*, which follows Symeon's description of King Guthred's election and his subsequent grant of the lands between Tyne and Wear to St Cuthbert, describes how Guthred, together with King Alfred, established a fine of ninety-six pounds against anyone who violated St Cuthbert's sanctuary and also established protections for the saint's property:

---

134 See Blair, 'Observations', p. 88.
135 See Craster, 'Patrimony', p. 199.
136 For further discussion of the *Historia*'s sequence of composition and the place of *HSC* 33–4 in that sequence, see above, pp. 29 and 35.
137 For the full text of this passage in the *LDE*, see below, Appendix I.3.

it was decreed by the common resolve of the aforesaid kings [Alfred and Guthred] and of the whole people that if anyone should give land to St Cuthbert, or if land should be bought with the saint's own money, no one should thenceforth dare to arrogate to themselves from it any right of service or custom, but that the church alone should possess it perpetually in undisturbed liberty and freedom from claims, with all its customary rights and with (as it is called in the vernacular) sake and soke and infangentheof. Anyone who by whatever effort presumed to infringe these laws and statutes was condemned by the judgement of all, unless he mended his ways, to anathema and perpetual punishment in the fires of hell.   (*LDE* II.13)

The fact that this section of the *Historia* survives only in L, which was not copied until the fifteenth century, may suggest that this is a later addition to the text and is based on the passage in the *LDE*. However, this section apparently followed *HSC* 33 in the copy of the *Historia* contained in the lost Prior's Book, which seems to be the earliest recorded copy of the text.[138] This suggests that it was integral to *HSC* 33 and that the two texts joined the *Historia* at the same time, either during the original composition of the text or shortly thereafter. On the other hand, there is no obvious reason why the scribe of O would have omitted this section from his copy of the text if it had been available to him. If Gullick is correct in identifying this scribe as Symeon of Durham, the same man who would compose the *Libellus de exordio* later in his life, then it is hard to imagine why he would have omitted this passage, which we know to have been of interest to him, from his copy of the *HSC*. At any rate, although Craster described it as 'a genuine privilege of uncertain origin',[139] there seems in fact to be no way to substantiate whether Oswiu, Guthred, Alfred or any other Anglo-Saxon king actually gave to the community of St Cuthbert the sort of formal royal immunity over its holdings which is implied in this passage.

---

[138] For the Prior's Book and its contents, see above, pp. 26–7.
[139] Craster, 'Red Book', p. 523, n. 4

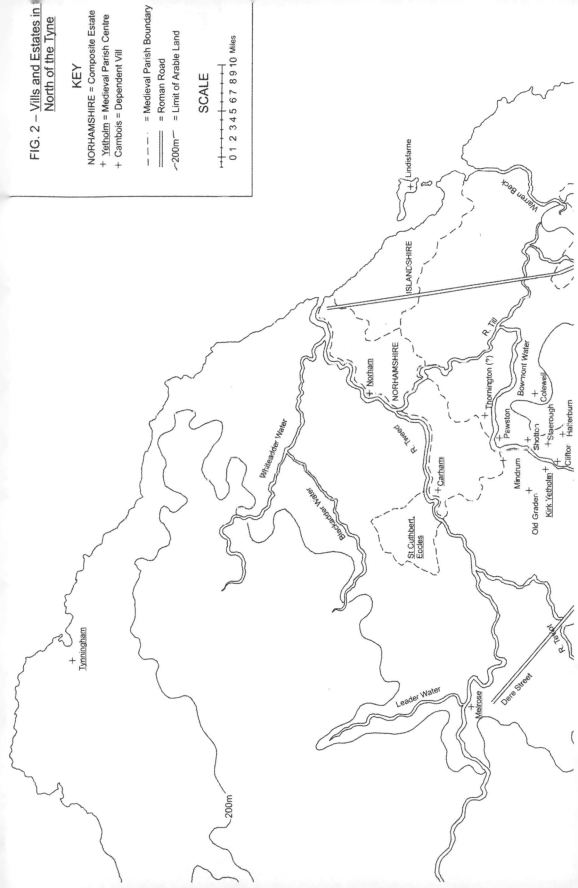

FIG. 2 – Vills and Estates in
North of the Tyne

KEY

NORHAMSHIRE = Composite Estate
+ Yetholm = Medieval Parish Centre
+ Cambois = Dependent Vill

– – . = Medieval Parish Boundary
═══ = Roman Road
⌐200m⌐ = Limit of Arable Land

SCALE

0 1 2 3 4 5 6 7 8 9 10 Miles

Tynningham +

Whiteadder Water

Blackadder Water

Leader Water

200m

Melrose +

Dere Street

R. Teviot

St Cuthbert
Eccles

R. Tweed

Carham +

Kirk Yetholm +

Old Graden +

Mindrum +

NORHAMSHIRE

Norham +

ISLANDSHIRE

Lindisfarne +

Warren Beck

R. Till

Thornington (?) +

Bowmont Water

Pewston +

Shotton +

Staerough +

Cliffor +

Halterburn

Colewell

KEY

+ GAINFORD = Composite
+ Seaham = Medieval Paris[h]
+ Raby = Dependent Vill

= Composite Est[ate]
= Medieval Paris[h]
= Roman Road
~200m~ = Limit of Arable

SCALE

0 1 2 3 4 5

Vallum

River Tyne

River Derwent

Dere Street

CHESTER-LE-STREET

Great Lumley

(Durham)

River Wear

BISHOP
WEARMOUTH

Westun?

Offerton

Ryhope Colliery (?)

Silksworth

Burdon

Seaton

Ryhope

Seaham

Dalton-le-Dale

Daldene

Cold Hesledon

EASINGTON

Little Thorp

Yoden

Shotton Colliery (?)

Shotton

Harden Hall

Castle Eden

Monk Hesleden

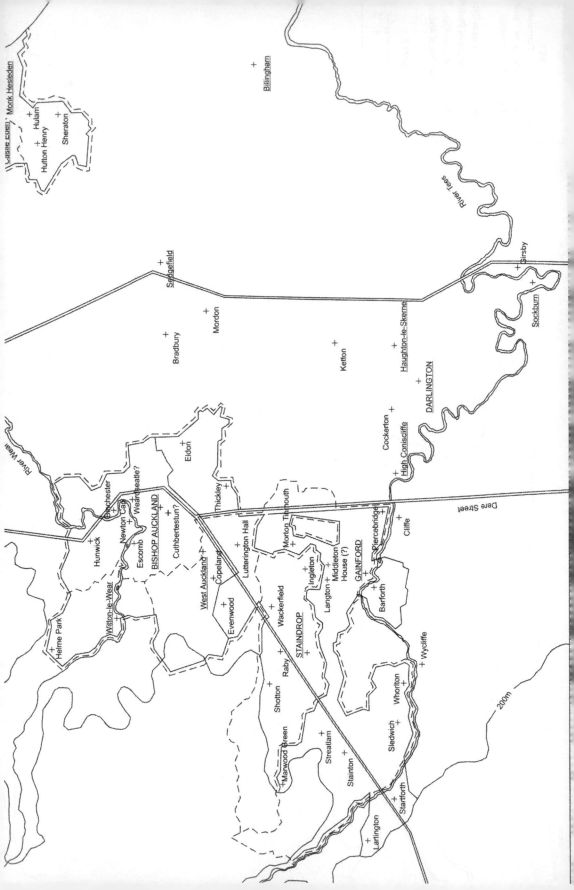

Appendix I: Related Texts

1. *Description of the Property of Lindisfarne in the 'Historia regum'* (HR*iii* 89)[1]

Anno .DCCCLIV., natiuitatis regis Elfredi .vi., Wlfere, regnante rege Osberto super Northimbros, suscepto pallio confirmatus est in archiepiscopatum Eboracensem, et Eardulf suscepit episcopatum Lindisfarnensem. Quo pertinebant Lugubalia, id est Luel, nunc dicitur Carliel, et Northam, quæ antiquitus Vbbanford dicebatur. Omnes quoque ecclesiæ ab aqua quæ uocatur Tweda usque Tinam australem, et ultra desertum ad occidentem, pertinebant illo tempore ad præfatam ecclesiam, et hæ mansiones, Carnam et Culterham, et duæ Geddewrd ad australem plagam Teinetæ quas Ecgredus episcopus condidit: et Mailros, et Tigbrethingham, et Eoriercorn ad occidentalem partem, Edwinesburch, et Pefferham, et Aldham, et Tinnigaham, et Coldingaham, et Tillemuthe, et Northam supradictam. [*See HSC 4*] Werchewurd quoque ipsius ecclesiæ possessio erat, donante rege Ceolwlfo cum omnibus appendentiis suis. [*See HSC 8*] Hanc enim mansionem ipse rex, abrenuntians mundo, secum ecclesiæ Lindisfarnensi contulit, in qua monachus effectus coelesti regno militauit. Cuius corpus postea delatum in ecclesiam supradictæ uillæ Northam multis ibidem, ut fertur ab habitatoribus ipsius loci, claruit miraculis [*See HSC 9*] . . . Præterea memoratus Ecgredus episcopus ædificans ecclesiam in loco qui dicitur Geineforde, donauit eam sancto Cuthberto. Condidit etiam Billingeham in Heorternysse et duas alias uillas, Ileclife et Wilegeclife ad australem plagam fluminis Taisæ, quas sancto Cuthberto ad uictum sibi seruientium dedit; [*See HSC 9*] similiter et Wudecestre, et Hwitingeham, et Eadulfingaham, Egwiluingeham, donante rege Ceolwlfo antiquitus S. Cuthberti fuerunt. [*See HSC 11.*]

2. *The Election of King Guthred in the 'Cronica monasterii Dunelmensis'* (lines 17–50)[2]

Anno ab incarnacione Domini octingentesimo septuagesimo quinto, Halfden, sumpta parte exercitus Paganorum, qui totam Angliam occupauerat, multa cum classe Tinam ingrediens, circa Tynemuth applicuit. Vnde prosiliens flamma et ferro in exterminium omnia duxit, sed non impune. Nam cum

---

[1] Adapted from Arnold, ed., *Symeonis opera* II, 101–2.
[2] Adapted from Craster, ed., 'Red Book', pp. 523–4.

insania mentis grauissimus corpus eius inuasit cruciatus. Unde etiam foetor exhalens intolerabilis omnibus Anglis et Danis eum reddidit exosum. Contemptus ergo ab omnibus cum tribus tantum nauibus de Tina profugit, nec uspiam postea apparuit. [*See HSC 12*] Inter hec, Anglis et Danis in unum populum compaginatis, cum regimen regale deesset, beatus Cuthbertus cuidam Abbati, nomine Eadredo, ualde religioso, per sompnum astitit; eique precepit omnibus dicere, quatinus Guthredum, Hardecnuti Regis filium, qui a Paganis captus atque in Angliam traductus, cuidam uidue apud Huityngham fuerat ab eis in seruum uenditus, hunc, dato uidue digno redempcionis precio, Angli et Dani in regem eleuarent. Qua uisione manifestata, illico omnes perquisitum iuuenum regium seruum inueniunt, moxque, iusto redemptum precio, in loco qui dicitur Oswiesdun omnes in Regem unanimi fauore sustollunt. Qui liberatori suo beato Cuthberto uicem repedens, pacem, sicut ipse sanctus ei per predictum Abbatem mandauit, ad refugium miserorum qui ad illus corpus confugerint instituit; et quicumque pacem illius infregisset, ita ei, quemadmodum Regi, emendaretur, sua pace infracta, uidelicet ad minus mille ducentis oris. Leges quoque ipsius, et que proprie Sancti Cuthberti dicuntur consuetudines, imperpetuum seruandas instituit. Tunc quoque, precipiente ipso sancto per memoratum Abbatem, Rex totam terram inter Weor et Tynam donauit ipso Sancto, ad subsidia illorum qui ei seruiebant et seruituri essent. Cui scilicet predicte terre adiecerunt, tam ipse Guthredus quam Alfredus Rex Australium Anglorum, terram inter Tesam et Weor, in augmentum Episcopatus beati Cuthberti. Nam multo ante defecerant Episcopi Haugustaldensis ecclesie. Per quinquaginta enim quatuor annos ante deuastacionem prouincie Northumbrorum sedes ibidem episcopalis cessauerat. Hec statuta et has donaciones duo reges, Alfredus scilicet et Guthredus, cum consensu tocius populi statuentes firmauerunt, et quicumque ex hiis aliquid presumpserit infringere, perpetuo illum anathemate dampnarunt. [*See HSC 13*]

3. *King Guthred's Grant in the 'Libellus de exordio' (LDE II.13)*[3]

Denique memorato abbati [Eadredi] per uisum astans ipse sanctus [Cuthbertus]: 'Dicito', inquit, 'regi [Guthredo], ut totam inter Weor et Tine terram mihi et in mea ecclesia ministrantibus perpetue possessionis iure largiatur, ex qua illis ne inopia laborent, uite subsidia procurentur. Precipe illi preterea ut ecclesiam meam tutum profugis locum refugii constituat, ut quicunque qualibet de causa ad meum corpus confugerit, pacem per triginta et septem dies nulla unquam occasione infringendam habeat.' Hec per fidelem internuntium abbatem audita, tam ipse rex Guthredus quam etiam rex

---

3   From Rollason, ed., *Symeon of Durham*, pp. 124–6.

potentissimus (cuius superius mentio facta est) Aelfredus declaranda populis propalarunt, eaque toto non solum Anglorum sed etiam Danorum consentiente atque collaudante exercitu in perpetuum seruanda constituerunt. Eos autem qui institutam ab ipso sancto pacem quoquomodo irritare presumpserint, dampno pecunie multandos censuerunt, ut scilicet quantum regi Anglorum pace ipsius fracta debeant, tantundem ipsi sancto uiolata eius pace persoluant, uidelicet ad minus octoginta et sedecim libras. Terra quoque quam preceperat inter memorata duo flumina mox ei donata, communi regum supradictorum et totius populi sententia decretum est, ut quicunque sancto Cuthberto terram donauerit, uel pecunia ipsius empta fuerit, nemo deinceps ex ea cuiuslibet seruitii aut consuetudinis sibi ius aliquod usurpare audeat, sed sola ecclesia inconcussa quiete ac libertate, cum omnibus consuetudinibus et (ut uulgo dicitur) cum saca et socne et infangentheof perpetualiter possideat. Has leges et hec statua quicunque quolibet nisu infringere presumpserint, eos in perpetuum, nisi emendauerint, gehenne ignibus puniendos anathematizando sententia omnium contradedit. [*See HSC 13*]

4. *Later History of Lindisfarne in the 'Gesta Pontificum Anglorum'* (GPA III.128–30)[4]

Item ad Edelredum regem: 'Ecce ecclesia sancti Cuthberti, sacerdotum Dei sanguine aspersa, omnibus spoliata ornamentis, locus cunctis in Britannia uenerabilior, paganus gentibus datur ad debellandum. Et ubi primum post discessum sancti Paulini ab Eboraco Christiana religio in Northanhimbrorum gente sumpsit exordium, ibi miseriæ et calamitatis cepit initium.

Quapropter, pensato consilio, decretum est, ut ab insula illa quæ esset maritimorum predonum hiatibus exposita, corpora sanctorum in continentem transferrentur. Tunc beatem magni Cuthberti corpus cum quidam religioso, ut putabant, furto Hiberniam transuehere ambirant, perdiderunt fructum operæ, dum aut multis diebus uentum operirentur in litore, aut flatu aliquantum concitatiore in altum provecti statim repellerentur. [*See HSC 20*] Quocirca cum honore debito sacrum corpus apud Ubbenford, incertum an episcopatus sedem, deposuere iuxta amnem Twda. [*See HSC 9*] Iacuit ibi multis annis, usque ad aduentum Ethelredi regis. Nec tamen interim in adiutorio prouintialium feriabatur, sed per totam Angliam uagabatur miraculis; quorum unum si retulero, non ab re, ut estimo, fecero. Eo insignius, quo illud in clarissima persona ostensum totius Angliæ libertatem reduxit, seruitutem exuit.

Erat rex Elfredus barbarorum infestatione ad hoc redactus inopiæ, ut in insula quadam paruissima, quæ uocatur Adelingenie, lateret inglorius. Dixi

---

4 Adapted from Hamilton, ed., *Gesta pontificum Anglorum*, pp. 268–9.

superius de hac insula in Gestis pontificum Wellensium. Ibi ergo quadam die cum domi soporatus iaceret, dolor enim animi somnum imperauerat, sotiis per oram fluminis dispersis, ecce beatus Cuthbertus dormientem alloquitur: 'Ego sum Cuthbertus, Lindisfarnensis quondam antistes. Misit me Deus, ut prospera tibi annuntiem. Quia enim Anglia iamdudum peccatorum penas enormiter luit, modo tandem indigenarum sanctorum meritis super eum misericordiæ suæ oculo respicit. Tu quoque tam miserabiliter regno extorris, gloriose post paucum tempus in solio reponeris. Atque adeo signum eximium tibi dabo. Venient hodie piscatores tui, magnam uim grandium piscium corbibus euehentes. Quod eo erit mirabilius, quia his diebus, gelante aqua, stagnum asperatum nichil tale sperare permittit. Super hæc gelido rore stillans aer omnem piscantium artem eludit. Verum tu fortunæ secundæ ueri compos, regaliter feceris, si adiutorem tuum Deum et me eius nuntium competenti deuotione demerueris.' Hæc dicens sanctus regem soporatum sollicitudinibus exuit, matremque prope cubantem eiusdem nuntii letitia confortauit. Experrecti ambo unum et idem se somniasse frequenti recursu uerborum iterabant, cum piscatores ingressi copia innumerabili piscium fidem somnio fecere. Nec multo post ille et regnum et regni gloriam recepit, sicut latius in gestis eius diximus. [*See HSC 14–16*]

5. *Description of Cnut's Pilgrimage in the 'Cronica monasterii Dunelmensis' (lines 148–68)*[5]

Deinde Cnut, regno Anglorum potitus, multo uenerabatur honore ecclesiam sancte Dei genitricis et sancti Cuthberti, in tantum ut nudis pedibus per quinque miliaria incedens, a loco qui Garmundi uia dicitur, unde primum de suth uenientibus Dunelmum uideri potest, ad sepulchrum incorrupti corporis beati patris Cuthberti ueniret, et ei suisque seruitoribus mansionem Staynedroppe, cum omnibus suis appendiciis, scilicet Cnappetune, Scottune, Raby, Wakerfeld, Hefenwuda, Alclit, Luteryngton, Elledon, Ingeltune, Thiccele et Middelton, libere et quiete imperpetuum possidendam donaret et redderet, sicut ipse eam habuit in sua propria manu, ita quietam et liberam. [*See HSC 32*] Has quoque terras quas sanctus Cuthbertus ex antiquiorum regum et principum tradicione in Euerwicshire habuerat, scilicet Segger, Horbodyby, Hotun, Hograve, Norton, Suthton, Hulm, Throp, Eueneton, Foxton, Gryssiby, Dicton, Neowiton, Osmunderle, Herleseie, Alrebec, Siggeston, et ecclesiam de Cucewald terraque adiacente, et ecclesiam de Smittona cum duabus carucatis terre, et ecclesiam de Gressiby, tribuens de suo proprio supradicte ecclesie uillam que Bromtune uocatur, que uiginti quatuor carucatas terre tenet. Hec omnia, cum saca et socne et plena libertate

5   Adapted from Craster, ed., 'Red Book', pp. 527–8.

et quietudine donauit, et ipse, cum Edmundo tunc illius loci Episcopo, omnes, qui hec infringere uel auferre uel minuere presumerent, excommunicauit et excommunicando in die iudicii maledictus in ignem eternum discessuris associauit.

Appendix II: Estate Structure in the *Historia*

The Vill

The basic unit of land holding in the *Historia* is the *uilla* or vill, and nearly all of the over one hundred particular places named in the *HSC* are in fact vills. The evidence of the *Historia* makes it clear that the term is used to describe a resource-area rather than a discrete settlement site. As David Austin has pointed out, we must be careful to distinguish between vill and village, if the latter is understood as being a single settlement at a specific geographic location:

> The *uillæ* of the *HSC* and *Domesday Book* are in fact economic, social and legal units involving both extensive space, that is lands and buildings, and exploitable population. By now this should be axiomatic in settlement studies and if any translation for *uilla* is permissible, it must be, in the north, 'township' with whose boundaries one suspects the limits of the medieval and perhaps the late Anglo-Saxon unit were coterminous.[1]

The term *uilla* thus describes a resource-area rather than simply a settlement site; it refers to a block of land comprising arable fields, pasture, waste and woods as well as dwellings. There is little evidence in the *HSC* itself concerning the relative size of this resource-area beyond the reference to Crayke as a vill with a circumference of three miles (*HSC* 5).[2] However, many of the vills mentioned in the *Historia* are described in further detail in *Boldon Book*, compiled in 1183, and this can give us at least a rough idea of the scale of a typical vill. Most vills in the Boldon survey are assessed at somewhere between two and six carucates of arable land, with the average being somewhere in the neighborhood of four carucates. (Vills which had served as estate centres, however, such as Bedlington or Sedgefield, might be assessed at ten carucates or more.) Since the size of a single tenancy in the Boldon survey is usually two bovates, and there are eight bovates in a carucate, this means that a typical vill might have contained one to two dozen households, at least by the time of *Boldon Book*.

It is not always clear whether the farmsteads of these households were grouped together in a nucleated settlement or scattered throughout the vill's

---

1 Austin, 'Settlement Patterns', p. 202.
2 Although they do not usually preserve the outlines of individual vills, the resuorce-areas of groups of adjacent vills can often be approximated using surviving township and parish boundaries; see below, pp. 126–8.

area in a dispersed pattern. Austin suggests that a Celtic pattern of dispersed settlement generally persisted in County Durham until upset by Norman manorial requirements;[3] recent research, however, suggests that in some regions the Celtic pattern was replaced by open fields with nucleated settlements in the Middle Saxon period.[4] A number of the vills named in the *Historia* are now associated with planned nucleated villages, but Robert's survey of Aucklandshire suggests that many of these villages were only given their present form in the aftermath of the Norman Conquest. On the other hand, Roberts also notes the existence of a number of irregular nucleated villages which date back to the time of the *Historia*.[5] Speaking very broadly, it seems safe to say that the vills described in the *Historia* included both nucleated villages on the one hand and scattered farmsteads and hamlets on the other, and that in general the percentage of villages probably decreased as one moved from the coast up into the less fertile hill country. This is certainly the pattern which survived the Middle Ages and is recorded in the earliest maps of the region.

It is also worth noting that none of the hundred-odd vills recorded in the *Historia* is associated with a site above 200m in altitude. When we turn to the modern Ministry of Agriculture Land Use Classification Map we find that the 200m contour provides a reliable boundary between 'good to fair' (classes 2 and 3) and 'poor to awful' (classes 4 and 5) agricultural land. Furthermore, known settlement sites above this altitude from the Anglo-Saxon period are limited to shielings associated with seasonal grazing and to marginal Anglo-Scandinavian sites.[6] All the evidence therefore suggests that the system of vills described in the *Historia* confined itself to the relatively productive agricultural land below 200 m; this does not, of course, preclude the grazing of animals on common land above this altitude.

The Composite Estate

The majority of the lands claimed for St Cuthbert in the *Historia* do not consist of individual vills, but rather of vills organized into distinct groups. Estates consisting of groups of vills include Bowmont Water (*HSC* 3 – twelve vills), Monk Hesleden (*HSC* 19b – seven vills), Bedlington (*HSC* 21 – six vills), Easington (*HSC* 22 – twelve vills), Bishop Wearmouth (*HSC* 26 – twelve vills), Gainford (*HSC* 31 – thirteen vills), Bishop Auckland (*HSC* 31 – twelve vills), and Staindrop (*HSC* 32 – twelve vills).

---

3   See Austin, 'Settlement Patterns', p. 206.
4   See, for example, Hall, 'Late Saxon Countryside', pp. 103 and 120–1.
5   See Roberts, 'Rural Settlement', pp. 312–13.
6   A good example of this type of site is Simey Folds; see Coggins and Fairless, 'Excavations'.

Several facts stand out when we examine these eight groups of vills. First, there is a remarkable regularity of size among these lists; each group consists of six/seven or twelve/thirteen vills. Second, when we map each group of vills according to the earliest surviving township boundaries, we find that each list occupies a number of adjacent early townships and forms a contiguous block of territory. This is the case even though two or more vills often occupy the same township, and although the vills in question are not necessarily the heads of townships any longer; indeed, they may survive only as single farmsteads or abandoned sites. Although townships might be consolidated over the years, or the head of a township might shift from one location to another, the actual boundaries of surviving townships could have been changed only with great difficulty, if at all. This phenomenon has been discussed for northern England in general by D. J. H. Michelmore:

> Although the Norman Conquest resulted in a revolution in English land-holding patterns, it appears to have had little effect on township organization which, with the possible exception of peripheral areas such as Cumberland, dates to no later than the Middle Saxon period . . . It would have been inconvenient if the territorial unit within which the peasant communities of northern England organized their daily lives and economies had been constantly changing . . . it is therefore not surprising that the pattern of townships should have continued with little alteration from century to century, landowners making use of the township organization when exploiting the potential wealth of their estates.[7]

Austin has argued that the estates described in the *Historia* cannot be mapped because they are conceptual, not real; they do not actually describe discrete blocks of territory on the ground. He takes the original grant of Gainford (*HSC* 9, later described in *HSC* 31–2 as the three estates of Gainford, Staindrop and Auckland) as his example:

> It is not possible to draw a line around [the estate] and say that all the land within it belonged to the estate. There are large numbers of villæ not appearing in documents until the twelfth or thirteenth centuries which lie in and amongst the listed villæ and which as units of land at least must have existed at the same time as the estate holdings.[8]

While Austin's criticism is true for general geographic descriptions of estates such as the 'bounds of Lindisfarne' (*HSC* 4) or the original Gainford grant (*HSC* 9), it does not hold for those estates described in the *HSC* by specific lists of vills. In the argument cited above, Austin blurs the distinction between the large tract of land around Gainford claimed by the community in the ninth century (*HSC* 9) and the specific estates claimed by the community

7 Michelmore, 'Reconstruction', pp. 8–9.
8 Austin, 'Settlement Patterns', p. 202.

in the eleventh (*HSC* 31–2). The ninth-century description constitutes a vague general claim to a whole block of territory, while the eleventh-century lists record the consitituent vills of three specific composite estates. The outlines of these two areas are different, and the majority of Austin's 'in and amongst' vills lie inside the former but outside the latter and thus have nothing to do with the composite estates we wish to study.[9]

In fact, when we map out the constituent vills of the Gainford, Staindrop and Auckland estates as described in *HSC* 31–2 using the earliest surviving township boundaries, we find solid, contiguous blocks of territory which show none of the 'false lacunae' to which Austin refers. This same conclusion also holds true for all of the other estates described by lists of vills in the *Historia*; the constituent vills of each estate lie adjacent to one another and define discrete blocks of territory. Furthermore, these blocks of territory seem to display a certain regularity of size. When reconstructed according to early township boundaries, the *Historia*'s six full-size composite estates all contain between 6,500 and 8,000 hectares of relatively productive agricultural land below 200m in altitude. This regularity reinforces the suggestion that these estates were not abstractions, but were conceived and laid out as physical territories with distinct borders.

There is also a noteworthy correspondence between the outlines of these eight composite estates and early parish boundaries. When mapped according to the earliest surtviving township boundaries, the estates described by lists of vills in the *Historia* each follow the outlines of one or more early parishes with surprising closeness. Furthermore, the first vills in each list are all early parish centres. The only exception to these rules is the Bowmont Water estate; this is presumably because the estate straddles the Anglo-Scottish border, which was established in the late tenth century and which would have disrupted any earlier boundaries.

This correspondence between Late Saxon estate boundaries and later parish boundaries is not unique to the *Historia*, but has been observed throughout the Anglo-Saxon kingdoms. The continuity of parish and township boundaries has recently been observed by Michelmore in pre-Conquest

---

9   For example, the ninth-century grant described in *HSC* 9 includes much land above 200m; we can assume that this high land was not initially settled, since none of the vills listed in the *Historia* are located above 200m. The vills above this altitude which Austin cites, like Hamsterly, were most likely the results of later colonization and probably did not exist before the twelfth or thirteenth centuries. Austin also points to lowland vills like Winston and Headlam, which would indeed have been covered by the ninth-century grant, but which do not appear in the eleventh-century lists, and which had apparently been alienated by the community (as were Cliffe and Wycliffe on the south bank of the Tees) during the course of the tenth century. The rest of Austin's vills consist of places like Witton Park and St Helen Auckland, which mark the later expansion of a single vill in the *Historia* into two discrete vills, again probably in the twelfth or thirteenth century.

Yorkshire, by Roffe in Lincolnshire, and by Hooke in the west Midlands, among others; all three scholars have concluded that pre-ninteenth-century parish boundaries can often preserve the outlines of late-Saxon estates.[10] In the case of the composite estates preserved in the *Historia*, it seems likely that each estate centre also contained an early church, and that the estate also functioned as a *de facto* parish. Parish boudaries generally remained stable, and the estate's boundaries would therefore have been preserved in later medieval parish boundaries, although a single early estate-parish might have been subdivided into two or three smaller parishes by the time parish bounds came to be recorded.

Finally, the eight lists of vills in the *Historia* demonstrate a certain level of internal organization. Three lists make a specific distinction between the first vill named, described as a *uilla*, and subsequent vills in the list, called *appendici*; these are the Bedlington, Bishop Wearmouth and Staindrop lists. All the lists with the exception of the Bowmont Water are organized in a geographic pattern which places emphasis on the first vill, regardless of whether it is given a distinguishing label.[11] We have already seen that each of these primary vills (again with the exception of the Bowmont Water) eventually became the heads of early parishes, suggesting that they had special administrative importance. Furthermore, each of these vills is located below the 100m contour, is sited on a coast or river, and generally controls the estate's best agricultural land. Together, this evidence suggests that for each of our estate-lists with the exception of the Bowmont Water we can make a distinction between the first vill on the list, which we can think of as a primary vill or estate centre, and the remaining *appendici* or dependent vills.

What we find in the *Historia*, then, are a group of eight composite estates with a number of common traits. Each estate contains roughly a dozen (or half a dozen) vills. These estates formed self-contained blocks of territory of which were fairly regular in size and which seemed to have formed the basis of later parish structure in their regions. Internally, each estate consisted of an estate centre and a number of dependent vills. These estates are sometimes identified in the *Historia* by the phrase *uilla . . . cum suis appendiciis*, and it seems likely that whenever this phrase occurs in the *Historia* it refers specifically to a composite estate of this type. Another term for these same composite estates seems to have been *scir* or 'shire'. *Boldon Book* in partic-

---

10 See Michelmore, 'Reconstruction', p. 8; Roffe, 'Pre-Conquest Estates', p. 117; Hooke, 'Estates in the Midlands', pp. 233–4.

11 This pattern varies depending on where the first vill lies in relation to the other vills on the list. In the Bishop Wearmouth and Easington lists, for example, the primary vill is also the northernmost, and the list proceeds from north to south. In the Bedlington, Gainford and Staindrop lists the primary vill is near one edge of the estate, and the list proceeds clockwise from this starting point. Bishop Auckland is near the centre of its territory, and its dependent vills are listed in a series of rays projecting out from this central point.

ular makes reference to several shires and two of these, Bedlingtonshire and Aucklandshire, contain some or all of the same vills given in the *Historia*.[12] Although it is beyond the scope of the present study, much interesting work remains to be done in analysing the composite estates preserved within the patrimony of St Cuthbert and comparing them with similar structures in the rest of Northumbria and elsewhere.[13]

[12] Bedlingtonshire in *Boldon Book* consists of six vills, including all the same vills as the composite estate of Bedlington in the *Historia* with the exception of *Grubbatwisle*; Aucklandshire consists of four of the twelve vills listed in the *Historia*. For further discussion see above, Commentary, *HSC* 21 (Bedlington) and *HSC* 31 (Bishop Auckland).

[13] The most notable studies of the Northumbrian shire in general are Jolliffe, 'Northumbrian Institutions', and Kapelle, *Norman Conquest*, ch. 3. The suggestion has been made, particularly by Jolliffe and Glanville Jones, that these shires are local examples of a pre-feudal estate type that can be found in other British and Anglo-Saxon kingdoms. For a partial listing of Jones' work see Bibliograpy below; see also Gregson, 'Multiple Estate', for a recent summary and critique of Jones. For a recent study which attempts to place these structures in their broader social and economic context, and which also points out the importance of distinguishing between the *scir* as a political unit and the composite estate as a unit of ownership and production, see Faith, *English Peasantry*.

Appendix III: Catalogue of Place Names
in the *Historia*

Unless otherwise noted, the modern identification of each listed place-name has been agreed on by all scholars concerned. Works consulted include Hinde's edition of the *HSC* (*Opera et Collectanea* I, 138–52), Arnold's edition of the *HSC* (*Symeonis opera* I, 196–214), Craster's 'Patrimony', Ekwall's *Concise Dictionary*, Barrow's *Kingdom of the Scots*, Hart's *Early Charters* and Gill's *Bishop Auckland*. I am especially grateful to Victor Watts for information from his unpublished survey of Northumbrian place-names.

ALCLIT (I) = Bishop Auckland NZ2029   (*HSC* 31)
    Description: *terra* (primary vill of composite estate)
ALCLIT (II) = West Auckland NZ1826   (*HSC* 31 and 32)
    Description: *terra* (dependent vill – Bishop Auckland and Staindrop estates)
BEDLINGTUN = Bedlington NZ2681   (*HSC* 21)
    Description: *uilla cum suis appendiciis* (primary vill of composite estate)
BEREFORD = Barforth NZ1616   (*HSC* 31)
    Description: *terra* (dependent vill – Gainford)
    Note: Ekwall explains the name Barforth as 'a late modification of Barford'. This identification is geographically preferable to the otherwise appealing Barford Moor (NZ1017), which lies on the north bank of the Tees and thus violates the geographical order of the list in *HSC* 31.
BILLINGHAM = Billingham NZ4522   (*HSC* 9 and 22)
    Variant: Billigaham (*HSC* 9, C)
    Description: *uilla* (*HSC* 9); *uilla cum suis appendiciis* (*HSC* 22) (probable estate centre)
BRINCEWELE = lost site near Brinkburn   (*HSC* 8)
    Description: *ciuitas* (element of Warkworth estate)
    Note: Craster identifies this as an early form of the place-name which subsequently became Brinkburn, located on the river Coquet. In fact, as Watts points out, the two names are different and presumably referred to two places distinct from one another yet close together. *Brincewele* is OE 'Brynca' (personal name) + 'wella' (well) or 'wæl' (pool in a river), while Brinkburn derives from OE Brynca + 'burn' (stream). Watts also notes that there is a promontory fort adjacent to Brinkburn which might be the 'civitas' mentioned in the *HSC*.

BROMTUN = Brompton SE3796   (*HSC* 32)
    Description: *[uilla] cum saca et socna* (possible estate centre)
BRYDBYRIG = Bradbury NZ3128   (*HSC* 30)
    Description: *terra* (possible dependent vill – Sedgefield estate)
BYNCEASTRE = Binchester NZ2031   (*HSC* 31)
    Variant: Bincestre (L)
    Description: *terra* (dependent vill – Bishop Auckland)
BYNNEWALLE = Benwell on Tyne NZ2164   (*HSC* 24)
    Description: *uilla* (single vill)
BYRDENE = Burdon NZ3851   (*HSC* 26)
    Description: *appendicium* (dependent vill – Bishop Wearmouth estate)
CARRUM = Carham NT7938   (*HSC* 7)
    Description: *[uilla] et quicquid ad ea pertinet* (probable estate centre)
CARTMEL = Cartmel SD3878   (*HSC* 6)
    Variant: Ceartmel (L)
    Description: *terra et omnes Brittani cum ea*
CEATTUNE = Ketton NZ3019   (*HSC* 29)
    Description: *.ii. carrucatae terrae cum suca et socna* (dependent vill –
    Darlington estate)
    Note: Hart leaves this unidentified; Hinde identifies it as Seaton near
    Stranton. Ketton lies near Darlington, as do the remainder of the vills in
    this grant, and the vill of Ketton is similarly associated with Darlington in
    Boldon Book. It is called Ketton in *BB* and Chettune in the *Feodarium
    prioratus Dunelmensis.*
CEBRINGTUN = Choppington NZ2583   (*HSC* 21)
    Description: *appendicium* (dependent vill – Bedlington estate)
CEDDESFELD = Sedgefield NZ3528   (*HSC* 21)
    Description: *uilla et quicquid ad ea pertinet* (probable estate centre)
CINGRESCLIFFE = High Coniscliffe NZ2215 (*HSC* 29)
    Variant: Cingcesclife (O)
    Description: *.iiii. carrucatas terrae* (dependent vill – Darlington estate)
CLETLINGA = Cleatlam NZ1118   (*HSC* 31)
    Variant: Cleclinga (L)
    Description: *terra* (dependent vill – Gainford estate)
    Note: This is Hinde's identification; Hart has Cleatham, possibly a typo-
    graphical error.
CLIFTUN = Clifton NT8126   (*HSC* 3)
    Description: *uilla* (dependent vill – Bowmont Water estate)
CNAPATUN = lost site near Staindrop   (*HSC* 32)
    Description: *appendicium* (dependent vill – Staindrop estate)
    Note: Hart leaves this unidentified, while Hinde notes that Hutchinson has
    proposed Snotterton, and himself suggests Keverston. Both of these places
    are in the right geographical area, being close to Staindrop; however, as

Watts notes, neither presents a plausible phonological development from
Cnapatun.

COCERTUNE = Cockerton NZ2715 (*HSC* 29)
Description: *.iiii. carrucatas terae* (dependent vill – Darlington estate)

COLWELA = Colewell (lost) near NT8930 (*HSC* 3)
Description: *uilla* (dependent vill – Bowmont Water estate)
Note: Hart's identification of Colwell near Hexham is geographically
untenable. It was Barrow who first noted the mention of a Colewell in
West Newton township in a document of 1328; see Barrow, *Kingdom of
the Scots*, p. 34, n. 133.

COMMES = Cambois NZ3083 (*HSC* 21)
Variant: Commer (C)
Description: *appendicium* (dependent vill – Bedlington estate)
Note: this town's name is still pronounced 'Cammus' by its inhabitants.

COPLAND = Copeland NZ1626 (*HSC* 31)
Description: *terra* (dependent vill – Bishop Auckland estate)

CRECA = Crayke SE5670 (*HSC* 5)
Description: *uilla et tria milliaria in circuitu* (single vill)

CUNCECEASTRE = Chester-le-Street NZ2751 (*HSC* 20, 21 and 24)
Variants: Cuncacestre (*HSC* 24 OL); Cuncecester (*HSC* 20 L);
Cuncecestre (*HSC* 21 C)
Description: *terra*; bounds given (estate centre)

CUTHBERTESTUN = St Andrew Auckland? NZ2128 (*HSC* 31)
Description: *terra* (dependent vill – Bishop Auckland estate)
Note: Although this has been identified by both Hinde and Hart as
Cotherstone in Teesdale, this would place it far outside the bounds of
Aucklandshire; furthermore, Watts demonstrates that Cotherstone is in
fact a development of OE *Cultherestun*. Gill tentatively identifies
Cuthbertestun with St Andrew Auckland, citing archaeological evidence
which shows that the latter was an ecclesiastical site by the late eighth or
early ninth century; it soon became the site of the mother-church of
Aucklandshire, which may explain its early association with the name of
St Cuthbert.

DALDENE = Dawdon NZ4248 (*HSC* 26)
Description: *appendicium* (dependent vill – Bishop Wearmouth estate)

DALTUN = Dalton-le-Dale NZ4048 (*HSC* 26)
Description: *appendicium* (dependent vill – Bishop Wearmouth estate)

DEARTHINGTUN = Darlington NZ2914 (*HSC* 29)
Variant: Dearningtun (L)
Description: *uilla cum saca et socna* (probable estate centre)

EADWULFINCHAM = Edlingham NU1109 (*HSC* 11)
Variant: Eadwulfingham (L)
Description: *uilla* (possible estate centre)

EBORACUM = York SE5951   (*HSC* 5 *et passim*)
    Variant: Æboracum (O)
    Description: *in Eboraca ciuitate totam terram quæ iacet . . .* (urban
    parish)
ECGWULFINGHAM = Eglingham NU1019   (*HSC* 11)
    Variant: Ecgwulfincham (*HSC* OL)
    Description: *uilla* (possible estate centre)
EDISCUM = Escomb NZ1830   (*HSC* 31)
    Description: *terra* (dependent vill – Bishop Auckland estate)
EFENWUDA = Evenwood NZ1525   (*HSC* 32)
    Description: *appendicium* (dependent vill – Staindrop estate)
ELLEDUN = Old Eldon NZ2427   (*HSC* 32)
    Description: *appendicium* (dependent vill – Staindrop estate)
ELTHERBURNA = Halterburn NT8427   (*HSC* 3)
    Description: *uilla* (dependent vill – Bowmont Water estate)
ESINGTUN = Easington NZ4143   (*HSC* 22)
    Description: *uilla* (primary vill of composite estate)
GATHAN = Kirk Yetholm NT8228   (*HSC* 3)
    Variant: Gethan (L)
    Description: *uilla* (possible primary vill – Bowmont Water estate)
GEDWEARDE = Jedburgh NT6520   (*HSC* 9)
    Description: first of *duas uillas . . . et quicquid ad eas pertinet* (estate
    centre)
alteram GEDWEARDE = Old Jeddart NT6614   (*HSC* 9)
    Description: second of *duas uillas* (dependent vill – Jedburgh estate)
GEAGENFORDA = Gainford NZ1716   (*HSC* 9, 24 and 31)
    Variants: Gegnford (*HSC* 9 OC); Ganford (*HSC* 9 L); Genforda (*HSC* 24
    L); Gegenford (*HSC* 31 O); Gegenforde (*HSC* 31 L)
    Description: *uilla et quicquid ad ea pertinet* (*HSC* 9 and 24); *terra* (*HSC*
    31) (primary vill of composite estate)
GREATADUN = Old Graden NT7929   (*HSC* 3)
    Variant: *Grstatadun* (C)
    Description: *villa* (dependent vill – Bowmont Water estate)
    Note: this name was rendered as *Gistatatun* by Hinde, and on this basis
    has traditionally been identified as Gateshaws near Morebattle. The evolu-
    tion of the name Graden is similar to that of Gratton in Devon, which also
    had its origins in OE *greate dun* = 'great hill'; see Ekwall, p. 203.
GRISEBI = Girsby NZ3508   (*HSC* 30)
    Description: *terra cum saca et socna* (vill; paired with Sockburn)
GRUBBATWISLE = Twizell? NZ1578   (*HSC* 21)
    Variants: Grubba, Twisle (C); Grubbatwise (L)
    Description: *appendicium* (dependent vill – Bedlington estate)
    Note: Hinde interpreted this as two separate names and identified

'Grubba' as Gubeon (NZ1783), but Watts points out that this seems instead to be named after a Norman feudal tenant called Gubion.

HALHTUNE = Haughton-le-Skerne NZ3116   (*HSC* 29)
Description: *.iiii. carrucatas terra* (dependent vill – Darlington estate)

HEALME = Helme Park NZ1236   (*HSC* 31)
Variant: Helme (L)
Description: *terra* (dependent vill – Bishop Auckland estate)
Note: Although Hinde and Hart identify Healme with modern Helmington (NZ1833), Watts notes that this is recorded as Holmeden in medieval documents, while Helme Park is (le) Helme in records of the twelfth and thirteenth centuries.

HESTERHOH = Staerough Hill NT8227   (*HSC* 3)
Variant: Hetteshoh (L)
Description: *uilla* (dependent vill – Bowmont Water estate)
Note: in Hinde's time the hill between Kirk Yetholm and Halter Burn was still known as Hesterheugh; it is now called Staerough. The name today is attached to a hilltop over 300m in height; the actual settlement site must have been below this, probably on the southern flank of the hill, where a high valley runs down toward the Bowmont Water.

HESELDENE = Cold Hesledon NZ4146   (*HSC* 26)
Description: *appendicium* (dependent vill – Bishop Wearmouth estate)

HOLUM = Hulam NZ4336   (*HSC* 19 and 22)
Description: *uilla* (dependent vill – Monk Hesleden and Easington estates)

HORETUN = Horden Hall NZ4342   (*HSC* 19 and 22)
Variant: Horedene (*HSC* 22)
Description: *uilla* (dependent vill – Monk Hesleden and Easington estates)

HOTUN = Hutton Henry NZ4236   (*HSC* 19 and 22)
Variant: Hotoun (L)
Description: *uilla* (dependent vill – Monk Hesleden and Easington estates)

HUNEWIC = Hunwick NZ1832   (*HSC* 31)
Description: *terra* (dependent vill – Bishop Auckland estate)

HWITINGHAM = Whittingham NU0611   (*HSC* 11)
Variants: Hwitincham (O); Bwitingham (L)
Description: *uilla* (possible estate centre)

ILECLIF = Cliffe NZ2015   (*HSC* 9)
Description: *uilla* (part of original territory of Gainford)

INGELTUN = Ingleton NZ1720   (*HSC* 32)
Description: *appendicium* (dependent vill – Staindrop estate)

IODENE = Yoden (now Peterlee) NZ4341   (*HSC* 19 and 22)
Variant: Geodene (*HSC* 19)
Description: *uilla* (dependent vill – Monk Heslesen and Easington estates)

Note: This is Watts' identification; Hinde has Little Eden. Yoden is called Eden Hall on the First Edition one-inch map.

IODENE AUSTRALEM = Castle Eden NZ4238   (*HSC* 19, 21 and 22)
   Variant: [alter] Geodene (*HSC* 19)
   Description: *uilla* (dependent vill – Monk Hesleden and Easington estates)

LANGADUN = Langton NZ1619   (*HSC* 31)
   Description: *terra* (dependent vill – Gainford estate)

LINDISFARNENSIS monasterium = Lindisfarne NU1241 (*HSC* 4 *et passim*)
   Description: *monasterium . . . cum terra suis* (estate centre)

LUEL = Carlisle NY3955   (*HSC* 5)
   Description: *ciuitas quæ habet in circuitu xv miliaria* (probable estate centre)

LUMMALEA = Great Lumley NZ2949   (*HSC* 29)
   Description: *.ii. carrucatas terræ* (vill)

LUTERINGTUN = Lutterington Hall NZ1824 (*HSC* 32)
   Description: *appendicium* (dependent vill – Staindrop estate)

LYRTINGTUN = Lartington NZ0117   (*HSC* 31)
   Description: *terra* (dependent vill – Gainford estate)

MARAWUDA = Marwood Green NZ0522   (*HSC* 31)
   Variant: Marauuda (*HSC* L)
   Description: *terra* (dependent vill – Gainford estate)

MEILROS = Melrose NT5434   (*HSC* 3)
   Variants: Melros (C); Mailros (L)
   Description: *monasterium cum omnibus suis appendentiis* (probable estate centre)

MIDDELTUN = Middleton House? NZ1719   (*HSC* 32)
   Description: *appendicium* (dependent vill – Staindrop estate)
   Note: This site is tentative, given the lack of evidence that Middleton House is a pre-Conquest settlement site.

MORDUN = Mordon NZ3226   (*HSC* 30)
   Description: *terra* (probable dependent vill – Sedgefield estate)

MORTUN = Morton Tinmouth NZ1821   (*HSC* 31)
   Description: *terra* (dependent vill – Gainford estate)

MYNETHRIM = Mindrum NT8432   (*HSC* 3)
   Description: *uilla* (dependent vill – Bowmont Water estate)

NEDERTUN = Nedderton NZ2381   (*HSC* 21)
   Description: *appendicium* (dependent vill – Bedlington estate)

NEOWATUN = Newton Cap NZ2030   (*HSC* 31)
   Description: *terra* (dependent vill – Bishop Auckland estate)

NORTHHAM = Norham NT9047   (*HSC* 9)
   Variant: Norham (L)
   Description: *uilla* (probable estate centre)

NORTHMANNABI = lost   (*HSC* 29)
    Description: *.iii. carrucatas terrae* (dependent vill – Darlington estate)
    Note: Hinde has identified this with Normanby over Tees, but this seems
    unlikely given that the vills with which our Normanby is listed
    (Coniscliffe, Cockerton, Haughton-le-Skerne and Ketton) are all located
    in the vicinity of Darlington.
PACRESTUN = Pawston NT8532 (*HSC* 3)
    Variant: Perstun (L)
    Description: uilla (dependent vill – Bowmont Water estate)
    Note: This name was transcribed as *Waquirtun* by both Hinde and Arnold;
    on this basis it was identified as Whitton by Hinde and as a lost site near
    Wackerage Cairn, Kirknewton, by Barrow. This mistranscription was
    caused by three ambiguities: first, the scribe of Ms. C (the only manuscript
    of *HSC* 1–8 known to Hinde and Arnold) uses the same symbol for both *p*
    and *w*; second, this *p* is followed by a complex symbol which Hinde and
    Arnold interpreted as a *qi* ligature, but which seems instead to be a *cr* liga-
    ture; this ligature is followed by a letter which Hinde and Arnold read as
    an *r*, but which is in fact the long-stemmed Anglo-Saxon *s* which the
    scribe of C uses regularly in proper names. (The reading *Perstun* in L also
    suggests that these letters should be read as *p* and *s*.) The same *cr(e)* liga-
    ture can be seen again in C in the name *Hwæcreddinci* (*HSC* 24). Pawston
    occurs in later medieval manuscripts as *Pachestenam* and *Palloxton*,
    leading Watts to suggest that it derives from OE *Pælloces-tun* or
    Pæcces-tun; the evidence of C suggests that *Pæccestun* may be the correct
    derivation.
PERSEBRIGCE = Piercebridge NZ2115   (*HSC* 31)
    Variant: Persebrige (L)
    Description: *terra* (dependent vill – Gainford estate)
QUEORNINGTUN = Whorlton NZ1014   (*HSC* 31)
    Variant: Cueornington (L)
    Description: *terra* (dependent vill – Gainford estate)
    Note: This is the identification accepted by Craster and Ekwall, based on
    the fact that Whorlton is called *Quernington* in later medieval records.
    Hinde's identification with Quarrington near Durham must be mistaken,
    since this name is rendered *Querendun* in a document of the twelfth
    century.
RABY = Raby NZ1222   (*HSC* 32)
    Description: *appendicium* (dependent vill – Staindrop estate)
REOFHOPPA (I) = Ryhope NZ4152   (*HSC* 26)
    Variant: Reophoppa (C)
    Description: *appendicium* (dependent vill – Bishop Wearmouth estate)
REOFHOPPA (II) = Ryhope Colliery? NZ4053 (*HSC* 26)
    Variant: Reophoppa (C)
    Description: *appendicium* (dependent vill – Bishop Wearmouth estate)

SÆHAM = Seaham NZ4250 (*HSC* 26)
    Variant: Saham (L)
    Description: *appendicium* (dependent vill – Bishop Wearmouth estate)
SÆTUN = Seaton NZ3949 (*HSC* 26)
    Variants: Setun (O); Satun (L)
    Description: *appendicium* (dependent vill – Bishop Wearmouth estate)
SCEOTADUN = Shotton NT8430 (*HSC* 3)
    Description: *uilla* (dependent vill – Bowmont Water estate)
SCEOTTUN (I) = Shotton NZ4139 (*HSC* 22)
    Variants: Scotun (C); Sceotton (L)
    Description: *uilla* (dependent vill – Easington estate)
    Note: Hinde seems mistaken in his identification of Seaton here; later
authors agree on Shotton, although Ekwall has Shotton near Grindon
instead.
SCEOTTUN (II) = Shotton Colliery? NZ3940 (*HSC* 22)
    Variants: Scotun (C); Sceotton (L)
    Description: *uilla* (dependent vill – Easington estate)
    Note: This site is tentative, given the lack of evidence that Shotton
Colliery is a pre-Conquest settlement site.
SCERBÆDLE = Shereburgh Hill? NT8226 (*HSC* 3)
    Variant: Scerbedle (L)
    Description: *uilla* (dependent vill – Bowmont Water estate)
    Note: Hinde has 'a misspelling of Mcrbedle, now Morbattle'; the same
confusion of *s* and *m* in both C and L seems unlikely. On the other hand,
Morebattle is geographically attractive, since several of the Bowmont
Water vills lie in Morebattle parish. Barrow's identification with
Shereburgh Hill is perhaps more plausible (although, as in the case of
Herteshoh above, we would have to assume that the hilltop preserves the
name of a nearby valley settlement, now lost); however, as Watts notes, it
is phonologically difficult to explain a transition in endings from *-bedle*
(meaning unclear) to *-burh*.
SCOTTUN = Shotton NZ1023 (*HSC* 32)
    Description: *appendicium* (dependent vill – Staindrop estate)
SCURUFATUN = Sheraton NZ4435 (*HSC* 22)
    Variant: Scrufatun (L)
    Description: *uilla* (dependent vill – Easington estate)
SELETUN = prob. Monk Hesleden NZ4537 (*HSC* 19, 22)
    Description: *uilla* (primary vill of composite estate; later part of
Easington estate)
    Note: This is the identification given by Hinde, Hart and Craster. Watts
points out that Seletun is OE *sele* + *tun* (*tun* with a hall), while Hesleden
derives from OE *hesel* + *dene* (hazel valley); he concludes that the two
names are not related, and that Seletun must be a lost site. However, it
seems to me that, given the phonetic similarity between the two names and

the presence of nearby Cold Hesleden, that phonetic confusion could cause the two names to merge. This conclusion is supported by strong geographic evidence, since Seletun begins a list of place-names that lie within the parish of Monk Hesleden.

SLICEBURN = West Sleekburn NZ2885 (*HSC* 21)
Variant: Scliceburn (L)
Description: *appendicium* (dependent vill – Bedlington estate)

SLIDDEWESSE = Sledwich NZ0915 (*HSC* 31)
Description: *terra* (dependent vill – Gainford estate)

SOCCEBURG = Sockburn NZ3407 (*HSC* 30)
description: *terra* (vill; paired with Girsby)

STANDROPA = Staindrop NZ1220 (*HSC* 32)
Variant: Standrope (L)
Description: *uilla cum suis appendiciis* (primary vill of composite estate)

STANTUN = Stainton NZ0718 (*HSC* 31)
Description: *terra* (dependent vill – Gainford estate)

STRETFORD = Startforth NZ0416 (*HSC* 31)
Variant: Strecforde (L)
Description: *terra* (dependent vill – Gainford estate)

STRETLEA = Streatlam NZ0819 (*HSC* 31)
Variant: Streclea (L)
Description: *terra* (dependent vill – Gainford estate)

SUGARIPLE = Sourhope? NT8420 (*HSC* 3)
Description: *uilla* (dependent vill – Bowmont Water estate)
Note: This is Barrow's identification; Hinde has Sowerhopeshill, a hilltop cairn, while Hart has Saughtree. Watts notes that *-iple* is meaningless in OE, and there is no phonological mechanism to explain a shift in endings from *-iple* to *-hope*. The name may be garbled in both C and L, and any identification is shaky at best.

SUTHGEDLING = Gilling? NZ1804 (*HSC* 6)
Variant: Suthgedluit (C)
Description: *uilla et quicquid ad ea pertinet* (possible estate centre)
Note: This identification is Craster's, on the basis of the similarity between Suthgedling and Bede's *Ingetlingtum*. Hinde, working from C alone, could offer no identification, while Arnold could only suggest that 'one of the Yealands near Morecambe Bay is perhaps intended': Arnold, *Symeonis opera* I, 200, note c.

SYLCESWURTHE = Silksworth NZ3752 (*HSC* 26)
Description: *appendicium* (dependent vill – Bishop Wearmouth estate)

THICCELEA = Thickley NZ2224 (*HSC* 31 and 32)
Variant: Ticcelea (L)
Description: *terra* (*HSC* 31); *appendicium* (*HSC* 32) (dependent vill – Bishop Auckland and Staindrop estates)

THOREP = Little Thorp NZ4242   (*HSC* 22)
    Description: *uilla* (dependent vill – Easington estate)
THORNBURNUM = Thornington? NT8833   (*HSC* 3)
    Description: *uilla* (dependent vill – Bowmont Water estate)
    Note: Neither Hinde nor Barrow could identify this, while Hart's sugges-
    tion of Thorneyburn near Bellingham lies nowhere near the Bowmont
    Water. Thornington, which lies on the Bowmont Water downstream from
    Pawston, is geographically sound but etymologically suspect, as Watts
    notes, since Thornburnum is OE *thorn* + *burnum* (dat. pl. of *burna*,
    stream), while Thornington probably derives from OE *thornegn*
    (thorn-copse) + *tun*. However, Watts also observes that the two names
    may be related, since an OE *thorning* may also have existed, meaning
    'stream where thorn-trees grow'.
TWILINGATUN = lost   (*HSC* 19, 21 and 22)
    Variant: Twinlingtun (*HSC* 22)
    Description: *uilla* (dependent vill – Monk Hesleden and Easington
    estates)
    Note: Hinde suggests Willington near Brancepeth, while Craster suggests
    Willington near Wallsend, but its position in the lists of vills in *HSC* 19
    and 22 indicates that Twilingatun was probably located within the early
    parish of Monk Hesleden to the south of Hutton Henry, since Hotun
    precedes Twilingatun in both lists, which proceed from north to south.
UFFERTUN = Offerton NZ3455   (*HSC* 26)
    Variant: Uffentun (C)
    Description: *uppendicium* (dependent vill – Bishop Wearmouth estate)
WACARFELD = Wackerfield NZ1522   (*HSC* 32)
    Description: *appendicium* (dependent vill – Staindrop estate)
WEARDSEATLE = lost (Bishop's Palace, North Auckland?)   (*HSC* 31)
    Description: *terra* (dependent vill – Bishop Auckland estate)
    Note: Hinde (followed by Hart) suggests Warsull in Teesdale, but this lies
    outside Aucklandshire and, as Watts points out, it follows an unrelated
    derivation from OE *Wirces-halh*. The list of vills in *HSC* 31 suggests that
    Weardseatle must lie between Bishop Auckland and Binchester. Gill and
    Roberts suggest that the place-name, meaning 'high or guarded seat',
    could refer to the site where the bishop's palace was later built. This
    hypothesis conforms to the evidence of the *HSC*, but has yet to be
    confirmed archaeologically; see Roberts' Appendix ii in Gill, *Bishop
    Auckland*.
WERCEWORTHE = Warkworth NU2406   (*HSC* 8)
    Variant: Werkeworde (L)
    Description: *uilla cum suis appendiciis*; bounds given (estate centre)
WESTUN = lost (near Bishop Wearmouth)   (*HSC* 26)
    Variant: Wertun (C)
    Description: *appendicium* (dependent vill – Bishop Wearmouth estate)

Note: Hinde (followed by Hart) has Westoe near South Shields, but this lies outside the shire of Bishop Wearmouth. The list of vills in *HSC* 26 places Westun between Bishop Wearmouth and Offerton, which lies some three miles west of Bishop Wearmouth. This suggests that Westun got its name from the fact that it lay just west of the estate-centre of Bishop Wearmouth.

WIGECLIF = Wycliffe NZ1114   (*HSC* 9)
Description: *uilla* (part of original territory of Gainford)

WIREMUTHE AUSTRALEM = Bishop Wearmouth NZ3956   (*HSC* 26)
Description: *uilla dilecta . . . cum suis appendiciis* (primary vill of composite estate)

WUDACESTRE = Woodhorn? NZ3088   (*HSC* § 1)
Description: *uilla* (possible estate centre)
Note: Craster states that Wudacestre 'is now Woodhorn, having, like Brinkburn, changed its suffix': Craster, 'Patrimony', p. 185. However, any name-change must have taken place by the twelfth century, since Woodhorn is called *Wudehorn* in a document of 1176. Reasons for assuming the identity of Wudacestre and Woodhorn are thus circumstantial; they include the facts that, like the other three vills of *HSC* 11, Woodhorn was an early church-site and parish centre, and that, like that cluster of vills, it is adjacent to, and partially overlaps, the estate of Warkworth as described in *HSC* 8.

WUDUTUN = Witton-le-Wear NZ1431   (*HSC* 31)
Variant: Wudetun (L)
Description: *terra* (dependent vill – Bishop Auckland estate)

Bibliography

Arnold, T., ed., *Symeonis monachi opera omnia*, 2 vols., Rolls Series 75 (London, 1883–5)

Austin, D., 'Fieldwork and Excavation at Hart', *Archaeologia Æliana* 5th ser. 4 (1976), 72–5

——, 'Late Anglo-Saxon Settlement Patterns in the North-East of England', in *Studies in Late Anglo-Saxon Settlement*, ed. M. Faull (Oxford, 1984), pp. 197–207

——, ed., *Boldon Book: Northumberland and Durham*, Domesday Book Supplementary Volume 35 (Chichester, 1982)

Baker, D., 'Scissors and Paste: Corpus Christi, Cambridge, MS 139 Again', in *The Materials, Sources and Methods of Ecclesiastical History* (Studies in Church History 11), ed. D. Baker (Oxford, 1975), pp. 83–123

Barrow, G. W. S., *The Kingdom of the Scots: Government, Church and Society from the Eleventh to the Fourteenth Century* (London, 1973)

Birch, W. de G., *Cartularium Saxonicum*, 3 vols. (London, 1885–93)

Blair, P. H., 'Some Observations on the Historia Regum Attributed to Symeon of Durham', in *Celt and Saxon*, ed. N. K. Chadwick (Cambridge, 1963), pp. 63–118

Blake, E. O., ed., *Liber Eliensis* (London, 1962)

Brooks, N. P., 'England in the Ninth Century: the Crucible of Defeat', *Transactions of the Royal Historical Society* 5th ser. 29 (1978), 1–20

Cam, H. M., 'Manerium cum Hundredo: the Hundred and the Hundredal Manor', in her *Liberties and Communities in Medieval England* (Cambridge, 1944), pp. 64–91

Campbell, A., ed., *Chronicon Æthelweardi* (Edinburgh, 1962)

Campbell, J., *Essays in Anglo-Saxon History* (London, 1986)

——, ed., *The Anglo-Saxons* (Oxford, 1982)

Clack, P., and Gill, B. H., 'Land Divisions of County Durham in the Early Medieval Period', in *The Uplands: Medieval Village Research Group Annual Report* 28 (1980), 30–4

Coggins, D., and Fairless, K., 'Excavations in Upper Teesdale 1972–7', *University of Durham Archaeological Reports for 1977 I* (Durham, 1978)

Colgrave, B., 'The Post-Bedan Miracles and Translations of St Cuthbert', in *The Early Cultures of North-West Europe*, ed. C. Fox and B. Dickins (Cambridge, 1950), pp. 307–25

——, ed., *Two Lives of St Cuthbert* (Cambridge, 1940)

——, ed., *Eddius' Life of St Wilfrid* (Cambridge, 1927)

——, and Mynors, R. A. B., eds., *Bede's Ecclesiastical History of the English People* (Oxford, 1969)

Craster, H. H. E., 'The Red Book of Durham', *English Historical Review* 40 (1925), 523–9

————, 'The Patrimony of St Cuthbert', *English Historical Review* 69 (1954), 177–99

Darlington, R. R., 'Æthelwig, Abbot of Evesham', *English Historical Review* 48 (1933), 1–22 and 177–98

Davis, R. H. C., *The Kalendar of Abbot Samson of Bury St Edmunds and Related Documents*, Camden 3rd ser. 84 (London, 1954)

————, 'East Anglia and the Danelaw', *Transactions of the Royal Historical Society* 4th ser. 5 (1955), 23–39

Dolley, M., *Viking Coins of the Danelaw and of Dublin* (London, 1965)

Dumville, D. N., 'The Corpus Christi "Nennius" ', *Bulletin of the Board of Celtic Studies* 25 (1972–4), 369–80

————, 'Celtic-Latin Texts in Northern England, c. 1150 – c. 1250', *Celtica* 12 (1977), 19–49

————, 'The Sixteenth-Century History of Two Cambridge Books from Sawley', *Transactions of the Cambridge Bibliographical Society* 7 (1980), 427–44

Ekwall, E., *The Concise Oxford Dictionary of English Place-Names* (Oxford, 1960)

Faith, R., *The English Peasantry and the Growth of Lordship* (Leicester, 1997)

Faull, M. L. and Stinson, M., eds., *Domesday Book: Yorkshire* (Chichester, 1986)

Finberg, H. P. R., ed., *Early Charters of the West Midlands* (Leicester, 1961)

Fleming, R., 'Rural Elites and Urban Communities in Late-Saxon England', *Past and Present* 141 (1993), 3–37

Foster, M., 'Custodians of St Cuthbert: the Durham Monks' Views of their Predecessors, 1083–c.1200', in *Anglo-Norman Durham 1093–1193*, ed. D. Rollason, M. Harvey and M. Prestwich (Woodbridge, 1994), pp. 53–65

Garmonsway, G. N., ed., *The Anglo-Saxon Chronicle* (London, 1972)

Gerchow, J., *Die Gedenküberlieferung der Angelsachsen* (Berlin, 1988)

Gill, B. H., *Bishop Auckland: an Archaeological Survey* (Durham, 1976)

Gransden, A., *Historical Writing in England c. 550 to c. 1307* (London, 1974)

Greenwell, W., ed., *Feodarium prioratus Dunelmensis*, Surtees Society 58 (Durham, 1872)

Gregson, N., 'The Multiple Estate Model: Some Critical Questions', *Journal of Historical Geography* 11 (1985), 339–53

Gullick, M., 'The Scribes of the Durham Cantor's Book (Durham, Dean and Chapter Library, MS B.IV.24) and the Durham Martyrology Scribe', in *Anglo-Norman Durham 1093–1193*, ed. D. Rollason, M. Harvey and M. Prestwich (Woodbridge, 1994), pp. 93–109

————, 'The Hand of Symeon of Durham: Further Observations on the Durham Martyrology Scribe', in *Symeon of Durham: Historian of Durham and the North*, ed. D. Rollason (Stamford, 1998), pp. 14–31

Hall, D., 'The Late Saxon Countryside: Villages and their Fields', in *Anglo-Saxon Settlements*, ed. D. Hooke (Oxford, 1988), pp. 99–122

Hall, D. J., 'The Community of St Cuthbert – Its Properties, Rights and Claims from the Ninth Century to the Twelfth' (unpubl. Ph.D. dissertation, Oxford Univ., 1984)

Hamilton, N. E. S. A., ed., *Willelmi Malmesbiriensis monachi gesta pontificum Anglorum*, Rolls Series 52 (London, 1870)

Hardwick, C., *et al.*, *A Catalogue of Manuscripts Preserved in the Library of the University of Cambridge*, 5 vols. (Cambridge, 1856–67)

Hart, C. R., *The Early Charters of Northern England and the North Midlands* (Leicester, 1975)

——, *The Danelaw* (London, 1992)

Harvey, P. D. A., 'Rectitudines Singularum Personarum and Gerefa', *English Historical Review* 108 (1993), 1–22

——, 'Boldon Book and the Wards between Tyne and Tees', in *Anglo-Norman Durham 1093–1193*, ed. D. Rollason, M. Harvey and M. Prestwich (Woodbridge, 1994), pp. 399–405

Hearne, T., *Hemingi chartularium ecclesiæ Wigorniensis* (Oxford, 1723)

Hinde, J. H., ed., *Symeonis Dunelmensis opera et collectanea*, 2 vols., Surtees Society 51 (Durham, 1868)

Hooke, D., 'Pre-Conquest Estates in the West Midlands: Preliminary Thoughts', *Journal of Historical Geography* 8 (1982), 227–44

Hudson, B. T., 'Cnut and the Scottish Kings', *English Historical Review* 107 (1992), 350–60

James, M. R., *The Ancient Libraries of Canterbury and Dover* (Cambridge, 1903)

——, *A Descriptive Catalogue of the Manuscripts in the Library of Corpus Christi College, Cambridge*, 2 vols. (Cambridge, 191?)

Jensen, G. F., 'The Vikings in England: A Review', *Anglo-Saxon England* 4 (1975), 181–206

John, E., *Orbis Brittaniæ and Other Studies* (Leicester, 1966)

——, 'The Social and Political Problems of the Early English Church', in *Land, Church and People*, ed. J. Thirsk (Reading, 1970), pp. 39–63

Jolliffe, J. E. A., 'Northumbrian Institutions', *English Historical Review* 41 (1926), 1–42

——, *Pre-Feudal England: The Jutes* (Oxford, 1933)

——, 'The Era of the Folk in English History', in *Oxford Essays in Medieval History Presented to Herbert Edward Salter*, ed. F. M. Powicke (Oxford, 1934), pp. 1–32

Jones, G., 'The Pattern of Settlement on the Welsh Border', *Agricultural History Review* 8 (1960), 66–81

——, 'Basic Patterns of Settlement Distribution in Northern England', *Advancement of Science* 18 (1961), 192–200

——, 'Early Territorial Organization in Northern England and its Bearing on the Scandinavian Settlement', in *The Fourth Viking Congress*, ed. A. Small (Edinburgh, 1965), pp. 67–84

——, 'The Multiple Estate as a Model Framework for Tracing Early Stages in the Evolution of Rural Settlement', in *L'habitat et les paysages rureaux d'Europe*, ed. F. Dussart (Liège, 1971), pp. 251–67

——, 'Early Territorial Organization in Gwynedd and Elmet', *Northern History* 10 (1975), 3–27

——, 'Multiple Estates and Early Settlement', in *English Medieval Settlement*, ed. P. Sawyer (London, 1976), pp. 9–34

Kapelle, W. E., *The Norman Conquest of the North* (Chapel Hill, NC, 1979)

Ker, N. R., 'Hemming's Cartulary', in *Studies in Medieval History Presented to*

F. M. Powicke, ed. R. W. Hunt, W. A. Pantin and R. W. Southern (Oxford, 1948), pp. 49–75
———, *English Manuscripts in the Century after the Norman Conquest* (Oxford, 1960)
———, *Medieval Libraries of Great Britain*, 2nd ed. (London, 1964)
———, *Medieval Manuscripts in British Libraries I: London* (Oxford, 1969)
Keynes, S., and Lapidge, M., eds., *Alfred the Great* (Harmondsworth, 1983)
Keynes, S., 'King Athelstan's Books', in *Learning and Literature in Anglo-Saxon England*, ed. M. Lapidge and H. Gneuss (Cambridge, 1985), pp. 143–201
———, *Anglo-Saxon Charters: Archives and Single Sheets* (Oxford, forthcoming)
Kirby, D. P., 'The Genesis of a Cult: Cuthbert of Farne and Ecclesiastical Politics in Northumbria in the Late Seventh and Early Eighth Centuries', *Journal of Ecclesiastical History* 46 (1995), 383–97
Klingelhofer, E., *Manor, Vill and Hundred: The Development of Rural Institutions in Early Medieval Hampshire* (Toronto, 1992)
Knowles, D., *The Monastic Order in England*, 2nd ed. (Cambridge, 1963)
Lapidge, M., 'Bryhtferth of Ramsey and the Early Sections of the *Historia Regum* attributed to Symeon of Durham', *Anglo-Saxon England* 10 (1982), 97–122
———, ed., *The Anglo-Saxon Chronicle: a Collaborative Edition vol. 17: Annals of St Neots with Vita prima S. Neoti* (Cambridge, 1985)
Lawrie, A. C., *Early Scottish Charters prior to 1153* (Glasgow, 1905)
Lawson, M. K., *Cnut: The Danes in England in the Early Eleventh Century* (London, 1993)
Lee, B. E., ed., *Records of the Templars in England in the Twelfth Century: The Inquest of 1185 with Illustrative Charters and Documents* (London, 1935)
Levison, W., 'Die Annales Lindisfarnenses et Dunelmenses', *Deutsches Archiv für Erforschung des Mittelalters* 17 (1961), 447–506
Liebermann, F., ed., *Die heiligen Englands* (Hannover, 1889)
———, ed., *Die Gesetze der Angelsächsen*, 3 vols. (Halle, 1903–16)
Lyte, H. C. M., ed., *Liber feodorum: The Book of Fees Commonly Called Testa de Nevill* (London, 1920)
Mac Airt, S., and Mac Niocaill, G., *Annals of Ulster* (Dublin, 1983)
Macray, W. D., ed., *Chronicon abbatiæ de Evesham ad annum 1418*, Rolls Series 29 (London, 1863)
Madan, F., and Craster, H. H. E., *A Summary Catalogue of Western Manuscripts in the Bodleian Library at Oxford* (Oxford, 1922)
Maitland, F. W., 'Northumbrian Tenures', *English Historical Review* 20 (1890), 625–32
Mawer, A., 'The Scandinavian Kingdom of Northumbria', *Saga-Book* 7 (1910–11), 38–64
Meehan, B., 'Outsiders, Insiders, and Property in Durham around 1100', in *Church, Society and Politics* (Studies in Church History 12), ed. D. Baker (Oxford, 1975), pp. 45–58
———, 'Durham Twelfth-Century Manuscripts in Cistercian Houses', in *Anglo-Norman Durham 1093–1193*, ed. D. Rollason, M. Harvey and M. Prestwich (Woodbridge, 1994), pp. 439–49

Michelmore, D. J. H., 'The Reconstruction of the Early Tenurial and Territorial Divisions of the Landscape of Northern England', *Landscape History* 1 (1979), 1–9

Morris, C. D., 'Northumbria and the Viking Settlement: the Evidence for Land-holding', *Archaeologia Æliana* 5th ser. 5 (1977), 81–103

——, 'Viking and Native in North England: a Case Study', in *Proceedings of the Eighth Viking Congress*, ed. H. Bekker-Nielsen (1981), pp. 223–44

——, 'Aspects of Scandinavian Settlement in Northern England: a Review', *Northern History* 20 (1984), 1–22

Nelson, J. L., ' "A King Across the Sea": Alfred in Continental Perspective', *Transactions of the Royal Historical Society* 5th ser. 36 (1986), 45–68

Norton, C., 'History, Wisdom and Illumination', in *Symeon of Durham: Historian of Durham and the North*, ed. D. Rollason (Stamford, 1998), pp. 61–105

Offler, H. S., ed., *Durham Episcopal Charters*, Surtees Society 179 (Gateshead, 1968)

Piper, A. J., 'The First Generations of Durham Monks and the Cult of St Cuthbert', in *St Cuthbert, His Cult and His Community to AD 1200*, ed. G. Bonner, D. Rollason and C. Stancliffe (Woodbridge, 1989), pp. 437–46

Raine, J., *History of North Durham* (Durham, 1852)

Roberts, B. K., 'Rural Settlement in County Durham: Forms, Pattern and System,' in *Social Organization and Settlement*, ed. D. Green, C. Haselgrove and M. Sprigs (BAR International. Ser. 47, 1978), pp. 291–322

Robinson, P., *A Catalogue of Dated and Datable Manuscripts in Cambridge Libraries, 737–1600* (Cambridge, 1988)

Roffe, D., 'Pre-Conquest Estates and Parish Boundaries: A Discussion with Examples from Lincolnshire', in *Studies in Late Anglo-Saxon Settlement*, ed. M. Faull (Oxford, 1984), pp. 115–22

Rollason, D., 'Lists of Saint's Resting-Places in Anglo-Saxon England', *Anglo-Saxon England* 7 (1978), 61–93

——, 'St Cuthbert and Wessex: The Evidence of Cambridge, Corpus Christi College Ms. 183', in *St Cuthbert, His Cult and His Community to AD 1200*, ed. G. Bonner, D. Rollason and C. Stancliffe (Woodbridge, 1989), pp. 413–24

——, *Saints and Relics in Anglo-Saxon England* (Oxford, 1989)

——, 'Symeon of Durham and the Community of Durham in the Eleventh Century', in *England in the Eleventh Century: Proceedings of the 1990 Harlaxton Symposium*, ed. C. Hicks (Stamford, 1992), pp. 183–98

——, 'Symeon's Contribution to Historical Writing in Northern England', in *Symeon of Durham: Historian of Durham and the North*, ed. D. Rollason (Stamford, 1998), pp. 1–13

——, ed., *Symeon of Durham: Libellus de exordio atque procursa istius, hoc est Dunhelmensis, ecclesie* (Oxford, 2000)

Sawyer, P., 'The Density of the Danish Settlement in England', *University of Birmingham Historical Journal* 6 (1958), 1–17

——, *The Age of the Vikings*, 2nd ed. (London, 1971)

——, *From Roman Britain to Norman England* (London, 1978)

——, *Kings and Vikings* (London, 1982)

Seebohm, F., *The English Village Community*, 4th ed. (London, 1890)

Sigal, P. A., 'Un aspect du culte des saints: le châtiment divin aux XIe et XIIe siècles d'après la litterature hagiographique du Midi de la France', *Cahiers de Fanjeaux* 11 (1976), 39–59.

Simpson, L., 'The King Alfred/St Cuthbert Episode in the Historia de Sancto Cuthberto: Its Significance for mid-tenth-century English History', in *St Cuthbert, his Cult and his Community to A.D. 1200*, ed. G. Bonner, D. Rollason and C. Stancliffe (Woodbridge, 1989), pp. 397–411

Skene, W. F., ed., *Chronicles of the Picts, Chronicles of the Scots, and Other Early Memorials of Scottish History* (Edinburgh, 1867)

Smyth, A. P., *Scandinavian York and Dublin*, 2 vols. (Dublin, 1975)

———, *Scandinavian Kings in the British Isles 850–880* (Oxford, 1977)

———, *Alfred the Great* (Oxford, 1995)

South, T. J., 'Competition for King Alfred's Aura in the Last Century of Anglo-Saxon England', *Albion* 23 (1991), 613–26

———, 'The Norman Conquest of Durham: Norman Historians and the Anglo-Saxon Community of St. Cuthbert', *Journal of the Charles Homer Haskins Society* 4 (1992), 85–95

———, 'Changing Images of Sainthood: St Cuthbert in the Historia de Sancto Cuthberto', in *Saints: Studies in Hagiography*, ed. S. Sticca (Binghamton, 1996), pp. 81–94

Stenton, F. M., 'Types of Manorial Structure in the Northern Danelaw', in *Oxford Studies in Social and Legal History* 2, ed. P. Vinogradoff (Oxford, 1910), pp. 3–96

———, *Anglo-Saxon England*, 3rd ed. (Oxford, 1971)

Stevenson, J., ed., *Liber uitæ ecclesiæ Dunelmensis*, Surtees Society 13 (London, 1841)

———, trans., *Church Historians of England*, 5 vols. in 8 (London, 1853–8)

Stevenson, W. H., ed., *Asserius de rebus gestis Aelfredi* (London, 1904)

Thompson, A. H., ed., *Liber uitæ ecclesiæ Dunelmensis* I, Surtees Society 136 (Durham, 1923)

Todd, J. H., ed., *The War of the Gaedhil with the Gaill*, Rolls Series 48 (London, 1867)

Twysden, R., ed. *Decem scriptores* (London, 1652)

Unwin, T., 'Towards a Model of Anglo-Scandinavian Rural Settlement in England', in *Anglo-Saxon Settlements*, ed. D. Hooke (Oxford, 1988), pp. 77–98

Wainwright, E. T., 'The Battles at Corbridge', in his *Scandinavian England* (Chichester, 1975), pp. 163–80

Ward, B., *Miracles and the Medieval Mind* (Philadelphia, 1982)

Watson, A. G., *A Catalogue of Dated and Datable Manuscripts in the British Museum* (London, 1979)

———, *A Catalogue of Dated and Datable Manuscripts in Oxford Libraries* (Oxford, 1984)

Watts, V., 'Place-Names', in *Durham County and City with Teesside*, ed. J. C. Dewdney (Durham, 1970)

Whitelock, D., ed., *English Historical Documents I, c. 500–1042*, 2nd ed. (London, 1979)

———, trans., *The Anglo-Saxon Chronicle* (London, 1961)

Index

Note: entries within the text of the *Historia de sancto Cuthberto* itself are given in bold type.

Anglo-Saxon Texts 3

HISTORIA DE SANCTO CUTHBERTO

While it retains many of the trappings of a traditional saint's life, the *Historia de Sancto Cuthberto* is also a remarkable record of the political activities and property acquisitions of a powerful Anglo-Saxon monastery, and it vividly demonstrates the ongoing relationship between the monks and their patron saint. Written in Northumbria in the tenth or eleventh century, the *Historia* presents a striking contrast with earlier lives of Cuthbert such as Bede's, and is a valuable teaching text. The present edition is the first to make use of all three surviving manuscripts of the *Historia*, and is also the first English translation of this brief but important text. It includes a reassessment of the text's purpose and date, a detailed historical commentary, excerpts from related texts, and a discussion of the patrimony of St Cuthbert, including maps of estates and a catalogue of the more than one hundred vills listed in the text.

TED JOHNSON SOUTH is Associate Professor of History, Western New England College.

Anglo-Saxon Texts

ISSN 1463–6948

Series editors
ANDY ORCHARD
MICHAEL LAPIDGE

Editors' preface

Anglo-Saxon Texts is a series of scholarly editions (with parallel translations) of important texts from Anglo-Saxon England, whether written in Latin or in Old English. The series aims to offer critical texts with suitable apparatus and accurate modern English translations, together with informative general introductions and full historical and literary commentaries.

Lightning Source UK Ltd.
Milton Keynes UK
UKOW06n2217180315

248109UK00001B/80/P